MASCULINE FEMININE OR HUMAN?

An Overview of the Sociology of the
Gender Roles
Second Edition

By Janet Saltzman Chafetz
University of Houston

 F. E. PEACOCK PUBLISHERS, INC., ITASCA, ILLINOIS

Table of Contents

Preface to the Second Edition

More than four years have passed since I completed work on the first edition of this book. These four years have both heartened and discouraged me.

I am heartened by the reception the first edition received. It served to demonstrate to me that interest in gender roles has burgeoned, despite the fears of the many publishers I approached who said there was "no market for this type of book," before I had the luck to connect up with Ted Peacock and F. E. Peacock Publishers, Inc. This subject matter is no passing fad. Indeed it is now institutionalized as a subdiscipline and has its own formal specialty section within the American Sociological Association.

I am heartened also by the tremendous wealth of published material that has appeared in the area since I first wrote this book. My task in revising the book has been made much more difficult by this outpouring, but my joy in the fact that so many scholars are taking these issues seriously more than makes up for the added work.

I am heartened by the fact that texts in other areas of sociology, and occasionally even professors' lectures, are changing to incorporate material concerning gender roles heretofore lacking. Moreover, it has become routine to find papers addressing gender role issues and a large variety of other substantive sociological matters in all types of sessions at professional meetings.

Finally, I am heartened by the social, cultural, political, educational, and economic changes we have witnessed in this society in the past several years. Since the first edition was written, men's awareness groups have begun to spring up to address the same general issues that the growing Women's Movement has been raising. Both sexes have a long way to go in the evolution from stereotyped gender roles to new forms of humanness, and the road to change is not as rapid as many of us would like, nor is it without its pitfalls, detours, and stop signs. However, change has begun and continues to occur, if only we have enough patience and longevity.

Ironically, I am discouraged by the relative lack of competition for this book. When I first published it there was virtually no book that attempted to survey the full range of topics relevant to the academic study of both gender roles from a sociological perspective. I assumed that there would soon be a number of such books. Four years later the situation is not much improved. The vast majority of the material available for teaching is still about women only, and, secondarily, there are now some books about men. Many of these books are collections of papers. There is still no more than a handful of books (excluding edited readers) that look at both roles as they interact and create problems for members of both sexes. As I maintained then I do now: One cannot understand either gender role without understanding both. The need for a full-blown, integrated text in the area has yet to be met.

Just as I am heartened by the social changes I have witnessed, I am discouraged (though scarcely surprised) at some of the failures and reversals which have occurred. I am discouraged that I must still write "*if* the E.R.A. passes. . . ." I am discouraged with the growing movement against abortion, and, among some of our colleagues as well as other people, against the presumed "quotas" entailed in affirmative action. I am discouraged by the adverse effects of the recent economic recession on the employment gains and opportunities of women, by the Supreme Court decision to allow pregnancy benefits to be exempted by employers from general health benefits, and by its decision to permit the government to withhold Medicaid payments for abortion. I am discouraged finally by the periodic infighting and general dispiritedness of some of the major feminist organizations.

My general purpose and orientation, as set forth in the Preface to the First Edition, have not changed. New data and theoretical and conceptual developments have led to alteration or expansion of some of my views. These changes, as well as facts and figures that are more recent than those used in the first edition, are incorporated into this version. However, my basic ideas have not changed to contradict those set forth in the earlier edition. I hope this new edition will prove to be at least as helpful as the old one to those who teach and learn about the sociology of gender roles at the undergraduate level.

I would like to thank Mary Helen Neville, who served as my research assistant for part of the revision work. Maradee Davis did extensive library work for me as my research associate, and without her help the revisions would have been virtually impossible. I would also like to thank the countless students who, over the past several years, have challenged me to develop my thinking about the sociology of gender roles during hundreds of hours of classroom and office discussion. The critical comments of many faculty members who have used the first edition of this book were also quite helpful in revising it. Finally, I would especially like to thank my publisher, Ted Peacock, who took a risk in publishing the first edition, and without whose nagging there would be no second edition.

JANET SALTZMAN CHAFETZ

Fall, 1977
Houston, Texas

Preface to the First Edition

Since I am not a "value-free scientist," this book is not a "value-free" endeavor. I am deeply committed to the basic goal of maximizing the opportunities for all human beings to develop to the fullest extent possible their own unique talents, interests, and predilections. My particular interest is in bringing about changes that will encourage males and females to explore and develop their human potentials more fully, as opposed to maintaining the stereotyped masculine and feminine roles foisted upon them by virtually every aspect of this society—as well as most others. In short, I am concerned not merely with "women's liberation," but with "human liberation," although I profess to be a "member" of the former social movement.

This book comprises an effort to delineate the parameters of the newly emerging field of the sociology of sex roles. I am attempting to describe the present and recent past state of affairs in this connection, and at the same time to prescribe much needed changes in that state of affairs, some of which have already been begun. A virtual mountain of recent publications exists pertaining to the problems of females in contemporary American society, and the genesis and possible solutions of these problems. Parallel literature about the male role comprises little more than an ant hill. Moreover, literature examining the two sex roles in their complementary aspects is practically nonexistent. Yet it would appear that when two role complexes are as tightly interwoven and interdependent as the sex roles, it makes no sense to explore one in isolation from the other.

In my view, both roles are constrictive and costly for many, if not most, human beings, although for very different kinds of reasons. To the extent that there are social problems relating to one sex, it is inconceivable that they would not involve counterparts in the other, and to begin to understand and cope with the problematic aspects of either sex role necessitates a broad view of the entire area. It is crucial first to understand the nature of these stereotyped roles, how they are sustained and transmitted, what their implications or human "costs" are for all of us, and who profits (and in what ways) by their continued existence. Such issues of "social statics" comprise a large segment of this book. It is also important to examine emerging trends that may (hopefully) undermine traditional sex roles and allow for the emergence of a society of *humans* whose lives are based on achieved rather than ascribed characteristics. In this I am exploring phenomena of social change.

This book is designed primarily for undergraduates, to be used as a brief overview and starting point in newly developing courses throughout the nation in the sociology of sex roles. It arises chiefly out of my own experiences in trying to teach such a course; I have found it difficult to locate reading that is other than polemical and/or centered almost exclusively on the feminine sex role. I am also of the opinion that this topic should not be tucked away in courses of its own, into which people already committed to the values implicit in the subject matter recruit themselves. Rather, it must find its way into the broader curriculum. Thus this text should be useful supplementary reading in education, counseling and social work curricula, and other sociology courses such as Introductory, Social Problems, Minorities, Stratification, Social Movements, Social Psychology, and Marriage and Family. In light of this, I have attempted to integrate as many relevant broadly sociological theories and concepts as possible.

Sociology has long been primarily a male field. Courses in it are usually taught by males, utilizing texts written by males. If we take our own discipline seriously, we should understand that all human knowledge (including our own) is partial in that it represents perceptions from some particular vantage point. Given contemporary social definitions, males and females tend to learn to perceive reality in somewhat different ways. Therefore, a masculine point of view will logically be partial, as will a feminine one; both are ultimately needed. Materials in virtually all courses must be expanded to comprise an understanding of reality as it appears from a wide variety of perspectives. It is my hope that by integrating material from the sociology of sex roles into the broader curriculum the discipline may begin to overcome its myopia. To the extent that this endeavor is a success, those of us who specialize in sex roles and women's studies should find ourselves superfluous. The true measure of this subfield is how long it takes for the "normal" curriculum to expand to take account of sex role phenomena, thus making our courses unnecessary.

Intellectual debts for a work such as this cannot be counted. How can I thank the scores of women whose frank discussions during various feminist meetings have inspired many of my ideas? Or the 75 students who put up with my first fumbling efforts at teaching the sociology of sex roles at Trinity University, and whose papers, as well as class participation and out-of-class discussions, contributed so much to my thinking and to the material presented herein? There are countless other students as well who, knowing of my interests, have contributed ideas and references. I specifically thank the secretarial staff of the Graduate School of Social Work, University of Houston for their help; Patricia Sampson for her work as research assistant; Barbara Brown, Henry Chafetz, Richard Vogel, and Kathleen Kemp for their careful reading and comments on early drafts of this book; and Kathleen Kemp for devoting hours to discussing many of the issues raised in the text and, most of all, for calling my attention to yet more material I should read and consider. I am particularly indebted to my friend and colleague Barbara Polk for the challenging and stimulating ideas she expressed during many delightful hours of discussion running the course of four years. Finally, my deepest appreciation goes to the University of Houston, whose Faculty Research Initiation Grant and Publications Committee Grant provided me the leisure and resources with which to write this book.

JANET SALTZMAN CHAFETZ

Houston, Texas
May, 1973

Chapter 1

Is Biology Destiny?

If, 10 years ago, you tried to predict the lives 25 years hence of a group of newborn babies, half snuggled under blue blankets and half under pink, two rather specific sets of images would have come to mind. While the last decade has witnessed some change in these sets of images, we are all sufficiently shaped by our recent sociocultural history that we must first examine what those images were before we can understand how they may be changing. A decade ago most American observers of that group of babies would have envisioned that those wrinkled little creatures under the pink nylon might become young wives in their computerized kitchens fixing a high protein soybean gruel for their toddlers or teachers facing 20 youngsters at their desk-console computers. They might be scurrying around some hospital in white pantsuits administering the doctor's orders, or sitting at a typewriter transcribing a boss's letters. That's about it. The babies under the blue blankets, however, would be envisioned as engaged in so many different pursuits it would be difficult to describe them all. There they would be, building, reading, lecturing, writing, barking orders, peering down microscopes, fixing machines, fighting fires, standing in a courtroom, a shop, a hospital, an office, a factory, a field. They would not, however, be caring for children, typing, or dusting furniture.

It can be imagined that a doctor or physical scientist would have commented on such images as follows:

> I never cease to marvel that nature has provided so marvelously for the different kinds of needs humans have by allowing for two sexes of such radically different physical and mental structures. The natural compassion, passivity, and nurturing instincts of women, arising from their childbearing and child-rearing functions and sustained by a delicate hormonal system, harmonize so beautifully with the innately greater aggressiveness, strength, and energy of the male of the species. *Vive la difference!*

A social scientist, on the other hand, might have been more likely to observe:

> What a crime that our culture dictates so strongly the possibilities of individuals on their birth day! For no inherent reason these infants have already been started on a long and complex path of learning designed to ensure that each sex will be restricted in a variety of ways from fulfilling the potentialities of its individual members. But times are changing. . . .

Such images and reactions point up two issues. First, there is the obvious importance of the ascribed characteristic of sex in determining many, if not most, aspects of the future life of every individual. While this is changing, it is still a fairly accurate picture of contemporary reality. Our society pays constant lip service to an equal-opportunity ethic in which achieved statuses are supposed to be all-important. From the very start of life, however, we in fact run two separate but not equal competitions, one for males and one for females (as we do with other groups with immutable characteristics, such as race). This phenomenon, indeed, comprises the substance of most of the rest of this book. The second issue is whether or not such ascribed differences are in any way necessary, given some innate nature for each of the two sexes. This chapter seeks some answers to this question.

Differentiating Biological Sex and Sociocultural Gender Roles

To begin such a discussion, it is necessary to make the crucial distinction, often obliterated in everyday thinking, between *sex* and *gender role*. Almost all human beings (and, for that matter, all animals above a very low order on the evolutionary scale) are born with a more or less clearly identifiable sex as male or female. For most people, the minute they are born the fact of their maleness or femaleness is obvious, as indicated by physical attributes including distinctions in gonadal, chromosomal, and hormonal characteristics. When, occasionally, these various indicators of sex do not agree, it is an indication that such individuals are not totally of one or the other sex. In some cases, infants with consistent sex characteristics can be misidentified at birth due to distortions of the genitals. Raised as members of the other sex, they find it difficult if not impossible to function like other members of their own sex when the mistake is later discovered. This problem attests to the strength of gender role identification in determining human behavior (see Money & Ehrhardt, 1972, for a detailed discussion of this phenomenon).

Gender role is a different order of phenomenon than sex. The relevant terms are not "male" and "female," which are sex terms, but "masculine" and "feminine." It does not require a very astute social observer to notice that from very early childhood to death, people act differently according to sex. Most females display, to a greater or lesser extent, a set of behavioral, temperamental, emotional, intellectual, and attitudinal characteristics identified, in a given culture at a given time, as feminine. Similarly, most males display, to a greater or lesser extent, a set of different characteristics defined as masculine. These learned characteristics can be conceptualized together under the general rubric of "gender roles."

Sociologists attach a specific meaning to the term "role." Most introductory texts define it in terms of a cluster of socially or culturally defined expectations that individuals in a given situation are expected to fulfill. At any given time for any given individual born into a culture, the roles are a given in the sense that they exist outside of that individual. Confronted by a set of socially and culturally prescribed roles, the individual is pressured, rewarded, and punished to accept and internalize certain roles and not others during the process of socialization. This process will be discussed at length in Chapter 3. Here, it is sufficient to understand that the concept "role" centers on two fundamental phenomena: (1) roles are defined more or less precisely by society and presumed to apply to all individuals in a given category (e.g., all people who sign up to take a course are expected to accept the prescribed role of student), and (2) roles are more or less well-learned responses by individuals. The main implication of these two aspects of the definition of "role" is that specific role definitions are subject to change over time and space. The expectations centered around the role of student in our society today differ in significant ways from those associated with that role here 100 years ago, or in China today, or, probably, at some future date in America. Also, it should be noted that roles are *more or less* well defined. They vary on at least two continua: they may be more or less precise in the expectations they prescribe, and the number of such expectations may be many or few. Moreover, individuals vary according to the extent to which they learn or internalize their roles. The more completely they do so, the more conformist they are.

The term "role" usually refers to relatively specific expectations and situations. Thus people are said to play many roles (e.g., student, worker, son or daughter, spouse, friend, lover). Strictly speaking, gender roles are not single roles. Rather, the use of the concept "gender roles" implies that a number of specific roles tend to cluster together, depending on whether the individual is male or female. Moreover, a variety of personal traits also tends to attach to one or the other cluster. In short, the term "gender roles" is somewhat of a misnomer. Nonetheless, the concept is valuable in an attempt to understand why and how males usually come to be more or less masculine, and females come to be more or less feminine. Therefore, in the absence of a better term, the concept "gender roles" will be used to convey the sociocultural components that are typically associated with each sex.

It should be clear that when the terms "masculine" and "feminine" are used, it is assumed that the characterics in question are socially prescribed and individually learned, and hence changeable, phenomena; they are not innate to the organism. Since they are not innate, they cannot be directly related to sex in any necessary fashion. Thus, if passivity is considered part of femininity, as opposed to femaleness, it is conceived as learned and, therefore, potentially unlearnable.

The points of view expressed at the beginning of the chapter by the physician and the social scientist might be reconceptualized to a question: Where does sex leave off and gender role begin? Are some behavioral and temperamental differences innate to the two sexes, or are they all aspects of gender role? The argument in the pages to follow will be this: Given present evidence, no precise line between organism and environment, sex and gender, can be drawn. However, the burden of proof rests with those who would argue for the innate quality of virtually any behavioral, attitudinal, emotional, or intellectual trait.

The term "instinct," when used in reference to humans, has long been in disrepute among students of human behavior. Indeed, many are reluctant to apply the term to any of the higher primates. Instead, terms such as "need disposition," "behavior tendencies," and so on are currently employed. This is not merely a matter of semantics. According to a dictionary's primary definition of an instinct, it is "an inborn tendency to behave in a way characteristic of a species; natural, unacquired mode of response to stimuli. . . ." Conceptually, an instinct can be viewed as a behavioral pattern programmed into the genetic structure of a species, much as a computer is programmed to respond in given ways to particular stimuli. There is virtually no important *adult* human behavior that is so programmed. Sucking, on the part of an infant, probably is; the mode of acquisition, preparation, and consumption of food by human adults certainly is not. Sexual behavior patterns among monkeys, apes, and humans are learned, not innate, behaviors. Where in human behavior do we find a counterpart of the elaborate and, within species, identical, mating rituals of many birds? Or the work patterns innate to the ant or bee?

Humans can survive so well in a wide variety of environments and under conditions of drastic change precisely because they lack such rigidly patterned responses; they are a highly adaptable species. It is imperative that humans eat, drink, reproduce, and so forth, but the ways in which they go about doing these things are culturally developed and transmitted, and they vary tremendously from one culture to another. Humans are provided with a diffuse sexuality, but there is no innate mechanism that specifies the appropriate sexual partner, not to mention the form of sexual behavior. The history of the ways in which human mothers have treated their children seems to present ample evidence that there is no such thing as a "maternal instinct." Moreover, "needs," unlike "instincts," can with a very few exceptions (e.g., nutritive and eliminative needs) be ignored, unfulfilled, or sublimated by individuals, and, although there will always be some sort of psychic and/or physical "cost" involved in ignoring them, it will not normally destroy the organism.

The question, then, isn't whether males and females are innately different at the instinctual level—whether males are instinctively "aggressive" and females innately "passive" or "maternal." A more sophisticated approach considers whether the two sexes are equipped with divergent need dispositions which could be ignored or culturally mitigated. Not only is the evidence on this issue obscure, but it is very difficult to devise methods of study that yield the kind of data necessary to answer such questions with any degree of surety. Humans are brought up by other humans, and after a very short period of time it is virtually impossible to separate the learned from any unlearned components of the behavior of an individual. However, on the basis of cross-cultural and even cross-species studies, some individuals have tried to distinguish sex and gender role components. A few of these formulations will be considered in the following section.

Speculations on Need Dispositions

Social theorists have often grounded their work in certain assumed innate tendencies common to humans. In Marx's assumption of a "species being" by which humans must be creative in their labor to be fully human, W.I. Thomas's "four wishes" of new experience, security, recognition and response, or even Pareto's "residues," to mention but a few, there is a common theme: humans do not come to the world with a complete *tabula rasa.*

Although the majority of social scientists in the past half century or so have tended to deny in practice virtually any influence other than "environment" on the development of the individual, only a second of thought would show such an approach to be preposterous. The human species represents no radical break in the evolutionary chain; it is not a species apart. Humans have some attributes that are more highly developed than other species (e.g., brains), and others that are less so (e.g., sense of smell). But all aspects of the human body are distinctly related to other species, particularly, of course, other primates. It is also clear that many animals, including most primates, have some sort of rudimentary "culture" in the sense that they learn certain behavior patterns from other members of their communities. Moreover, it is obvious that most, if not all, species do in fact possess certain innate behavioral tendencies, whether instinctual or less rigidly patterned. To assume that there are no remnants of such tendencies in *Homo sapiens* is simply anthropocentric. But even if we are more humble in our approach, the virtually unanswerable questions remain: What is the nature of these behavioral tendencies in humans? How strong are they? And, for the present text, the crucial question: Do they vary within the species by sex?

Margaret Mead: Tweedle Dee and Tweedle Dum

Margaret Mead has been directly and indirectly concerned with such questions for over 35 years. Indeed, the vacillations of her ideas have been a pretty accurate gauge of public opinion on the "woman question" during this period. For this reason, she is amply discussed and lampooned by many "feminist" authors (Bird, 1968, p. 176; Friedan, 1963, chap. 6). But for a long time she was also one of the few scholars to devote much attention to trying to cope with these issues. Her two most important works for the present purposes are *Sex and Temperament in Three Primitive Societies,* published originally in 1935, and *Male and Female,* which appeared nearly 15 years later. Her more recent views have been presented in a variety of speeches, interviews, and articles in popular magazines.

The overriding impression gained from her study of three "primitive societies" in New Guinea (Mead, 1935/1969) is one of virtually total cultural conditioning of human "temperament." In two of three cultures males and females do not seem to differ in temperament, while strong sex-linked behavior patterns are evident in the third. Division of labor along gender lines is evident in all three. Mead argues that individuals differ innately in temperament along a continuum. A given culture takes only one or two parts of that continuum and makes it the norm for one or both sexes, condemning those who fall elsewhere on it to life as a deviant. However, sex is not relevant to one's place on the continuum, and, thus, members of both sexes may find themselves deviant in any given society. The same individuals, of course, would not necessarily be deviant in another culture.

The general nature of the similarities and differences between the genders in these three cultures comes as a shock to those who assume the Western pattern to be "natural" and somehow inviolate. At the risk of distortion, the simplest way of characterizing the genders in these cultures is as follows: among the Arapesh, both genders resemble our stereotypical contemporary femininity; among the Mundugamor, they both appear to approximate our norm of masculinity; and finally, among the Tchambuli, the females are "masculine," the males "feminine."

The Arapesh of both sexes are peaceful, cooperative, and passive, overwhelmingly concerned with "growing" things and people. Males as well as females are said to "bear children." Long before the actual birth of a child, the fetus is believed to grow and develop during the first several weeks only by the continual participation of the father in adding his sperm to mix with the mother's blood, thus producing the individual in the womb. Postnatal rituals pertaining to the growth and development of the infant also involve the father as intimately as the mother.

The Arapesh male's "maternal" behavior doesn't begin with the fathering of a child. While still little more than a boy, after his initiation, he receives a young girl as a bride. His task is then to "grow" her— namely, feed her, protect her, and train her. Eventually they engage in sexual intercourse when both are ready, and they thus are married. His authority over her then is no more or less than that of a parent over the child it has nurtured. Where this arrangement breaks down due to premature death of one of the partners or for some other reason, a later marriage is never really successful, because the husband has not "grown" his wife and, therefore, has no truly legitimate claim to her.

Mead makes it clear that barring a few exceptions who find themselves truly outcast, both male and female Arapesh "are neither strongly nor aggressively sexed . . ." (p. 157). Even the role of authority figure is so repugnant to the Arapesh that they have institutionalized ways of selecting an individual male and, from childhood, training him to be more aggressive. He is more pitied than envied by those whom he will eventually lead.

The formerly cannibalistic Mundugamor present a picture that is almost diametrically opposed to the Arapesh. Mead summarizes the Mundugamor ideal of character as "identical for the two sexes; . . . both men and women are expected to be violent, competitive, aggressively sexed, jealous, and ready to see and avenge insult, delighting in display, in action, in fighting" (1969, p. 213).

The family structure of the Mundugamor is such that intense animosity between husband and wife, father and son, mother and daughter, same-sexed siblings, and co-wives is institutionalized. Moreover, the hostility, distrust, and aggressiveness formalized in the family structure extend outward and pervade the entire community, giving it a highly competitive and even violent atmosphere. The Mundugamor are well prepared for this by their early childhood. Pregnancy is viewed by both the future parents as a disaster, and the future mother is ignored by her husband, who often uses this opportunity to find a new wife. When the infant arrives, the father is prepared to virtually hate a male; similarly, the mother will despise a female. Moreover, the mother is less than attached to the idea of being mother at all. She rarely comforts the child or has warm bodily contact with it (unlike the Arapesh); she suckles it as little as possible and then weans it early and abruptly.

Very little attention is given to the third tribe of this study, the Tchambuli. The image of the two genders that emerges, however, is one of differentiation along lines essentially opposite to our own. Artistic ability, petty jealousy, sensitivity, nervousness, and emotional dependence are descriptive of the males. The females are casual but efficient and competent, virtually running all necessary domestic and economic functions. They have *de facto* control of the important real property, in spite of the existence of formally patrilineal institutions. Moreover, it is the female who plays the role of sexual aggressor; the male "holds his breath and hopes . . ."; he is "not so urgently sexed" as the female (pp. 241-42).

From these findings Mead concludes that

> . . . many, if not all, of the personality traits which we have called masculine or feminine are as lightly linked to sex as are the clothing, the manners, and the form of head-dress that a society at a given period assigns to either sex . . . the evidence is overwhelmingly in favor of the strength of social conditioning (1969, p. 260).

About 15 years later, in 1949, Mead came to somewhat different conclusions. In *Male and Female* (1949/1970), she reviews her work on four tribes in addition to the three discussed above, paying particular attention to comparisons and contrasts to gender roles in then-contemporary America. In this long, rambling, and often contradictory work, psychoanalytic thought (which will be discussed later) is influential. Mead is now concerned to show how basically different bodies and reproductive functions *must* affect other aspects of the personalities (temperaments) of the two sexes. Here she talks about "the different gifts of each sex" and the "special superiorities" of each. She is not convincing. Nowhere does she present serious cross-cultural evidence that any *particular* personality trait is necessarily sex linked.

Mead's arguments pertaining to females seem to rest on the invalid assumption that mothers must do the child rearing. Given the present state of science, all children must be borne by females, but raising children is certainly not a sex-linked function by biological necessity. Other than breast feeding, females are no better equipped to raise children than males. Mead argues from the basis of this fallacious assumption that women have a "special superiority in those human sciences which involve that type of understanding which until it is analyzed is called intuition." (We all "know" from folk culture that women are "naturally intuitive"!) The point is, whoever actually raises a child probably becomes more "intuitive," "sensitive," "humane" and so forth in the process. But anatomy does not dictate that it be the female who does the child raising, society does, and especially today when so few women nurse their young for very long, if at all.

Mead's discussion of males gives further evidence of her essentially nonbiological assumptions. She assumes that because men are not tied to the act of reproduction in anything but a very passing manner, they must "compensate" by being creative in everything else. Doubtless there is an element of veracity to this reasoning; "womb envy" will be a topic of further comment. It is a desire to be *creative* that is here basic to the organism, however, and presumably this is a *human* characteristic, not a male one. Many, but by no means all, females are able to fulfill this need via motherhood, especially in cultures that define motherhood as creative. Presumably, however, those females who, for whatever reason, do not procreate are as competent and creative as males in everything else but reproduction.

Mead is also concerned with ensuring male sexual desire. Her argument is that sexual intercourse and hence reproduction of the species does not require sexual desire on the part of the female, while, for obvious anatomical reasons, it does for the male. Therefore, anything that systematically reduces male sexuality is to be avoided. The question to be asked of Mead is: What kinds of things destroy male sexual desire in otherwise "normal" heterosexuals? The answer is that essentially anything that males perceive as threatening to their *masculinity* tends to have that effect. As discussed earlier, masculinity, as a gender role term, is defined by a given culture and thus is subject to change. In short, I suggest that concern for male sexual desire indicates support for the gender role status quo. Since any systematic deviation from gender role definitions, particularly by females, will often be perceived by males as a "threat" to masculinity and may result in impotency, Mead's orientation necessarily sees such deviations as "bad." This is a crucial point and one worth exploring a little further.

Assume for now that we really are concerned with ensuring human reproductivity (which might seem questionable at this point in history), or at least with heterosexual sexuality. Obviously, males must achieve and sustain erections to accomplish sexual intercourse; no such limitation is placed on the ability of the female to function as a sexual partner—at least minimally. The literature on male impotence is vast, but most of it is medical or psychological. The problem here is sociological. We are not concerned with why one man may be impotent, but with cases where impotence may be widespread in a society. In an era of changing gender roles, especially for females, is it not conceivable that widespread male impotence will result? Certainly it is, in the short run. If, for instance, millions of females become the primary source of income, when masculinity has heretofore been defined as provider and femininity as homebody, then their male mates and co-workers may find themselves similarly threatened and similarly impaired sexually. Whether or not this has in fact occurred recently in our society is a moot question, but the issue involved is important.

The problem is the confusion of sex and gender role by society. The only 100 percent sure component of maleness in all societies is male sexuality, that is, sexual satisfaction via erection of the penis and subsequent ejaculation. When other components are added to the definition of masculinity, the potential for trouble begins. (This same logic also applies to the feminine role.) Thus, for instance, in our society the artistic or sensitive male, the male who adores children and would like to teach kindergarten or stay home and raise his own, the male who has a mate in a higher status and better paid job than his (to mention but a few) begins to wonder about his essential maleness. He doesn't ask whether he deviates from "society's arbitrary norms," but rather whether he deviates from "nature's rules." He has confused society's (temporary) definition of masculinity with the essentially unchangeable reality of his maleness. His ability to function as a male thus suffers—unnecessarily. It is only when we sort things out and separate sex from gender role that the latter can change without affecting the functioning of the former.

Judging by the evidence presented by Mead in the two works considered here, the conclusions of the second can be all but ignored. The impression remains that although "temperaments" vary between individuals and different cultures institutionalize vastly different "ideal temperaments" for each or both sexes, there is no innate core temperament that can be attributed to one sex as against the other. Mead, the *cultural* anthropologist, remains just that.

Sigmund Freud: Biology Is Destiny—Almost*

No chapter concerning gender roles could ignore Sigmund Freud's theories of psychosexual development. His contributions to the study and understanding of human sexuality have had a profound impact on 20th-century Western thought. Many of Freud's concepts and principles are currently accepted as generalized knowledge, and his theories and vocabulary have found their way into the popular idiom. Unfortunately, such popularization can reduce theory to slogans, and the initial concepts become subject to severe distortions. Partly because of such distortions and partly on the basis of their own merits, Freud's ideas have been subject to angry rejection by many feminists, as will be reviewed more fully in Chapter 3. Here the discussion will be confined to trying to understand Freud's own notions of the relationship of biology to culture in psychosexual development.

Freud was a Victorian living in a Victorian age, and he displayed the paternalistic and authoritarian qualities characteristic of the role of the physician. That these personal qualities should be reflected in his writings is to be expected. However, his writings covered a period of over four decades during which he wrote prolifically, frequently reconceptualizing, reordering, and discarding earlier concepts which he felt did not hold up under scrutiny. In that vast corpus of writing,

*This section was written with the late Dr. Allyn Zanger.

statements may be found to support virtually any point of view on the subject at hand. It is impossible to follow here the development of Freudian thinking in any detail, but an effort will be made to highlight basic concepts as they relate to an understanding of sex and gender role. Brenner (1957), Jones (1961), Lidz (1968), and Waeldner (1964) give greater detail. Freud's own article "Three Contributions to the Theory of Sex" (1938) is the basis for part of the following discussion.

Freud postulated the existence of drives or "libido" which, when operative, produce a state of tension which impels the individual to activity. The activity itself is mediated by experience, learned behavior, and reflection. It is not predetermined. He conceived of drives as possessing three major components: a source, an aim, and an object. The source was conceived of as biological in nature; the aim as tension reduction; the object as the product of learned or environmentally determined experiences. Thus sex as a drive impels an individual to seek gratification through some sort of sexual activity. The plasticity of the object of the drives is important in understanding the readiness with which objects can be substituted for one another in the event that the original object becomes associated with anxiety. The object of the sexual drive may be a heterosexual object, a homosexual object, an inanimate object (as in fetishism), or any other kind of object which the individual has learned through his or her unique life experiences to regard as nonthreatening and gratifying. It is clear from Freud's writings, however, that all these responses are not equally "normal" and "healthy," thus implying more emphasis on biological than cultural components. At any rate, Freud tried to maintain the position that *both* constitutional or biological factors and experiential or cultural factors interact dynamically to produce behavior, "normal" as well as "neurotic."

Biological maturation unfolds from conception in a largely predetermined manner that is species specific. The sequence of maturation is a given, but it is somewhat variable in terms of individual differences and the impact of the family as representative of the cultural environment. Paralleling physiological maturation is psychosexual development, which is the emotional and mental aspect of personality as it is shaped by the interaction of biology and culture. The cultural element is conceived by Freud in narrow terms—namely, the family. In the course of development from infancy to adulthood the sexual activities motivated by drives change according to an inborn biological schedule, culminating in "mature" sexual needs that are normally characterized by heterosexuality. However, the evolution of sexuality is heavily influenced by parental inputs at every stage of development.

Freud conceived of sexual development as following approximately this scheme: (1) the three stages in early childhood, oral, anal, and genital, culminating in the Oedipus (including Electra) complex; (2) a latency period, namely a brief prepubertal stage evidencing a revival of oral and anal strivings; (3) puberty, and (4) a genital stage characteristic of adult sexuality. It is the prelatency stages that, in Freudian thinking, are crucial for determining adult behaviors.

In the first two stages of early childhood psychosexual development (oral and anal) there is no differentiation of the sexes, although genetic and hormonal influences may predispose the child at birth to basic patterns of passivity or activity which enter into the subsequent development of male or female gender role characteristics. At approximately three years of age the child begins the third and most important stage, the genital, having reached a stage of physiological development where erogenous gratification is clearly focused in the genital area. With the biological sensitization of the genitals, children develop a keen interest in their anatomy and begin to substitute genital masturbation for thumb sucking and to manifest curiosity around differences in sexual anatomy. These stages comprise the biological component in Freud's thinking.

Within the family parents find that the child is no longer asexual but a relatively uninhibited creature with clear sexual qualities. They generally can no longer relate to the child as a neuter but begin thinking of it as either a boy or a girl, and the "cultural" element enters the picture. Until this point, Freud thinks the psychosexual development of boys and girls is identical. Recent research indicates he was incorrect in this, a matter to be discussed more fully in Chapter 3.

According to Freud, the "Oedipus complex" arises out of the wish or expectation of the child that the mother, who has always gratified needs in the past, will also gratify these new drives in some fashion. The crucial variable is how both parents respond to this new development. Generally, the child soon becomes aware that parents do not respond with delighted enthusiasm to sexual overtures. Depending upon the quality of parental responses on the one hand and the primitive state of the child's cognitive development on the other, a boy will generally develop a fear that the parents will deprive him of the sexual organ which he now so highly prizes. This is "castration anxiety," according to Freudian theory, which helps to inhibit conscious expression of incestuous fantasies. At the same time, the boy begins to identify with the gender role of his father in an effort to emulate this person who possesses both the "bigger and better" penis and the object of the child's fantasies, namely, the mother. Such gender role identification elicits approval and thus reinforces the learning.

The girl (like the boy) receives gratification through masturbatory activities, becomes sexually curious, and so forth. Physiologically, it is the clitoris that is the area of greatest excitability. There is a tendency to compare herself unfavorably with the more obvious appendage of the boy. Children, at least in Western culture, have already assimilated a "bigger means better" mentality at that age—the essence of the Freudian concept of "penis envy." It is also quite likely that little girls associate the greater power and privilege of males with this obvious characteristic of maleness and thus envy the possessor of a penis and wish for one of their own. Freudian theory presents a tortuous scheme in an effort to describe the girl's shift of love object from mother to father, while yet retaining an identification with the mother. In essence, Freud said the girl renounces the mother for having deprived her of a penis and turns her interest to the father in a fantasy of possessing the father's penis. This is the "Electra complex." It is only when she later substitutes a desire for a (male) baby for the desire for a penis that she will have reached true "maturity" and, of course, mental "normalcy."

Freud repeatedly referred to the rather defective development of the superego (conscience) in females and its lack of stability, apparently convinced that women lacked the most important incentive for superego formation, namely, the castration fear. This was based on his observations that the girl does not usually repress her desire for the father as completely as the boy represses his erotic feelings for his mother. This deficit in superego development is supposedly reflected in the female's lack of a sense of social justice and in her narcissism. A feminine identity, Freud claimed, is established only when the wish for a penis is replaced by the wish for a child, which is directly related to female masochism, and when clitoral orgasm is renounced for vaginal orgasm (a nonsensical dichotomy, according to modern medical science). In many of Freud's writings activity is associated with masculinity and passivity with femininity, with frequent blurring of the distinction between sex and gender role. As a consequence of his biological orientation, it was never clarified whether these "feminine" qualities are biologically or culturally determined.

Freud did not consistently postulate radically different innate biological qualities for males and females, although many of his concepts were sufficiently ambiguous to leave that possibility open, and many of his followers have so interpreted them. Rather, he concentrated on the dynamic interplay between biological development and the reactions of those closest to the growing child, its parents. A critical analysis of his approach and those of the army of his followers will be left for a later section of this book.

Lionel Tiger: The Bond That Ties

One of the more contemporary targets for the wrath of feminists is Lionel Tiger's book *Men in Groups* (1970). In an impressive tour de force Tiger, another anthropologist, cites evidence from a large variety of social scientific and biological sources to support his basic contention that there is an innate, biological propensity for human males to "bond." Moreover, he argues that this bonding, resulting as it does in cohesive, all-male groups, is vitally linked to male dominance and political power.

Ethologists (students of nonhuman animal behavior) have produced a veritable outpouring of research papers in recent years. Much of their discussion has centered around two related phenomena, territoriality and status hierarchies within nonhuman communities. Beginning with Robert Ardrey's *The Territorial Imperative* (1966), some efforts have been made to generalize the findings of ethology to the human species. In Ardrey's book this was done primarily by analogy, and the resulting argument is weak and unconvincing. Tiger has presented a more cogent argument based on studies of various human groups and communities, as well as ethological evidence.

Tiger begins his analysis with the argument that Homo sapiens evolved as a basically hunting species which, given limited biological equipment, pursued game in groups. Since the rigors of childbirth and rearing preoccupied the female, these hunting groups were all male. The female who did pursue the hunt was less likely to pass on her genes since there was greater risk to her life, as well as to the lives of her young, than there was to her sisters who remained behind. Over time, Tiger argues, a nonerotic, male-male link parallel to and as important for the survival of the species as the male-female link developed and became biologically "programmed" into the genetic structure. Bonding became a general male genetic characteristic, he continues, because it would have resulted in a breeding advantage to individuals who had it. To the extent that bonded males were more efficient hunters and better able to protect their communities, they would be more successful in leaving offspring (Tiger, 1970, chap. 3). Given the lack of evidence substantiating the existence of an innate male-female "bond," I find it difficult to understand precisely what kind of mechanism Tiger might be referring to when he talks of male bonding. The concept appears quasi mystical.

Tiger has noted many ramifications of such male bonding. He claims that aggression "is directly a function and/or outgrowth of corporate male interaction" (p. 247). Aggression by a group of bonded males serves to strengthen in-group cohesion and cooperation, a general (i.e., not sex-linked) phenomenon long recognized by sociologists (Coser, 1964; Sumner, 1906/1959). There is also obvious stratification in male groups. Such groups, to be efficient for hunt, war or, in complex contemporary societies, economic, political, and religious enterprises, must be both cooperative and hierarchical; somebody needs to be more or less in charge, and others must be prepared to follow. According to Tiger, females are not found in positions of leadership because, given male bonding, they simply do not provide the "releasers" for followership behavior (pp. 96-97 and 258). In fact, he does not find women to be politically active in any context to any great extent, and he suggests that this may be because political activity rests on the basis of male groups and an innate, presumably male, territoriality.

Territoriality, a characteristic found in a number of animal species, consists of either individual (male) or community (both sexes, usually male-dominated) possession of a piece of real estate which is protected from invasion by other members of the same species. In the case of individual territoriality, a male, by virtue of the territory he holds, attracts one or more mates; he permits no other males access to his "turf." In communal territoriality, a groups holds a territory and defends it against invasion by other groups of the same species. In these species there is often a relatively elaborate status hierarchy, especially among mature males, with the breeding advantage going to the highest status males. Although most extant higher primate species do not seem to be territorial at all, Ardrey (1966) argues that Homo sapiens is. Moreover, although other species are either individually or communally territorial, Ardrey seems to suggest that humans may be both, with the home and the nation alike constituting territory to be defended. Tiger appears to accept tentatively Ardrey's unsubstantiated argument that Homo sapiens is innately territorial, and he links this to male bonding and male dominance of political activity.

The burden of Tiger's argument does not concern territoriality, however. It is best summarized in his own words:

> The hypothesis here is that in the most general political case, defense needs and those for social order are satisfied most effectively by soliciting subordinate or cooperative relationships with adult males. Thus, females of all ages and pre-adult males will seek subordinate relationships with adult males who will protect them when the group is attacked and who will enforce social order when internal disturbance occurs. . . . The hypothesis contains the proposition that the defenders and policemen must be males (1970, pp. 109-10).

From this it would seem that Golda Meir, Ella Grasso, Indira Gandhi, and other female leaders must be mistaken about their sex. Female subordination is nothing more or less than a fact of genetics, in this view. Of course, as an anthropologist Tiger cannot really accept such extreme conclusions. He pays due lip service to the strength of sociocultural phenomena and suggests that females may in fact function in ways perhaps more "natural" to males, given "explicit self-conscious provision of special facilities by a concerned, sensitive, and willing community" (p. 112).

The same logic applies to the occupational sphere, according to Tiger, in which there is virtually everywhere "an inverse relationship between the status of occupations and the participation of females" (p. 142). Moreover, "'Female' implies tasks involving specific interactions of a personal or quasi-personal kind [e.g., taking care of the family] while 'male' implies activities on a larger scale . . . with greater direct and active relevance for communal integrity and social dominance" (pp. 146-57). In arguing this Tiger ignores the fact that the greater physical strength of males could allow them to appropriate power and privilege, regardless of any quasi-mystical force such as bonding.

Most of the rest of *Men in Groups* is devoted to extensive documentation of the male bonding phenomenon as revealed in sports, secret societies, initiation rites, war, and so on. Tiger shows how males "court" other males and "validate" their maleness through interaction, often of an aggressive, even violent nature. Forms of communal female interaction and ceremony are virtually ignored. Tiger presents the reader with a large array of exemplary material, but nowhere does he make any pretense of really "testing" his hypothesis, let alone "proving" it. Moreover, research comparing male and female patterns of social participation fails to support Tiger's thesis (Booth, 1972).

George Gilder: Gender Roles or Social Suicide

Recently, and in a more popular, less scholarly vein, George Gilder has developed a thesis that relates almost all of the social ills of contemporary society to the decline of male dominance. His argument in *Sexual Suicide* (1973) is interesting inasmuch as it posits a view of the innate characteristics of males that is so negative that, if one took it seriously, the most logical conclusion to be drawn would be to advocate mass male infanticide! Indeed, if his view of males were propounded by a feminist, it would bring instant and vociferous charges of man-hating. Gilder's solution to the problem he poses is to resurrect clear distinctions between males and females which emphasize male dominance over females. Failure to do so, according to his view, will bring about mass violence and social chaos.

Gilder begins by expounding a Puritan ethic. He is deeply disturbed by every conceivable kind of change in American mores pertaining to both sexuality and gender roles. He bemoans pornography, *Playboy* magazine, homosexuality, decreasing birth rates, and increasing rates of "illegitimacy," "swinging," and "promiscuity." Indeed, all sexuality outside of marital sex, engaged in when procreation is at least a possible outcome, is regarded with disapproval.

Several basic assumptions concerning the sexes form the bases of his argument. First, he assumes the natural superiority of women because of their capacity to reproduce and suckle. He argues that these "powerful and fulfilling sexual experiences," which are of course precluded from men, make women more erotic and thereby give them a "primacy of the biological realm" (p. 15). Unlike males, females have a "clear and stable" identification arising from their biology; women can just relax and "be" (pp. 16 and 18). Men, on the other hand, are insecure and must constantly work at "becoming," at acquiring an identification.

Gilder goes on to assume that females control the sexuality of males, who must petition or bargain for sexuality. Thus, males are in an inferior position in sexual encounters (p. 22). Women's interest is "naturally" in the long-term involvements and cycles which supposedly result from their procreative functions. Thus, they grant men sexual experiences and progeny in return for male accommodation to long-term commitments and responsibilities. In short, predicated on these (dubious) assumptions about female sexuality, Gilder argues that women "domesticate" men.

"The crucial process of civilization," writes Gilder, "is the subordination of male sexual impulses and psychology to long-term horizons of female biology. . . . Modern society relies increasingly on predictable, regular, long-term human activities, corresponding to the female sexual patterns" (1970, p. 23). Males are assumed to possess innately a short-range perspective. They are inclined to sporadic flurries of activities, not to sustained, long-range planning and commitment. They are also innately disposed, it would seem, to violence, to a quick means of asserting their identity. When females cease to domesticate males—that is, when they fail to require faithful commitment to permanent marriage which produces offspring—males run amuck. They rape, steal, kill, abuse drug taking, and generally engage in antisocial, destructive behavior. They do not become integrated into a community or committed to steady work.

Male dominance over females in all contexts except the sexual one is necessary, according to Gilder, if men are to be motivated to give up their freedom for the domesticated life. A male who feels threatened by a female (as discussed earlier) often cannot perform sexually. If he cannot perform, he will not relinquish his freedom. If he remains free, he engages in antisocial behavior. Women's liberation, or any change in the feminine role, threatens men. Gilder's "logical" conclusion is that it therefore threatens the very fabric of civilized, orderly, social living. Indeed, this conclusion may well follow logically if we accept his very dubious assumptions about the primacy of biology in the life of females and the inherently antisocial nature of males. This is a new version of an ages-old stereotype which holds that women serve as the repository of morality and goodness, while men are self-serving and self-seeking. Gilder asks that females remain second-class citizens so that social chaos may be averted. An equally reasonable conclusion to be drawn from his premises is that males should be placed in concentration camps, if not made subject to extensive infanticide. Clearly, none of these "solutions" is palatable in a democratic society, but then it is highly unlikely that Gilder's assumptions are correct.

There are several contemporary authors who, in the process of attacking the Feminist Movement or changing gender roles, have used arguments which assume, to a greater or lesser extent, that biological differences between the sexes are crucial determinants of other noted differences. None are more credible than those discussed here. In this context, McCracken (1972), Decter (1972), and especially, Goldberg (1973) are relevant references.

Alternative Ideas on the Origin of Patriarchy

Tiger's and Gilder's biological explanations for male political and economic dominance constitute the sex-based approach to an analysis of gender-differentiated behavior. There is little question as to the existence of certain extraordinarily widespread regularities in the area of male dominance. Virtually everywhere there is division of labor by sex. The tasks assigned to females or males vary tremendously, so that what is masculine in one place and time is feminine in another, and vice versa (with a few possible exceptions). The division of labor is practically universal, however, and it seems to be related in almost all societies to the institution of patriarchy. The overwhelming majority of human societies about which we have any information have been patriarchal, at least to some extent. Even where cultures have been found to be matrilocal and/or matrilineal, in the definitions of male versus female tasks, the former are more prestigeful. Moreover, *final* authority for decision making seems virtually everywhere to be a male prerogative. There are some exceptions to this pattern, but they appear to be extremely limited in number.

The question is, why are prestige and authority nearly universally male prerogatives? Biology offers one set of explanations. An alternative explanation, while also based on biological considerations, concentrates more explicitly on sociocultural factors; this is the gender role approach. Any answer to this question must go back to the dawn of human development and therefore must be speculative. With this in mind, I offer the following conceptualization of the development of male dominance. It appears to make at least as much sense as Tiger's or Gilder's.

As humans evolved from their primate ancestors they lost many physical advantages. The prehensile tail that enables the monkey to scramble from tree to tree, safe from ground predators, disappeared; eyesight and hearing became markedly inferior to those of many mammals; protective fur coats and strong jaws and teeth were lost; and the size and strength characteristic of some higher primates were diminished. In short, humankind became the physically vulnerable creature called by Desmond Morris (1967) "the naked ape." All this was traded in for the apposite thumb and, most crucially, a markedly increased brain capacity.

Over the millenia, this vulnerable naked ape could only survive (not to mention thrive) by substantially increasing its brain capacity. The enlarged size of the skull necessary to contain the bigger brain presented a practical problem: How was such a skull to pass through the birth canal? One possible solution was for the pelvic region of the female to so broaden that she would be rendered virtually immobile throughout her life. But evolution followed another path: human infants were born in a relatively underdeveloped state. Thus, at birth the human brain is only 23 percent of its final adult size (Morris, 1967, p. 29). The extremely long dependence period of the human child is the result.

The consequence of this long-term dependency, however, was a different kind of immobility for the female. One need not postulate any maternal instinct to understand that the helpless child was primarily dependent on the mother, and only indirectly so on the father. As in all mammal species the infant lived on its mother's milk, and in humans this was true for a considerable period. Given almost constant pregnancies and biologically dependent children, females were often incapable of readily supplying themselves with the requisite food, shelter, and (especially) protection. In this connection, it is important to realize that Homo sapiens was evolving not in the lush jungles of its primitive herbivorous ancestors, but in the desolate savannas that were replacing them.

During the evolutionary process, another important biological change was occurring. In nonhuman species that reproduce sexually, the female of the species is sexually receptive only at certain periodic intervals, namely, during "heat." Perhaps because of the dependence of the human infant and thus of its mother, or perhaps for some other reasons, the human female evolved the capacity to receive sexually and enjoy a male at any time. The estrus cycle disappeared. Undoubtedly, this ability of humans of both sexes to enjoy sex at any time played an important role in the creation of relatively permanent mating bonds, a rare phenomenon among other species and absent in other primates. Essentially, then, the human family may have grown out of an exchange of sexual accessibility by females in return for provision of food, shelter, and protection by males (Morris, p. 54 ff.). This, in turn, would help to ensure the survival of the young during their long dependency. So far this approach offers little that Tiger would dispute. However, in her intriguing book *The Descent of Woman,* Elaine Morgan (1972) questioned this entire interpretation of human prehistory. She claims that neither sexuality nor economic dependence of females encouraged the creation of the mated pair in humans. In fact, many scholars note that females supplied the vast bulk of the total food supply by gathering fruits, nuts, roots, and so forth (Boulding, 1976). Moreover, in losing the estrus cycle, Morgan argues, human females lost much of their sexuality.

Assuming the more orthodox interpretation, the question arises how male dominance or patriarchy arose from the exchange of sexual accessibility for creature needs. By its very nature the exchange is somewhat unequal. Individual males (as well as females) could survive quite well without sex. Females with young, however, might not readily survive without male protectors. Thus, as Shulamith Firestone (1970, pp. 8-9) argues, a power differential is built into the human "biological family," whether that family is monogamous or structured in some other manner.

Without the reinforcing mechanisms of most cultures, this power differential might have remained negligible. Indeed, there seems to be good reason to believe that in the earliest societies females had a substantial amount of prestige and, perhaps, power (Gough, 1971, pp. 768-69). Many if not most major early deities were probably fertility goddesses. It is even likely that knowledge of the male's function in reproduction was lacking. After all, it is no mean intellectual feat to connect logically an act of sexual intercourse with some symptoms that appear a number of weeks later and a delivery occurring nine months after the fact!

It seems likely that to primitive humans the act of giving birth must have appeared to be a spectacularly mystical and creative phenomenon, although also quite frightening, as various taboos pertaining to postpartum and menstruating women in preliterate tribes attest. It is not at all farfetched to suggest that early males suffered acute "womb envy" (Stannard, 1970). It should be no cause of wonder that males, simultaneously frightened and strongly attracted by the birth process, attempted to appropriate virtually all other mystical, status-conferring, and culturally defined creative activity for themselves. They may have succeeded by default. It is from this "mass sublimation" that patriarchy, which was mildly inherent in the biological facts of life for the species, possibly gained a powerful grip. Cultural patterns were then established granting males, by virtue of their inability to bear children, all manner of rights and privileges, eventuating in the replacement of the fertility goddess by the male god of war and the hunt.

There is another possible explanation for the emergence of patriarchy which might supplement the one just described or might constitute an alternative explanation. The most primitive groups of humans just barely managed to accumulate enough necessities to enable group members to survive. Employing only the most simple technologies, they produced few surplus goods over and above minimal requirements (see Lenski, 1966). Under those conditions, private property was not likely to have existed. There would have been very little in the way of nonconsumable goods to be owned, not to mention to be passed on to heirs. With the development of technology came the creation of surplus goods which could be passed on from one generation to the next. Stated in another way, improved technology resulted in the institution of private property. Once private property existed, males would have wanted to know who their own offspring were in order to leave them their possessions. The only way males could be assured of knowing who their own children were was for females to be monogamous. Thus, males may have sought to dominate females in order to control their sexual behavior, thereby assuring that the paternity of children (heirs) would be known.

In fact, for a long time, even into the 19th century, Western patriarchal culture had produced a medical "science" convinced that the male carries a miniature but complete baby in his sperm, the female merely supplying an appropriate environment for its early development (Stannard, 1970, p. 28). The creativity of the reproductive act, having first been viewed (erroneously) as female, was made into an exclusively male function, with the resulting offspring being defined by law and custom as the father's possession. Thus to this day a legitimate child is an infant who bears its father's name. All infants have an identifiable mother; we only grant full status, however, to those whose paternity is well assured. As a friend quipped, "maternity is a fact, paternity only a rumor." Irrespective of the reason for the origin of patriarchy, once it was in existence, virtually every social and cultural institution was changed to support it.

The interesting possibility exists that even the size and strength differential between the sexes was, in origin, a culturally induced phenomenon. In many animal species the sexes are not differentiated by size or physical strength. Moreover, there are some human cultures where males and females are built about the same, such as the Balinese studied by Mead (1970, p. 106). It is conceivable that once patriarchy was instituted, culturally defined notions of beauty came to favor strength and large size in males, and weakness and petite structure in females. Such definitions of beauty, marvelously supportive of patriarchal social institutions, would lead to selective reproduction favoring small, weak females and big, strong males. This difference, then, would feed back and support male power and prestige.

Hormones, Chromosomes, and Behavior

No chapter considering the question of the extent to which male-female behavioral and psychological differences are innate or learned would be complete without a word about the possible effects of hormones. Three facts are clear in this respect: (1) males and females have different amounts of the various sex-related hormones in their systems, (2) sex hormones do enter the brain and affect its activity, and (3) research is inconclusive as to what the specific behavioral ramifications of nos. 1 and 2 might be. Judith Bardwick's *Psychology of Women* (1971, chap. 2) is a good source of information on this topic, as are Money and Ehrhardt (1972) and Barfield (1976).

Hormones are chemical substances secreted into the bloodstream by the endocrine glands. The primary male sex hormone is testosterone, one of a group of hormones known as androgens. Females secrete this hormone also, but in small amounts. In the female there are a number of important sex hormones, the release of each of which is related to the menstrual cycle. Two of the most important are estrogen and progesterone (which are also present in small amounts in males). The former is chiefly responsible for the development of female secondary sex characteristics and for preparing the uterus for ovulation and possible conception. The latter is important in maintaining a state of pregnancy and for signaling the end of the menstrual cycle if impregnation does not occur.

Right before menstruation the levels of both estrogen and progesterone are low. Given the repeated finding that most women experience premenstrual depression, irritability, fatigue, crying spells, hostility, anxiety, and so forth, regardless of their "normal" psychological state, it would appear that hormonal levels probably do influence the psyche. Specific reactions to the cycle vary according to the mental health of the individuals, but nearly all women seem to undergo substantial cyclical patterns of emotional variation. Moreover, the same psychological symptoms appear in most women at two other times when the estrogen and progesterone levels are low: during menopause and immediately after childbirth. Other findings cited by Bardwick reported "passive-receptive tendencies and a feeling of well-being correlated with progesterone production, and active heterosexual striving correlated with estrogen production" (1971, pp. 28-29). She also suggests that feelings of maternal nurturance toward infants are biologically grounded in the high levels of estrogen and progesterone present during pregnancy (pp. 33-35). It is, however, quite possible (especially in Western cultures) that females have been told since childhood that they can *expect* to experience these different mood swings during their cycles, during menopause, and after childbirth, and such information itself helps to create a self-fulfilling prophecy. If this is the case, cultures, not hormones, may create the emotional variation. This assertion is bolstered by the finding, reported by Ashton Barfield (1976, p. 88), that women in responsible jobs, who can't "afford" mood swings, are less likely than other females to report premenstrual symptoms.

The male has generally not been thought to undergo cyclic hormonal and related psychic changes, although recent research casts doubt on even this assumption. Estelle Ramey (1972) has presented evidence from a number of studies which suggest that males are also influenced by a hormone cycle of approximately 30 days which affects mood (see also Barfield, 1976, p. 87). At any rate, levels of testosterone definitely do vary among men, and it appears that there may possibly exist an important behavioral correlate of this variation. A study of a sample of prisoners (Kreuz & Rose, 1971) led to the following tentative conclusion: "The findings suggest that testosterone may be related to a history of assault, and to the occurrence of more violent or aggressive criminal behavior during childhood through adolescence" (p. 16). However, testosterone level did not appear to be related to adult behavior in this study. Bardwick offers some supporting evidence concerning the behavioral effects of male hormones on the behavior of rhesus monkeys. Baby female monkeys whose mothers had been injected with male hormones before giving birth "displayed much more 'rough and tumble' play than normal females and exhibited as much chasing behavior as males" (1971, p. 85). They also showed more aggressive behavior. Even more convincing is some research she cites with reference to humans: "If testosterone is administered to normal adult females we find that their . . . levels of physical activity and their general level of aggressiveness may increase to levels normally found in males" (p. 89).

Finally, a word should be added concerning sex chromosomes and behavior. The female of the species has her sex determined by the XX chromosome, the male by the XY. It has become common knowledge since Ashley Montagu wrote *The Natural Superiority of Women* in 1952 that because of the generally more important role of the larger X chromosome, of which females have two compared to only one for males, the latter are much more vulnerable to a wide variety of genetically transmitted disorders, such as hemophilia and color blindness (1952/1968, chap. 5). Montagu lists about 60 such disorders, 30 of which are "serious" (pp. 76-78). Males also die more frequently pre- and postnatally. But more important for our purposes are the recently emerging findings concerning those few males whose sex chromosomes are XYY. Preliminary studies seem to indicate that such men may be particularly prone to violence and aggressive behavior. Prison inmates seem to manifest this characteristic more frequently than a "normal" sample; one of the more notorious XYY's is mass murderer Richard Speck. These traits may, however, result from the psychological ramifications of the fact that such males are sterile and frequently somewhat abnormal in external sex-related characteristics. For an extremely detailed discussion of chromosomal abnormalities, see Money and Ehrhardt (1972).

The conclusions to be drawn from findings concerning hormones and chromosomes point once again to the need for keeping the biological component in mind when assessing human behavior—gender role or otherwise. On the basis of the research cited, there may be reason to say that males, or at least those with extra Y chromosomes or testosterone, have a greater inherent bent for aggressive, even violent behavior than females (which is not to deny the existence of these traits in the latter). Similarly, some aspects of maternal behavior, especially shortly after childbirth, may be innate to the female endocrine system.

One set of additional facts is relevant to this discussion. It seems evident that babies are born with somewhat differing "temperaments"— some are cranky, some pacific, and so forth. Most differences noted do not appear to be related to sex, but a few do. At birth it seems that, generally, females show greater motor passivity than males (i.e., they are less physically active), and they are more sensitive to a greater number of physical stimuli (Bardwick, 1971, p. 93; Lynn, 1972, p. 243; Barfield, 1976, pp. 73-75). Whether such differences are directly related to hormones, chromosomes, or something else has not been established, but surely they would tend to elicit different responses from parents and others in contact with the infant which might be expected to feed back, strengthening and reinforcing gender differences. Bardwick concludes:

> It is not, then, that children are born with a built-in set of responses that will determine their behaviors irrespective of environmental reactions. Nor is it true that children are 'tabula rasa,' or blank clay, destined to be molded solely by the imprint of a parental . . . hand. Predispositions to respond and to perceive similar stimuli may be significantly different between the sexes because of genetically determined differences that have their roots in physiology. The endocrine data and the infant animal and human studies lead to the assumption of general behavioral tendencies that are sex linked. . . . The behaviors of the organism, whether animal or human, will be responded to, rewarded, punished, or ignored in the process of socialization. I suggest that most cultures may be reinforcing behavior tendencies or predispositions *characteristic* of the sexes (1971, p. 95).

Heredity or Environment: Some Conclusions

During the course of this chapter a number of studies and hypotheses have been reviewed pertaining to the basic questions: What if anything inherently differentiates males and females? Are the only too obvious differences frequently noted no more than sociocultural whims? The answers to these questions are very little clearer now than they were at the outset; relevant research is highly inconclusive, while speculation abounds. In very general terms, however, it is possible to draw a few conclusions.

First, it is clear that the vast majority of the behavioral and psychological characteristics designated as masculine or feminine in any given culture are not innate to the sexes. If they were, the amount of cross-cultural variation noted by Mead, among others, would be virtually impossible to explain.

Second, the data pertaining to hormones, and chromosomes in particular, lead to the conclusion that some few innate tendencies probably do differ by sex. However, I think it is also safe to conclude, with Tiger, that sociocultural factors can be institutionalized to virtually obliterate the effects of any such innately different tendencies between the sexes. This is because such traits are not "instinctual" but, at most, predispositions to behave in certain ways, and they are therefore modifiable.

One other conclusion can be drawn. Whatever innate behavioral and psychological differences may exist between the sexes, they are a matter of degree, not kind. Males are not aggressive and females passive; if anything, males may be somewhat more *inclined* to aggressiveness than females. Similarly, females may be at times more inclined to nurturing behavior toward infants than males would be, although the latter presumably have some inclination in this direction as well. The issue of the nature and types of intergroup differences will be considered further in the next chapter.

These conclusions are best summarized in Bardwick's argument that most cultures reinforce those differences that may be inherent in the sexes. In effect, Freud's theories allow for much the same conclusion. It is my contention that such "reinforcement" is far and away the most important element in determining sex-linked behavior and psychology. Put simply, gender role is a much more crucial factor than sex.

References

Ardrey, Robert. *The Territorial Imperative.* New York: Delta Books, Dell Publishing Co., 1966.

Bardwick, Judith. *Psychology of Women: A Study of Bio-cultural Conflicts.* New York: Harper & Row, 1971.

Barfield, Ashton. "Biological Influences on Sex Differences in Behavior." In Michael Teitelbaum (ed.), *Sex Differences: Social and Biological Perspectives,* pp. 62-121. Garden City, N.Y.: Anchor Books, 1976.

Bird, Caroline. *Born Female: The High Cost of Keeping Women Down.* New York: David McKay Co., 1968.

Booth, Alan. "Sex and Social Participation." *American Sociological Review* 37 (April 1972): 183-93.

Boulding, Elise. "Familial Constraints on Women's Work Roles." *Signs* 1 (Spring 1976): 59-117.

Brenner, Charles. *An Elementary Textbook on Psychoanalysis.* Garden City, N.Y.: Doubleday & Co., 1957.

Coser, Lewis. *The Functions of Social Conflict.* Toronto, Canada: Free Press Paperback, 1964.

Decter, Midge. *The New Chastity and Other Arguments against Women's Liberation.* New York: Coward, McCann & Geoghegan, 1972.

Firestone, Shulamith. *The Dialectic of Sex.* New York: Bantam Books, 1970.

Freud, Sigmund. "Three Contributions to the Theory of Sex." In A. A. Brill (ed.), *The Basic Writings of Sigmund Freud,* pp. 553-632. New York: Random House, 1938.

Friedan, Betty. *The Feminine Mystique.* New York: Dell Publishing Co., 1963.

Gilder, George F. *Sexual Suicide.* New York: Quadrangle/The New York Times Book Co., 1973.

Goldberg, Steven. *The Inevitability of Patriarchy.* New York: William Morrow & Co., 1973.

Gough, Kathleen. "The Origin of the Family." *Journal of Marriage and the Family* 33 (November 1971): 760-70.

Jones, Ernest. *The Life and Work of Sigmund Freud.* Abridged and edited by Lionel Trilling and Steven Marcus. New York: Basic Books, 1961.

Kreuz, Leo, and Rose, Robert. "Assessment of Aggressive Behavior in a Young Animal Population." *Psychiatric Spectator* 7 (August 1971): 15-16.

Lenski, Gerhard. *Power and Privilege.* New York: McGraw-Hill Book Co., 1966.

Lidz, Theodore. *The Person.* New York: Basic Books, 1968.

Lynn, David B. "Determinants of Intellectual Growth in Women." *School Review* 80 (February 1972): 241-60.

McCracken, Robert. *Fallacies of Women's Liberation.* Boulder, Colo.: Shields Publishing Co., 1972.

Mead, Margaret: *Sex and Temperament in Three Primitive Societies.* New York: Dell Publishing Co., 1969; first published 1935.

Mead, Margaret. *Male and Female: A Study of the Sexes in a Changing World.* New York: Dell Publishing Co., 1970; first published 1949.

Money, John, and Ehrhardt, Anke. *Man and Woman, Boy and Girl.* Baltimore, Md.: Johns Hopkins University Press, 1972.

Montagu, Ashley. *The Natural Superiority of Women.* New York: P. F. Collier, 1968; first published 1952.

Morgan, Elaine. *The Descent of Woman.* New York: Stein & Day, 1972.

Morris, Desmond, *The Naked Ape.* New York: Dell Publishing Co., 1967.

Ramey, Estelle. "Men's Cycles." *Ms.,* Spring 1972, pp. 8-14.

Stannard, Una. "Adam's Rib, or the Woman Within." *Trans-Action* 8 (November-December 1970): pp. 24-35.

Sumner, William G. *Folkways.* New York: Dover Publications, 1959; first published 1906.

Tiger, Lionel. *Men in Groups.* New York: Vintage Books, Random House, 1970.

Waeldner, Robert. *Theories of Psychoanalysis.* New York: Schocken Books, 1964.

Chapter 2

Stereotypes and Their Costs

Human beings try to make sense out of their world by lumping together a variety of individual cases, labeling them, and then reacting to categories of phenomena. If they didn't do this, they might quite literally "blow their minds." It is certainly impossible for people to react to the myriad stimuli around them on an individual basis; their brains would overload and the circuits would burn out. Therefore they categorize phenomena on the basis of an outstanding attribute or a few salient features that a number of individual cases seem to have in common. Often they then proceed to react to the category rather than the individual phenomenon.

This process of prejudging or stereotyping is as true of reactions to other humans as it is of reactions to any other phenomenon. Particularly when we don't know people well, we tend to react to them on the basis of a small number of relatively obvious characteristics. Chief among these are probably sex, race (or ethnicity), dress (or life-style in general), occupation (or social class), and age. Up to a point, there is nothing the matter with this; indeed, we could hardly function socially without making some assumptions about people. Moreover, up to a point, stereotyping is "true." For whatever reasons, people who are similar on any one or more of those key characteristics *tend* to be similar in other ways as well. The problem arises when we take our categories too seriously; when we say that since females (blacks, old people, poor people, and so forth) tend to do so and so, a *particular* individual can be expected to do the same. It is worse yet when the characteristic is judged negatively by those doing the categorization. At this point, prejudgment becomes prejudice. When we behave toward an individual on the basis of that prejudice, we are guilty of discrimination.

In concrete terms, it is one thing to make the more or less factually accurate observation that most females in contemporary America are not ambitious for promotions entailing great amounts of authority and responsibility. It is quite another thing to say, on that basis alone, that Jane Doe doesn't want a promotion in her job. And it is inexcusable, in a society dedicated to equal opportunity for all, to then fail to promote Ms. Doe on that basis alone. An excellent detailed discussion of these distinctions is provided in Gordon Allport's classic work, *The Nature of Prejudice* (1958).

Categorical Differences

Allport (1958, p. 94 ff.) presents a useful fourfold distinction of types of categorical or intergroup differences. Two (or more) categories of people can differ in a given characteristic in these ways: (1) a J-curve of conformity behavior, (2) a rare-zero differential, (3) overlapping normal curves of distribution, and (4) a categorical differential. Most male-female differences are probably of the third type. The four categories are hypothetically illustrated in Figure 2.1.

The J-curve of conformity behavior occurs when practically all members of a group have a characteristic in common while a few do not. Thus, for instance, if most (say, 80 percent) young American males play football fairly regularly, 15 percent play it only occasionally, and 5 percent never do, a graph (frequency polygon) of this would resemble a J (Figure 2.1A). A J-curve shows that a particular attribute is highly characteristic of a specific population. It distinguishes one group from another when both do not behave in a like manner. Thus American females, relatively few of whom ever play football and almost none of whom play regularly, would not fit this curve.

The second type of difference is the rare-zero differential (Figure 2.1B). This occurs when a very small number in one group possesses a

FIGURE 2.1

FOUR TYPES OF CATEGORICAL DIFFERENCES*

A. J-curve depicting frequency of football playing among American males.

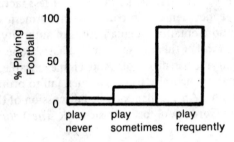

B. Rare-zero differential of hemophilia.

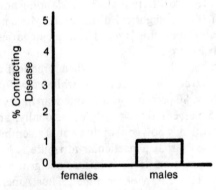

C. Overlapping normal curves of height distribution.

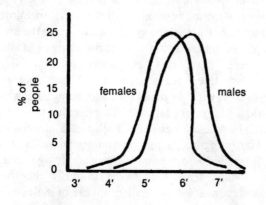

D. Categorical differential of suicide rates.

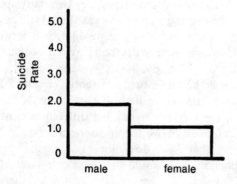

*All numbers are hypothetical.

given trait, but no one in the other group does. An example of this is the relatively rare disease hemophilia, which strikes only males (although females are carriers).

Probably the most common kind of difference between groups is that represented by overlapping normal curves (Figure 2.1C). The trait in question is distributed normally within each of two or more groups, but the arithmetic means of the various groups differ, as do the modes and medians. Examples of this are legion. Comparisons of height and weight between the sexes have this characteristic. "Passivity" and "aggressiveness" (whatever these may mean) are also probably distributed in this way, with the mean for males being somewhat lower on the former and higher on the latter than for females. Concretely, this means, in terms of aggressiveness, that both males and females vary between being highly aggressive and very unaggressive. However, the *group* average for males is somewhat higher, signifying that a greater number of males than females is found in the higher ranges of aggressiveness, and, conversely, a smaller number of males is found in the lower ranges. Nonetheless, a substantial number of females will be equally or more aggressive than a substantial number of males. How substantial this overlap is will depend on how far apart those group means fall and what the standard deviations are. Generally speaking, however, differences within one group (in this case a sex) will be greater than differences between groups; there is more difference between the most aggressive and least aggressive males than between most males and most females (see Brenton, 1966, pp. 48-50; Tresemer, 1975).

Allport's fourth type is the categorical differential (Figure 2.1D). In this case, the various groups compared all have some of the given characteristics (unlike the rare-zero type), but differences exist in the extent of the trait. It differs from overlapping normal curves by being a discontinuous variable; that is, it does not fit a normal curve. An example of such a phenomenon would be the suicide rates of males compared to that of females. Members of both groups kill themselves, but the rates differ.

Pinpointing and describing group differences and beliefs about them is a crucial first step in understanding how they arise, what they mean to members of the different categories, and how they are sustained. This chapter and the next will attempt to develop these understandings with reference to contemporary American gender roles.

Contemporary American Gender Role Stereotypes

Americans routinely employ a very telling term to refer to the sex which is not their own: "opposite." This term succinctly conveys the common view that to be masculine means to be not feminine, and vice versa. This fact alone gives tremendous insight into the gender role stereotypes that have long been characteristic of American culture. The number of traits on which males and females are said to differ is legion, but almost all are conceptualized as opposing dualities.

Recent research clearly demonstrates that the stereotyped approach, which conceptualizes masculinity and femininity as opposite poles, is simple-minded and inaccurate as a description of real people. In a famous series of studies, Sandra Bem (1974, 1975, 1977; Bem & Lenney, 1976) developed a "sex role inventory" (the BSRI) and applied it to numerous people. She found that "about 50 percent of the students [studied] are 'appropriately' sex-typed, about 35 percent are an-drogynous [mix traits from both genders], and about 15 percent are 'cross' sex-typed" (1977, p. 323). Thus, more than one third of her subjects had mixed traits which, according to the stereotype, are unmixably opposed to one another. Indeed, as Ann Constantinople (1973) has argued, masculinity and femininity are not even end points on a single continuum on which some or many people would fall at points in between. They are, rather, at least two entirely separate continua. This means that someone could be simultaneously very masculine *and* very feminine or, conversely, low on each characteristic, as well as having any other mixture of scores.

Despite the research evidence which demonstrates that the stereotypes are, for perhaps half or more of all people, descriptively inaccurate, these stereotypes do exist and do influence people's feelings and perceptions of self and others. What, then, are the components of the two gender role stereotypes? Table 2.1 lists a large number of such traits subdivided into six general types, plus a residual "other personal characteristics" category. This list grew out of the work done in 1971 by 13 small groups (five to six people per group) of students of both sexes who discussed the question: "What kinds of words and phrases do you think *most Americans* use to characterize males compared to females, or 'masculinity' versus 'femininity'?" In the years since 1971 no doubt the stereotypes have been altered somewhat, but in the main I think this list is still an accurate statement of cultural expectations.

TABLE 2.1

GENDER ROLE STEREOTYPE TRAITS

Characteristics	Masculine Traits	Feminine Traits
I. Physical	Virile, athletic, strong* Sloppy, worry less about appearance and aging Brave	Weak, helpless, dainty, nonathletic* Worry about appearance and aging* Sensual Graceful
II. Functional	Breadwinner, provider*	Domestic* Maternal, involved with children* Church-going
III. Sexual	Sexually aggressive, experienced* Single status acceptable; male "caught" by spouse	Virginal, inexperienced; double standard* Must be married, female "catches" spouse Sexually passive, uninterested Responsible for birth control Seductive, flirtatious
IV. Emotional	Unemotional, stoic, don't cry*	Emotional, sentimental, romantic* Can cry Expressive Compassionate Nervous, insecure, fearful
V. Intellectual	Logical, intellectual, rational, objective, scientific* Practical Mechanical Public awareness, activity, contributor to society Dogmatic	Scatterbrained, frivolous, shallow, inconsistent, intuitive* Impractical Perceptive, sensitive "Arty" Idealistic, humanistic*
VI. Interpersonal	Leader, dominating* Disciplinarian* Independent, free, individualistic*	Petty, flirty, coy, gossipy, catty, sneaky, fickle* Dependent, overprotected, responsive*

GENDER ROLE STEREOTYPE TRAITS—Continued

Characteristics	Masculine Traits	Feminine Traits
	Demanding	Status conscious and competitive, refined, adept in social graces*
		Follower, subservient, submissive
VII. Other Personal	Aggressive*	Self-conscious, easily intimidated, modest, shy, sweet*
	Success oriented, ambitious*	Patient*
	Proud, egotistical, confident	Vain*
	Moral, trustworthy	Affectionate, gentle, tender, soft
	Decisive	Not aggressive, quiet, passive
	Competitive	Tardy
	Uninhibited, adventurous	Innocent
		Noncompetitive

*Attribute listed by five or more of the groups.

All attributes listed were mentioned by at least 2 of the 13 groups. Group members were specifically instructed to ignore their own particular impressions, if possible, since they were assumed to be somewhat more sophisticated on the subject than "most Americans." The sample taking part was anything but random. First, the students had recruited themselves into a course entitled "Sociology of Sex Roles" given at a small, private university. They were overwhelmingly white, although there were a few blacks and Mexican-Americans. They were mostly middle to upper-middle class in family background, and about two thirds to three quarters were female. Finally, since the school is located in Texas, some regional biases were probably present. A somewhat less biased sample of graduate social work students at another Texas university arrived at almost the same stereotypes of masculinity and femininity when asked the same question, however. Moreover, the lists developed by other researchers and observers are very similar to this in the traits listed (see Williams & Bennett, 1975; Broverman et al., 1972; Heilbrun, 1976).

Given the biases of the sample, a number of interesting observations can still be made on the basis of this relatively comprehensive list of traits stereotypically assigned to the genders. The first of these is the manner in which some of these traits can be related to Allport's typology of categorical differences. Those words and phrases that were mentioned by at least five of the groups and had counterparts for both sexes are largely of the overlapping normal curves (ONC) variety, as shown in Table 2.2. This means that many, if not most, members of one sex will have at least some traits assigned stereotypically to the other. More precisely, a large proportion of each sex will have high levels or "scores" on variables assigned categorically (primarily as J-curves) in the popular imagination to the other sex. The potential confusion that

TABLE 2.2

TYPES OF CATEGORICAL DIFFERENCES BETWEEN
  SOME GENDER ROLE TRAITS

Masculine Traits	Feminine Traits	Categorical Difference Type
Athletic, strong	Weak, nonathletic	Overlapping normal curve (ONC) ONC
Worry less about appearance and aging	Worry about appearance and aging	ONC
Breadwinner	Domestic	Categorical difference
Sexually experienced	Virginal	Categorical difference
Unemotional, stoic	Emotional, sentimental	ONC
Logical, rational, objective, intellectual	Scatterbrained, inconsistent, intuitive	ONC
Leader, dominating	Follower, subservient	ONC
Independent, free	Dependent, overprotected	ONC
Aggressive	Passive	ONC
Success oriented, ambitious	Easily intimidated, shy	ONC

this can cause is obvious, as members of both sexes can be led to wonder "What's the matter with me? Why am I a 'masculine' female (or a 'feminine' male)?"

Making prejudgmental or stereotypical assertions about groups does not necessarily entail negative connotations. In the case of the gender role traits cited, however, a curious difference between the masculine and feminine lists is evident in this respect. In any language, words take on an emotional content over and above their definitions per se. This affective dimension is a function of prevailing cultural values. There are many more blatantly negative connotative words used to describe femininity than masculinity, and somewhat fewer positive terms. It must be recalled that one of the biases of the sample was overrepresentation of females. Among the words listed with reference to masculinity, only "sloppy" and "egotistical" are clearly negative in connotation in this society, and the former is trivial. "Proud," "ambitious," "aggressive," "dogmatic," and a few others are somewhat negative, depending on the context in which they are used and the values of the individuals using them. Consensus on the values represented by these terms is lacking. Large segments of our society would find these traits very agreeable, but substantial numbers would define them as disagreeable. Generally speaking, however, the words used to describe the masculine role are quite positive: "practical," "logical," "experienced," "brave," "adventuresome," "confident," "trustworthy," and so on.

The tone of the words used to describe femininity is considerably different. Such terms as "petty," "fickle," "coy," "sneaky," "status conscious," "frivolous," "shallow," and "vain" are very negatively charged in this society. The positively charged words are innocuous compared to their masculine counterparts. Females are said to be "idealistic, humanistic" rather than a "contributor to society"; "innocent" rather than "adventurous"; "patient" rather than "ambitious"; and "gentle, tender, soft" rather than "moral, trustworthy." Thus a general, if not too precise, impression emerges that the masculine gender role stereotype is a positive thing, and the feminine one either negative or passive. A basic dualism is, in fact, displayed toward the female, who is simultaneously held to be "sexually passive, uninterested" (the Virgin Mary image) and "seductive, flirtatious" (the wicked Eve tempting poor innocent Adam). This theme runs throughout the history of Western civilization, and our mores concerning "good" and "bad" females have no parallels for males. These findings concerning the more positive evaluation of masculine traits compared to feminine traits mirror those of other researchers (Broverman et al., 1972; Williams & Bennett, 1975). John Williams and Susan Bennett report that "of the 15 male evaluative adjectives 10 were scored 'favorable,' while 10 of the 15 female evaluative adjectives were scored 'unfavorable.'"

Other evidence exists that the gender role stereotypes depicted above are indeed held by Americans. I. K. Broverman et al. (1970) report that a study of 79 psychotherapists, 46 male and 33 female, revealed the following description of the "mentally healthy adult female": "submissive, emotional, easily influenced, sensitive to being hurt, excitable, conceited about appearance, dependent, not very adventurous, less competitive, unaggressive, and unobjective." Moreover, she "dislikes math and science." This description was generally agreed upon by both the male and female therapists. Clinicians have different standards of mental health for men, however. Indeed, their standards for a "healthy adult man" looked like those for a "healthy adult," but healthy women differed from both. In short, only men, not women, can be healthy adults and healthy in relation to their gender role at the same time!

Myron Brenton reviews common masculine stereotypes in a chapter in *The American Male* entitled "The Masculinity Trap" (1966, chap. 2). Some of the supposed masculine characteristics he discusses include "aggressive-sadism"; "violence"; a tendency to "stifle . . . intuition, tenderness, and sensitivity"; "stoicism"; "protectiveness" concerning females; a feeling that the financial burden is the male's alone; "mechanical ability"; "athletic prowess"; "courage" and "bravery." Similarly, Jerome Kagan and Howard Moss (1962) define the masculine role model in such terms as "sexually active," "athletic," "independent," "dominant," "courageous," and "competitive." Their feminine model includes the traits of "sexual timidity," "social anxiety," "fearing and avoiding problem situations," and "pursuing homemaking activities rather than career ones." In the introduction to their recent reader on males, *The Forty-Nine Percent Majority* (1976), Deborah David and Robert Brannon characterize the masculine man as one who never feels anxious, depressed, or vulnerable, never cries, is the tower of physical and emotional strength, is confident, determined, aggressive, tough, self-reliant, and, above all, not feminine. Thus, although some of the individual words differ, the general images of the two roles are quite consistent.

An exercise to show just how stereotyped our notions of the two sexes are involves taking some descriptive material pertaining to a member of one sex and systematically substituting the other sex in all references. Jennifer Macleod (1971) did this in an article "advising" new bridegrooms:

> Oh, lucky you! You are finally bridegroom to the woman of your dreams. But don't think for a minute that you can now relax and be assured automatically of marital happiness forever. You will have to *work at it*. While she may have eyes only for you *now,* remember that she is surrounded every day by attractive young men who are all too willing to tempt her away from you. And as the years go by, you will lose some of the handsome masculinity of youth. . . .

Macleod proceeds to state a number of specific recommendations for the husband to prevent the wife from being "tempted to stray," such as:

> . . . You should always be available to your wife whenever she wants you. It is of course your husbandly prerogative to say no, but you will be wise never to do so unless you are really ill, for that may tempt her to turn to other men. . . . She cannot do without sex. . . .
> . . . Now for a subject that may seem trivial: your appearance and dress. Don't overlook it. . . .
> Every woman likes to be proud of how attractive her husband is, so dress to please her. . . .

To reinforce the point (and also because these quotes are fun!), consider the following from a local newsletter for a women's liberation group in Albuquerque, New Mexico:

> Mr. Herb Dennish, an attractive young man of 27, spoke to the June meeting. . . . Mr. Dennish was informally attired in tan slacks and a navy blazer, with a lemon-yellow shirt. He wore a fashionably wide navy tie with yellow stripes centered by red pinstripes. His jewelry was all gold: watch, two sleeve buttons, a wide wedding band, and a class ring.
> Mr. Dennish spoke on the Model Cities program and the new Youth Opportunity program. He is the Assistant Model Cities Director. . . .
> Mr. Dennish is the husband of Janie Dennish, who has a doctorate fellowship. . . .

The gender role stereotypes reviewed are those most common in the dominant American culture. There is, however, some question as to the extent to which Americans who are other than white and middle class subscribe to the same stereotypes. Research on class and racial differences in this area is still very scanty. Betty Yorburg (1974) reports that, while all social classes learn the same stereotypes, "the more educated classes are less rigidly bound by these traditions" (p. 179). Members of the working class are more likely to endorse the concept of inequality of the sexes than members of the middle class (p. 180), as are first-generation Americans (i.e., immigrants) and migrants from rural areas (p. 181). However, black Americans have a less stereotyped concept of gender roles than do middle-class whites.

The Media and Gender Role Stereotypes

Perhaps the most generalized reflection of extant gender role stereotypes can be found in the mass communications media, which both reflect and reinforce various contemporary realities, including gender role definitions. These media include television, newspapers, magazines, movies, and popular music, among others.

In Chapter 2 of her classic *The Feminine Mystique,* Betty Friedan (1963) discussed findings from an analysis of women's magazines from the late thirties to 1960, especially *Redbook, McCall's,* and *Ladies' Home Journal.* She documented the rapid demise of "happily, proudly, adventurously, attractively career women" as heroines after World War II and their replacement by heroines with "Occupation: housewife." (The historical phenomenon involved here will be discussed in Chapter 6). During the fifties virtually all of the stories and articles centered around the housewife, who is told that in her role she is "expert in a dozen careers simultaneously," such as "business manager, cook, nurse, chauffeur, dressmaker, interior decorator, accountant, caterer, teacher, private secretary . . . [and] philanthropist" (p. 36). She is informed that "great men have great mothers," and warned that careers and higher education lead to "masculinization" and concomitant danger "to the home, the children dependent on it and to the ability of the woman as well as her husband to obtain sexual gratification" (p. 37). Typical titles of articles from this era were: "Femininity Begins at Home," "Have

Babies While You're Young," "How to Snare a Male," "Are You Training Your Daughter to Be a Wife?" "Why G.I.'s Prefer Those German Girls," "Really a Man's World, Politics," "How to Hold on to a Happy Marriage," "Don't Be Afraid to Marry Young," "Cooking to Me Is Poetry," and so on. Friedan notes that "by the end of 1949, only one out of three heroines in the women's magazines was a career woman— and she was shown in the act of renouncing her career and discovering that what she really wanted to be was a housewife." By 1958, Friedan could find no heroines "who had a career, a commitment to any work, art, profession, or mission in the world, other than 'Occupation: housewife.'" Moreover, "even the young unmarried heroines no longer worked except at snaring a husband" (p. 38).

Friedan goes on to state that the heroines get constantly younger "in looks, and a childlike kind of dependence." Their only vision of the future is to have more babies; the only "active growing figure in their world is the child" (p. 38). Their problems consist of how to get their allowances increased, how to fight those "devil" career women who threaten to steal their husbands, and, occasionally, how to squash their own dreams of independence and a life of their own (p. 40). "The end of the road," writes Friedan, "is the disappearance of the heroine altogether, as a separate self and the subject of her own story. The end of the road is togetherness, where the woman has no independent self . . .; she exists only for and through her husband and children" (p. 41).

Politics, national issues, science, and virtually every idea concerning the world beyond the family were absent from the only material that most females read, according to studies. Not surprisingly, where the magazine writers and editors of the preceding era were female, in the era of the "feminine mystique," as Friedan calls it, they were replaced by males (p. 47). A final, if subtle, insult, "the very size of their print is raised until it looks like a first-grade primer" (p. 58).

More recent studies of magazines tend to support Friedan's findings. In a brief study of fictional heroines in three women's magazines in 1957 and 1967, Margaret Lefkowitz (1972) found strong support of the "happy housewife" syndrome. She concluded that "changes in real-life American women" are not yet reflected in short-story heroines in women's magazines (p. 40). Lovelle Ray (1972) intensively studied four women's magazines and the men's magazine *Playboy* throughout the late sixties for their image of females and found considerably more diversity of role models than Friedan had earlier. These were mostly reflected in the nonfiction articles, in which females were portrayed in a variety of occupational fields. However, strong support for the traditional feminine stereotype was still obvious in all five magazines. Ironically, the supposed career-girl magazine *Cosmopolitan* was as guilty as the others or more so in its total emphasis on "catching a man" (pp. 47-53).

Dwayne Smith and Marc Matre (1975) studied romance and adventure magazines from the year 1973. They too found strong support for traditional gender role stereotypes in these working-class-oriented publications. Other studies of the content of magazines, newspapers, and TV conducted during the early 1970s demonstrated that, by and large, the mass media continued to present stereotyped portrayals of both sexes (Courtney & Whipple, 1974; O'Kelly & Bloomquist, 1976; Tedesco, 1974; Mills, 1974; Culley & Bennett, 1976). Indeed, especially on television, women were notable for their relative absence, especially in lead roles. A recent examination of the portrayal of women on television does show some change from the early seventies, when Mary Tyler Moore was one of the few women portrayed in a responsible job, to the midseventies, by which time the Bionic Woman, Charlie's Angels, and Police Woman had appeared. However, these women characters are usually controlled or helped by a male, and typically they "unmask the villain by accident or luck" rather than skill (Tarvis & Offir, 1977, p. 181).

The media of mass communications do appear to be gradually changing their portrayal of women, although the depictions offered of males usually remain stereotypic. However, the rate at which the image of women is changed seems to be considerably slower than the rate at which the reality of women's lives has been changing.

The stereotypes that are reflected so clearly in the media are reinforced and legitimized in a number of ways in our society, including the legal, religious, academic, scientific, linguistic, and medical realms. More detailed discussion of how gender role stereotypes are reinforced will be undertaken in Chapters 3 and 4. Some of the implications of gender role stereotypes for people pressured to conform to them are considered in the next section.

Some Individual Costs of Gender Role Conformity

It is probably true that very few individuals conform totally to their sex-relevant stereotypes. Roles of all kinds, as explained in Chapter 1, are sociocultural givens, but this is not to say that people play them in the same way. Indeed, individuals, like stage actors and actresses, interpret their roles and create innovations for their "parts." The fact remains that there is a "part" to be played, and it does strongly influence the actual "performance."

It is also important to recall that the precise definitions of gender role stereotypes vary within the broader culture by social class, region, race and ethnicity, and other subcultural categories. Thus, for instance, more than most other Americans, the various Spanish-speaking groups in this country (Mexican-American, Puerto Rican, Cuban) stress domesticity, passivity, and other stereotypical feminine traits, and dominance, aggressiveness, physical prowess, and other stereotypical masculine traits. Indeed, the masculine gender role for this group is generally described by reference to the highly stereotyped notion of *machismo*. In fact, a strong emphasis on masculine aggressiveness and dominance may be characteristic of most groups in the lower ranges of the socioeconomic ladder (McKinley, 1964, pp. 89, 93, 112; Yorburg, 1974). Conversely, due to historical conditions beyond its control, black America has had to rely heavily on the female as provider and, more often than in the rest of society, as head of the household. Thus, the feminine stereotype discussed above has traditionally been less a part of the cultural heritage of blacks than that of whites (Staples, 1970; Yorburg, 1974). It is also clear that, at least at the verbal level, both gender role stereotypes have historically been taken more seriously in Dixie than elsewhere (see Scott, 1970, especially chap. 1). Although today this difference is probably declining, along with most other regional differences, personal experience leads me to conclude that it nonetheless remains. The pioneer past of the Far West, where survival relied upon strong, productive, independent females as well as males, may have dampened the emphasis on some aspects of the traditional feminine stereotype in that area of the country.

Much research remains to be done by way of documenting differences in gender role stereotypes between various groups, but there is little doubt that such differences exist. It is important to note, however, that, with the exception of explicitly countercultural groups, such as the "hippies" of the 1960s, even among subcultures with relatively strong traditions of their own the cultural definitions of the dominant society exert substantial pressure toward conformity. Minorities—namely, all those who are not part of the socioculturally dominant white, northern European, Protestant, middle and upper classes—exist within a society that defines them to a greater or lesser extent as inferior. To some degree such definitions are internalized by many members of the various minority groups and accepted as valid, a phenomenon known in the literature on minority groups as racial or ethnic "self-hatred" (Adelson, 1958, pp. 486, 489; Allport, 1958, pp. 147-48; Frazier, 1957, pp. 217, 226; Simpson & Yinger, 1965, pp. 227-29).

To the extent that individual minority members engage in such group self-hatred, they are led to attempt, within the limits of opportunity and the resources allowed by the dominant group, to "live up to" the norms and roles of the dominant society. Given limited economic opportunities, the result is often a parody of the values and behaviors of the dominant society, as exemplified by the strong emphasis on aggression, sexual exploitation, and physical prowess by lower class males of most ethnic groups. Similarly, large numbers of blacks, many highly educated and involved in radical politics, have accepted the negative (and false) description of their family structure as "matriarchal" which has been propounded by Daniel Moynihan (1965) and other whites. Moreover, many black males and females are now engaged in efforts to change this structure to conform to the major cultural pattern of male as dominant partner and breadwinner, and female as subservient homemaker. However, less biased research (Hill, 1972; Rhodes, 1971; Stack, 1974; Myers, 1975; Dietrich, 1975) suggests that the traditional black family structure is and has been very functional in enabling the black to survive in this society. This structure is not the pathological, weak, disorganized entity usually conveyed by the term "matriarchy."

Individuals of all levels of society who reject traditional gender role stereotypes are labeled "nonconformist" and subjected to the wrath of most members of the society. The harsh treatment of longhaired males in the 1960s by police, possible employers, and ordinary citizens speaks eloquently of the "cost" of nonconformity, as does the "wallflower" status of competitive, intellectually gifted, or career-oriented females.

But costs are also paid by those who generally conform to gender role stereotypes (or any other kind, for that matter), and these are usually more "hidden."

Perceived Costs and Benefits

In 1971, students in a sex role class were asked to form single-sex groups to discuss the advantages of the other gender role and the disadvantages of their own. This exercise was a replication of the study done by Barbara Polk and Robert Stein (1972) at a northern university, using 250 students of highly diverse backgrounds, and the results parallel theirs almost exactly. Results of the class study are reported in Tables 2.3 and 2.4.

TABLE 2.3

DISADVANTAGES OF SAME GENDER ROLE AND ADVANTAGES OF OTHER ONE AS PERCEIVED BY MALES

Male Disadvantages	Female Advantages
Can't show emotions (P)	Freedom to express emotions (R)
Must be provider (O)	Fewer financial obligations; parents support longer (S)
Pressure to succeed, be competitive (O)	Less pressure to succeed (P)
Alimony and child support (O)	Alimony and insurance benefits (S)
Liable to draft (O)	Free from draft (S)
Must take initiative, make decisions (O)	Protected (S)
Limit on acceptable careers (P)	
Expected to be mechanical, fix things (O)	
	More leisure (S)
	Placed on pedestal; object of courtesy (S)

Note: Letters enclosed in parentheses refer to a fourfold categorization of roles (Polk & Stein, 1972):
P = Proscription
O = Obligation
R = Right
S = Structural benefit

TABLE 2.4

DISADVANTAGES OF SAME GENDER ROLE AND ADVANTAGES OF
OTHER ONE AS PERCEIVED BY FEMALES

Female Disadvantages	Male Advantages
Job opportunities limited; discrimination; poor pay (P)	Job opportunities greater (S)
Legal and financial discrimination (P)	Financial and legal opportunity (S)
Educational opportunities limited; judged mentally inferior; opinion devalued; intellectual life stifled (P)	Better educational and training opportunities; opinions valued (S)
Single status stigmatized; stigma for divorce and unwed pregnancy (P)	Bachelorhood glamorized (R)
Socially and sexually restricted; double standard (P)	More freedom sexually and socially (R)
Must bear and rear children; no abortions (in many places); responsible for birth control (O)	No babies (S)
Must maintain good outward appearance; dress, make-up (O)	Less fashion demand and emphasis on appearance (R)
Domestic work (O)	No domestic work (R)
Must be patient; give in; subordinate self; be unaggressive; wait to be asked out on dates (P)	Can be aggressive, dating and otherwise (O)
Inhibited motor control; not allowed to be athletic (P)	More escapism allowed (R)

Note: Letters enclosed in parentheses refer to a fourfold categorization of roles (Polk & Stein, 1972):
P = Proscription
O = Obligation
R = Right
S = Structural benefit

When the advantages and disadvantages of the gender roles are compared, the most striking finding relates to the relative length of the various lists. There seem to be many more disadvantages adhering to the feminine role as perceived by females than to the masculine role as perceived by males (or else the females were simply and stereotypically more loquacious!). Conversely, more advantages are seen as accruing to the masculine role by females than to the feminine role by males. More relevant to the question of costs, however, is the finding that the perceived advantages of one sex are the disadvantages of the other. If it is a masculine disadvantage not to be able to show emotions, it is a feminine advantage to be able to do so. Likewise, if it is a feminine disadvantage to face limited job opportunities, the converse is a masculine advantage. Summarizing similar findings, Polk and Stein (1972) conclude: "The extent to which this relationship exists strongly suggests that there is general agreement on the desirable characteristics for any individual, regardless of sex" (p. 16).

Polk and Stein's fourfold categorization of role components as rights, obligations, proscriptions, and structural benefits is useful in examining the nature of specific perceived costs and benefits of the two roles. According to Polk and Stein, "Rights allow the individual the freedom to commit an act or refrain from an act without receiving sanctions for either choice" (p. 19). Obligations and proscriptions are different in that individuals are negatively sanctioned, in the first case for not doing something, in the second for doing it. Structural benefits refer to "advantages derived from the social structure or from actions of others" on the basis of sex alone (p. 21). Each advantage and disadvantage listed in Tables 2.3 and 2.4 is followed by a letter in parentheses which represents my judgment as to whether that characteristic is a right (R), a proscription (P), an obligation (O), or a structural benefit (S). Masculine disadvantages consist overwhelmingly of obligations with a few proscriptions, while the disadvantages of the feminine role arise primarily from proscriptions, with a few obligations. Thus females complain about what they can't do, males about what they must do. Females complain that they cannot be athletic, aggressive, sexually free, or successful in the worlds of work and education; in short, they complain of their passivity. Males complain that they must be aggressive and must succeed; in short, of their activity. The (sanctioned) requirement that males be active and females passive in a variety of ways is clearly unpleasant to both.

The nature of the types of advantages seen as accruing to each of the two roles by the other sex supports the stereotyped dichotomy between activity and passivity still further. Females are seen as overwhelmingly enjoying structural benefits, namely, advantages that accrue to them without reference to what they do. Males believe females have only one right. Females believe males also enjoy structural benefits but have considerably more rights, namely, choices of action or inaction. These findings generally agree with those of Polk and Stein, who found that altogether the masculine role had 14 obligations compared to 8 for the feminine role; 6 rights compared to 0; 4 proscriptions compared to 15; and 6 structural benefits compared to 4 (pp. 20-21, Table 2).

The many costs of being female and feminine have, in the past half-dozen years, been extensively aired. The often less obvious costs of being male and masculine can be summarized in a student's own somewhat melodramatic and confused but deeply felt words:

> I, a 20th-century American male, feel trapped, suppressed, suffocated by an uncaring, stereotyping . . . society. My individuality is labeled queer and my interests unnatural because the idea of seeing a baseball game . . . does not send me into euphoric ecstasy. I feel bitterness for the conforming role nature has forced me to bear. Then again, nature is not to blame, it is our . . . society. . . . My problem [is that I am] . . . myself with a veneer of overt masculine, . . . emotionless behavior, all aimed toward the affirmation of my masculinity. By far the most tragic fact of this role playing which most American men portray is the fact that we lose sight of our true beings. If we concentrate on appearing as a brute masculine, bicep-oriented expanse of wall-to-wall ego, then we cease to be caring, compassionate human beings. . . . I feel compelled to display or affirm my masculinity. This in itself implies insecurity; but I am not insecure. . . . I do not need a football game, a wild boar hunt, or rippling biceps and triceps to prove my masculinity. I feel the societal pressure, however, and this embitters me.

> .   .   .   .   .

> I am a male. I am not uncaring. . . . I am not devoid of emotion. I can cry; I can laugh; I can feel. I cannot suppress these facts of my being and don the stereotyped male sex role.

> .   .   .   .   .

> Why is it that
> We cannot know
> Ourselves?
> We block out facets
> Of personal experience
> That could make
> Life worth living.
> What is going to be the
> Destruction of man?
> His war or his psyche?

Economic Costs and Benefits

How helpful or costly would the masculine or feminine gender role stereotype traits listed in Table 2.1 above be for a competitor in the highest echelons of our economy and society? One measure of such success is occupation. Robert Hodge, Paul Siegel, and Peter Rossi (1966) studied the relative prestige of a large number of occupations in the United States and found that the four most prestigious were: U.S. Supreme Court Justice, physician, scientist, and state governor. Table 2.5 summarizes the data on which stereotypical traits are clearly helpful in attaining and performing well in these occupational roles and which are harmful. While the designation as "helpful" or "harmful" for some few traits is debatable, the overall picture probably is not. Stereotypical feminine traits patently do not equip those who might try to live up to them to compete in the world of social and economic privilege, power, and prestige; the exact opposite is the case for masculine characteristics. Where 15 feminine traits are classified as "harmful," only 2 masculine

TABLE 2.5

GENDER ROLE TRAITS HELPFUL AND HARMFUL IN ACQUIRING AND PERFORMING WELL IN PRESTIGIOUS OCCUPATIONAL ROLES

Stereotyped Traits	Harmful	Helpful
Masculine	Sloppy	Breadwinner, provider
	Dogmatic	Stoic, unemotional
		Logical, rational, objective, scientific
		Practical
		Mechanical (for scientist and physician)
		Public awareness
		Leader
		Disciplinarian
		Independent
		Demanding
		Aggressive
		Ambitious
		Proud, confident
		Moral, trustworthy
		Decisive
		Competitive
		Adventurous

TABLE 2.5—Continued

GENDER ROLE TRAITS HELPFUL AND HARMFUL IN ACQUIRING AND
PERFORMING WELL IN PRESTIGIOUS OCCUPATIONAL ROLES

Stereotyped Traits	Harmful	Helpful
Feminine	Worry about appearance and age	Compassionate
	Sensual	Intuitive
	Domestic	Humanistic
	Seductive, flirtatious	Perceptive
	Emotional, sentimental	Idealistic
	Nervous, insecure, fearful	Patient
	Scatterbrained, frivolous	Gentle
	Impractical	
	Petty, coy, gossipy	
	Dependent, overprotected	
	Follower, submissive	
	Self-conscious; easily intimidated	
	Not aggressive, passive	
	Tardy	
	Noncompetitive	

Note: Traits from Table 2.1 which are not classifiable as either "helpful" or "harmful" are omitted.

ones are so designated. Conversely, where 17 masculine traits are classified as "helpful," the analogous number of feminine traits is 7. The cost of femininity for those who would enter the world outside the home could scarcely be more clear: The more a female conforms, the less is she capable of functioning in roles that are other than domestic.

Indeed, gender roles are so deeply ingrained that even among successful business executives, women, unlike men, often attribute their success to luck rather than their own hard work and competence. Moreover, women tend to understate the extent of their achievements (Hennig & Jardim, 1977). On the other hand, reared in a culture that emphasizes the myth that hard work and personal worth will result in job success, many males, especially in the middle class, suffer feelings of personal inadequacy and failure if they are not highly successful in a material sense. In short, the feminine role stereotype gears women for economic failure, and if that is not the case, women explain their success in terms external to themselves. The masculine role stereotype gears men for economic success, and if that is not forthcoming men perceive themselves as personally responsible for their "failure."

Health Costs*

A number of other problems—medical, psychiatric, educational, and legal—differ by sex and undoubtedly reflect the pressures of gender role stereotyping. Chapter 4 will provide a more thorough discussion of the direct costs of discrimination against females in economics, politics, and other institutional areas. Here, some of the health-related costs that males and females pay for conformity will be discussed. Basically, gender role stereotyping affects people's "heads." That is to say, a good many of the costs are mental, and other problems, medical and behavioral, result from the psychological effects.

The feminine stereotype fosters a view of women as being emotionally and physically weak, dependent, and in need of protection. In fact, however, women are healthier and live longer than men (Verbrugge, 1976a; Retherford, 1975; Preston, 1976; Waldron, 1976). Those very traits of masculinity that are most highly valued in our culture— independence, mastery of environment, aggressiveness, emotional restraint, and work orientation—help to undermine the health and longevity of males (Verbrugge, 1976b; Waldron, 1976; Fuchs, 1974; Preston, 1976). For those males who have the least opportunity to achieve socioeconomic success, namely, those in the lower classes and nonwhites, the mortality and morbidity (ill health) rates are the highest.

Throughout the world today, countries with life expectancy at birth greater than 55 years all report longer life expectancy for women than for men. Only nine countries report life expectancies equal for the sexes or greater for males, and these all have a low life expectancy for both sexes, as well as statistics of doubtful validity. In countries with longer male life expectancy—Nigeria, Upper Volta, Liberia, India, Cambodia, and Pakistan (United Nations, 1974)—the chief cause of higher female mortality is childbirth death. Where few women die in childbirth, as in all but the poorest nations, females enjoy a longer life expectancy than men. In 1973 the life expectancy in the United States was 67.6 years for men and 75.3 years for women. U.S. women ranked ninth in the "world women's life expectancy rankings," and U.S. men ranked 19th in the
*This section was written with Maradee Davis.

"world men's life expectancy rankings." For Sweden, the country with the highest life expectancy in the world, the 1973 expectancies were 72.1 for males and 77.7 for females. Sweden's male life expectancy is lower than that of the 20th-ranked nation's female life expectancy (U.S. Department of Health, Education, and Welfare, 1977). Thus, the data on mortality rates belie the notion that women are "the weaker sex."

Male fetuses are more likely to die, and there is a higher infant mortality rate for male babies. These differences are probably biologically caused. Of more importance in this context, in the age range of 15 to 35 males have a much higher mortality rate than females as a result of violence (motor vehicle accidents, work and sports accidents, homicides). Part of the definition of masculinity is personal bravery and adventuresomeness, traits which are, if anything, actively discouraged among females. Under the circumstances, it is little wonder that more males die for such reasons.

In middle age, the causes of more frequent male deaths than female deaths are primarily cardiovascular disease (heart attacks), lung cancer, and chronic pulmonary disease. Indeed, of the 15 leading causes of death in the United States, 14 cause more male than female deaths, and between 1958 and 1972 women's relative advantage increased in most of these categories (Verbrugge, 1976b). These diseases are linked to the life-style and psychic states of those who suffer from them. The pressures on males to "succeed" in a highly competitive world of work create tremendous stress; in the final analysis, few males can ever sit back and say "I've arrived; I am a success; now I can relax." So strong is the work and success ethic for males in our society that even millionaires feel compelled to "produce," in the sense of active participation in the economy. Among the large numbers of males doing less competitive but more repetitious labor, the pressure to persist day in, day out, year after year, in highly alienating work results from the gender role requirement that they provide for their families the best they possibly can in material terms, and such pressures can lead to illness. The proscription on expressing emotions entailed in the masculine role definition probably exacerbates the stresses inherent in the obligation to support a family—financially and emotionally—and to succeed in an often highly competitive "rat race."

Recent research (Rosenman, 1974; Waldron, 1976) suggests that a certain personality type is highly associated with coronary heart disease.

This type is characterized by some of the following traits: work orientation, ambition, aggressiveness, and competitiveness. These are, of course, some of the major traits which constitute the masculine stereotype. Similar factors probably also help to cause the higher rate of peptic ulcers suffered by males compared to females.

It has been noted that males die as a result of accidents more frequently than females do. Myths concerning women drivers to the contrary, males are involved in 130 percent more fatal car accidents than females and 30 percent more accidents per mile driven (Waldron & Johnston, 1976). Males, especially those in the lower-class and nonwhite categories, work in physically hazardous environments more often than females do. As part of the masculine, but not feminine, culture, guns contribute to male death rates through accidents as well as homicides. Indeed, homicide is a leading cause of death among black men through middle age (Fuchs, 1974; Erhardt & Berlin, 1974).

More frequent abuse of alcohol and most drugs by males increases their chances for ill health and, in some cases, early death. Until recently the same was true of cigarette smoking. Although females attempt suicide twice as often as males, men have a suicide rate three times as high as that for women. It would be noted, however, that suicide rates have in recent years increased more rapidly for females than for males (Verbrugge, 1976b). Suicidal men are prone to use guns, with often irreversible consequences, whereas women are more likely to use poisons, which can be treated by use of stomach pumps and antidotes. Ingrid Waldron and S. Johnston (1976) postulate that "Women apparently are better able to use a suicide attempt as a cry for help and it seems likely that this ability to some extent protects them from the need to actually kill themselves. In contrast, males see themselves as strong, powerful, dominant, potent and find it difficult to seek help."

As we have seen, the feminine role is clearly linked to domesticity, meaning, probably more than anything else, childbearing and child rearing. It is little wonder, then, that females suffer relatively high rates of mental breakdown and suicide at about the time their youngest children leave the "nest." Since this usually coincides with menopause, many have viewed these biological changes as directly or indirectly "causing" the breakdown. I think it is rather the fact that women lose their primary, indeed, almost sole functional role at this time of their life and see very little in their future. Pauline Bart's (1970) study of middle-aged women in mental hospitals showed that prior intense involvement with the mother role was closely related to serious depression. It is interesting to note that in highly traditional societies where the role of grandmother is revered and respected, females do not seem to suffer psychological problems at menopause (Dowty, 1972). Further supporting this interpretation is the fact that males undergo severe mental problems (and the highest suicide rate for men is recorded) at about 65 or during prolonged periods of unemployment, namely when stripped of their only important functional role, that of worker and provider. There is no relatively abrupt biological change that can serve as an explanation for this phenomenon among males (see Bart, 1971).

Myrna Weissman and Gerald Klerman (1977) suggest that alcoholism and depression are different but equivalent disorders. Women get depressed and seek the help of physicians. Men are reluctant to admit to being depressed or to seek treatment, and instead they mitigate their feelings by drinking. Thus men self-prescribe alcohol as a treatment for depression. Working-class men seek the local bar, while middle- and upper-class men seek the country club or cocktail lounge as settings for group psychopharmacological self-treatment. The end result is far more damaging to the health of men.

Women tend to seek out physicians and psychiatrists for help more frequently than men for virtually all complaints. In fact, the only health risk-taking behavior in which women exceed men is in the use of psychoactive drugs: tranquilizers, sedatives, and stimulants. Twice as many women as men receive prescriptions for these drugs, and doctors give women prescriptions for them twice as often as men, and for twice the length of time (Coser, 1975). During the later 1800s, when opium was widely available as a patent and prescription drug, women were opium addicts at a rate of 2 to 1 over men. Alcohol was incongruent with temperance, but opium-laden drugs were socially acceptable as nervines and tonics (Haller, 1975, pp. 275-92). It is important to note that this one area of female risk-taking is really an act that is dependent on the authority of a physician (usually male), while illicit drug use and alcohol consumption require independent action. The fact that physicians prescribe such drugs more frequently for females than for males probably reflects biases in diagnoses. Females' complaints may often be attributed to "nerves" or hypochondria, while the same complaints voiced by males are assumed to have an organic basis.

Because of their reluctance to admit weakness and to ask for help, males are probably less inclined to seek treatment for illness and, when they do seek it, may often be at a late stage of disease development when treatment is less effective. Thus, despite the fact that males suffer more from many major, chronic illnesses, females report more physical symptoms, visit doctors more often, spend more days in bed, and restrict their normal activities more often (Verbrugge, 1976a, 1976b; Waldron & Johnston, 1976; Mechanic, 1976; Nathanson, 1975). In part, this reflects the fact that adult males often cannot "afford the time" to be sick or to seek medical treatment unless their discomfort is severe. Employed women are in the same situation, but about half of all adult women are not employed. In addition, females are held responsible for the health of their families and are taught to be more sensitive to health issues. Finally, the stereotypic view of women as weak and frail (which resulted in a virtual "cult of invalidism" among Victorian ladies) encourages women to perceive themselves as ill more readily and to seek help.

Conformity to gender roles also influences mental illness. In a critical review of over 80 studies of psychiatric disorders, Bruce and Barbara Dohrenwend (1976) concluded that:

1. There are no consistent sex differences in rates of functional psychoses in general. This condition includes schizophrenia and other major psychotic conditions which usually have an organic or genetic basis.
2. Rates of neurosis are consistently higher for women.
3. Rates of personality disorder are consistently higher for men. Personality disorders include antisocial and psychopathic personalities.

It would appear, then, that women tend to turn their frustrations in upon themselves and thus suffer depression. Men tend to focus their frustrations outward and thus engage in antisocial and irresponsible behavior. Weissman and Klerman (1977) summarize the pathways through which women's social status contributes to depression. The first is via social discrimination against women, which makes it difficult for them to achieve mastery by direct action and self-assertion. Discrimination, including proscription against achievement and mastery, leads to economic helplessness, dependency on others, chronically low self-esteem, low aspirations, and ultimately clinical depression. The second pathway they call "learned helplessness," in which stereotypical images produce in women an inability to be assertive. Young girls learn to be helpless during their socialization and thus develop a limited response repertoire when under stress.

Young males, perhaps even more than their elders, suffer a number of psychological costs in the process of trying to establish their masculine identity. According to Patricia Sexton (1969, p. 6), as children males outnumber females in mental institutions at a rate of 2 to 1. This ratio is reversed in adulthood, according to Phyllis Chesler (1971, p. 747). Male youths are far more frequently adjudged delinquent; they comprise the vast majority of school discipline "problems"; they have reading and general learning problems about twice as frequently as girls (Sexton, 1969, p. 10). Sexton argues that the major cause of all these problems is to be found in the vast discrepancy between what boys are encouraged to be as masculine creatures and what they are required to do as students. School requires sitting still, rather passively, and carrying out the orders of an authority figure who is generally female. Meanwhile, male children are being urged to accept "values such as courage, inner direction, certain forms of aggression, autonomy. . . . adventure, and a considerable amount of toughness . . ." (p. 15). Moreover, they are learning that they are "better than girls," whom they must protect and help, while they are being subjected to the direct authority of female teachers. They conform either to their gender role stereotype and become learning and school "problems" or to school requirements and are considered by their peers to be "sissies," or they buckle under the pressure of conflicting expectations. Such pressures clearly do not exist for most girls, whose gender role stereotype dovetails nicely with the behavior required by schools.

Thus conformity to gender roles helps to create ill health, physically and mentally, for both sexes and probably contributes to a lower male life expectancy. Fifteen years ago Betty Friedan (1963, chap. 1) began to focus attention on this phenomenon as it affected middle-class, middle-aged, married women. She called it "the problem that has no name":

> It was strange stirring, a sense of dissatisfaction, a yearning that women suffered. . . . Each suburban wife struggled with it alone. As she made beds, shopped for groceries, matched slipcover material, ate peanut butter

sandwiches with her children, chauffeured Cub Scouts and Brownies, lay beside her husband at night—she was afraid to ask even of herself the silent question—"Is this all?" (1963, p. 11).

Basically, Friedan's argument is that conformity to stereotyped domesticity (the "feminine mystique") dearly cost large numbers of intelligent, educated, once-active, dynamic females. They fled to psychiatrists asking why, with all they had (lovely house, children, loving husband), they were dissatisfied with life, empty, bored, looking forward to nothing. They complained to their doctors of being tired all the time, a symptom usually regarded as psychosomatic, and many turned to tranquilizers, barbituates, and alcohol (although, as noted earlier, the vast majority of drug addicts and alcoholics are male). And, most tragically, as a result of their frustration a generation of children who were unable "to endure pain or discipline or pursue any self-sustained goal of any sort," children with "a devastating boredom with life" may have been produced (pp. 24-25).

It is clear that our society does in fact define stereotypically a host of traits as fitting almost exclusively one or the other gender roles. In short, it creates a radical dichotomy of human types, despite both the many differences between individuals of the same sex and the many similarities between people of "opposite" sexes. From birth on we are all encouraged to assume a self-definition and certain behaviors which may or may not be congruent with our natural proclivities and which, at any rate, express only half, if that, of our human potential. It is abundantly clear that this is a costly procedure for everyone involved, in a myriad of ways.

References

Adelson, Joseph. "A Study of Minority Group Authoritarianism." In Marshall Sklare (ed.), *The Jews: Social Patterns of an American Group,* pp. 475-92. Glencoe, Ill.: Free Press, 1958.

Allport, Gordon. *The Nature of Prejudice.* Garden City, N.Y.: Doubleday Anchor Books, 1958; first published 1954.

Bart, Pauline. "Mother Portnoy's Complaints." *Trans-Action* 8 (November-December 1970): 69-74.

Bart, Pauline. "Depression in Middle Aged Women." In Vivian Gornick and Barbara Moran (eds.), *Women in Sexist Society,* chap. 8. New York: Basic Books, 1971.

Bem, Sandra. "The Measurement of Psychological Androgyny." *Journal of Consulting and Clinical Psychology* 42 (1974): 155-62.

Bem, Sandra. "Sex-Role Adaptability: One Consequence of Psychological Androgyny." *Journal of Personality and Social Psychology* 31 (1975): 634-43.

Bem, Sandra. "Psychological Androgyny." In Alice Sargent (ed.), *Beyond Sex Roles.* St. Paul, Minn.: West Publishing Co., 1977.

Bem, Sandra, and Lenney, E. "Sex-Typing and the Avoidance of Cross-Sex Behavior." *Journal of Personality and Social Psychology* 33 (1976): 48-54.

Brenton, Myron. *The American Male.* Greenwich, Conn.: Fawcett Publications, 1966.

Broverman, I.K., et al. "Sex-Role Stereotypes and Clinical Judgments of Mental Health." *Journal of Consulting and Clinical Psychology* 34 (1970): 1-7.

Broverman, I.K., et al. "Sex Role Stereotypes: A Current Appraisal." *Journal of Social Issues* 28 (1972): 59-78.

Chesler, Phyllis. "Women as Psychiatric and Psychotherapeutic Patients." *Journal of Marriage and the Family* 33 (November 1971): 746-59.

Constantinople, Ann. "Masculinity-Femininity: An Exception to a Famous Dictum?" *Psychological Bulletin* 80 (1973): 389-407.

Coser, Rose. "Why Bother? Is Research on Issues of Women's Health Worthwhile?" In V. Oleson (ed.), *Women and Their Health: Research Implications for a New Era,* pp. 3-9. Department of Health, Education, and Welfare Publication 77-3138. Washington, D.C., 1975.

Courtney, Alice, and Whipple, Thomas. "Women in T.V. Commercials." *Journal of Communications* 24 (1974): 110-18.

Culley, James, and Bennett, Rex. "Selling Women, Selling Blacks." *Journal of Communications* 26 (1976): 160-74.

David, Deborah, and Brannon, Robert. *The Forty-Nine Percent Majority: The Male Sex Role.* Reading, Mass.: Addison-Wesley Publishing Co., 1976.

Dietrich, Kathryn. "The Re-examination of the Myth of Black Matriarchy." *Journal of Marriage and the Family* 37 (May 1975): 367-74.

Dohrenwend, Bruce, and Dohrenwend, Barbara. "Sex Differences and Psychiatric Disorders." *American Journal of Sociology* 81 (1976): 1447-454.

Dowty, Nancy. "To Be a Woman in Israel." *School Review* 80 (February 1972): 319-32.

Erhardt, Carl, and Berlin, Joyce (eds.). *Mortality and Morbidity in the United States.* Cambridge, Mass.: Harvard University Press, 1974.

Frazier, E. Franklin. *Black Bourgeoisie.* Glencoe, Ill.: Free Press, 1957.

Friedan, Betty. *The Feminine Mystique.* New York: Dell Publishing Co., 1963.

Fuchs, Victor. *Who Shall Live? Health, Economics and Social Choice.* New York: Basic Books, 1974.

Haller, John. "Abuses in Gynecological Surgery : An Historical Appraisal." In V. Oleson (ed.), *Women and Their Health: Research Implications for a New Era,* pp. 27-33. U.S.Department of Health, Education and Welfare Publication 77-3138. Washington, D.C., 1975.

Heilbrun, Alfred. "Measurement of Masculine and Feminine Sex Role Identities as Independent Dimensions." *Journal of Consulting and Clinical Psychology* 44 (1976): 183-90.

Hennig, Margaret, and Jardim, Anne. *The Managerial Woman.* New York: Anchor-Doubleday, 1977.

Hill, Robert B. *The Strengths of Black Families.* New York: Emerson Hall Publishers, 1972.

Hodge, Robert; Siegel, Paul; and Rossi, Peter. "Occupational Prestige in the United States: 1925-1963." In Reinhard Bendix and S.M. Lipset (eds.), *Class, Status and Power,* pp. 322-34. 2nd ed. Glencoe, Ill.: Free Press, 1966.

Kagan, Jerome, and Moss, Howard. *Birth to Maturity: A Study in Psychological Development.* New York: John Wiley & Sons, 1962.

Lefkowitz, Margaret. "The Women's Magazine Short-Story Heroine in 1957 and 1967." In Constantina Safilios-Rothschild (ed.), *Toward a Sociology of Women,* pp. 37-40. Lexington, Mass.: Xerox College Publishing Co., 1972.

Macleod, Jennifer. "How to Hold a Wife: A Bridegroom's Guide." *Village Voice,* February 11, 1971, p. 5.

McKinley, Donald G. *Social Class and Family Life.* Glencoe, Ill.: Free Press, 1964.

Mechanic, David. "Sex, Illness, Illness Behavior and the Use of Health Services." *Journal of Human Stress* (1976): 29-40.

Mills, Kay. "Fighting Sexism on the Airwaves." *Journal of Communications* 24 (Spring 1974): 150-56.

Moynihan, Daniel P. *The Negro Family: The Case for National Action.* Washington, D.C.: U.S. Department of Labor, 1965.

Myers, Lena Wright. "Black Women and Self-Esteem." In Marcia Millman and Rosabeth Kanter (eds.), *Another Voice,* pp. 240-50. Garden City, N.Y.: Anchor Books, 1975.

Nathanson, Constance. "Illness and the Feminine Role: A Theoretical Review." *Social Science and Medicine,* 1975, pp. 57-62.

O'Kelly, Charlotte, and Bloomquist, Linda. "Women and Blacks on T.V." *Journal of Communications* 26 (1976): 179-84.

Polk, Barbara Bovee, and Stein, Robert B. "Is the Grass Greener on the Other

Side?" In Constantina Safilios-Rothschild (ed.), *Toward a Sociology of Women,* pp. 14-23. Lexington, Mass.: Xerox College Publishing Co., 1972.

Preston, Samuel. *Mortality Patterns in National Populations.* New York: Academic Press, 1976.

Ray, Lovelle. "The American Women in Mass Media: How Much Emancipation and What Does it Mean?" In Constantina Safilios-Rothschild (ed.), *Toward a Sociology of Women,* pp. 41-62. Lexington, Mass.: Xerox College Publishing Co., 1972.

Retherford, Robert. *The Changing Sex Differential in Mortality.* Westport, Conn.: Greenwood Press, 1975.

Rhodes, Barbara. "The Changing Role of the Black Woman." In Robert Staples (ed.), *The Black Family,* pp. 145-49. Belmont, Calif.: Wadsworth Publishing Co., 1971.

Rosenman, R.H. "The Role of Behavior Patterns and Neurogenic Factors in the Pathogenesis of Coronary Heart Disease." In R.S. Eliot (ed.), *Stress and the Heart,* pp. 123-41. Mount Kisco, N.Y.: Futura Publications, 1974.

Scott, Anne Firor. *The Southern Lady.* Chicago: University of Chicago Press, 1970.

Sexton, Patricia Cayo. *The Feminized Male.* New York: Vintage Books, 1969.

Simpson, George E., and Yinger, J. Milton. *Racial and Cultural Minorities.* 3rd ed. New York: Harper & Row, 1965.

Smith, Dwayne, and Matre, Marc. "Social Norms and Sex Roles in Romance and Adventure Magazines." *Journalism Quarterly* 52 (Summer 1975): 309-15.

Stack, Carol. *All Our Kin: Strategies for Survival in a Black Community.* New York: Harper & Row, 1974.

Staples, Robert. "The Myth of the Black Matriarchy." *Black Scholar* 1 (January-February, 1970): 8-16.

Tarvis, Carol, and Offir, Carole. *The Longest War: Sex Differences in Perspective.* New York: Harcourt, Brace, Jovanovich, 1977.

Tedesco, Nancy. "Patterns in Prime Time." *Journal of Communications* 24 (1974): 119-24.

Tresemer, David. "Assumptions Made about Gender Roles." *Sociological Inquiry* 45 (1975): 308-39.

United Nations. *Demographic Yearbook.* New York, 1974.

U.S. Department of Health, Education, and Welfare. Statement by Dorothy Rice, director NCHS, before the U.S. Senate Subcommittee on Health and Scientific Research, Committee on Human Resources, March 31, 1977.

Verbrugge, Lois. "Females and Illness: Recent Trends in Sex Differences in the United States." *Journal of Health and Social Behavior* 17 (1976a): 387-403.

Verbrugge, Lois. "Sex Differentials in Morbidity and Mortality in the United States." *Social Biology* 23 (1976b): 275-95

Waldron, Ingrid. "Why Do Women Live Longer than Men? Part I." *Journal of Human Stress* 2 (1976): 2-13.

Waldron, Ingrid, and Johnston, S. "Why Do Women Live Longer than Men? Part II." *Journal of Human Stress* 2 (1976): 19-30.

Weissman, Myrna, and Klerman, Gerald. "Sex Differences and the Epidemiology of Depression." *Archives of General Psychiatry* 34 (1977): 98-111.

Williams, John, and Bennett, Susan. "The Definition of Sex Stereotypes via the Adjective Check List." *Sex Roles* 1 (1975): 327-37.

Yorburg, Betty. *Sexual Identity: Sex Roles and Social Change.* New York: John Wiley & Sons, 1974.

Chapter 3

The Bringing Up of Dick and Jane

A baby is born knowing nothing, but full of potential. The process by which an individual becomes a creature of society, a socialized human being reflecting culturally defined roles and norms, is complex and as yet imperfectly understood. It is evident, however, that most individuals eventually reflect societal definitions more or less well; most males born and raised in America will someday think and behave like other American males in many important ways and not, for instance, like their Japanese counterparts. Through the socialization process humans come to more or less completely internalize the roles, norms, and values appropriate to the culture and subculture within which they function. Cultural definitions become personal definitions of propriety, normality, and worthiness. Because internalization of cultural definitions is less than total for most people, social control mechanisms are brought to bear by some individuals and social groups to encourage others to conform to expectations. Control mechanisms range from such severe forms as physical punishment inflicted by the state (imprisonment and even execution), to social ostracism or unwillingness to hire job applicants, to such mild forms as ridicule.

Underlying both the socialization process and the concomitant use of social controls is the assumption that people learn to conform by the application of sanctions. Sanctions may be positive, in which case they are known as "rewards," or negative, when they are known as "punishments." Generally, people learn more completely and retain things longer when rewards rather than punishments are employed. By their nature, however, social control mechanisms utilize largely negative sanctions, and therefore they function as relatively ineffective teaching techniques. The socialization process itself is typically comprised of a mixture of both types of sanctions. The proportion of rewards to punishments during this process varies according to such factors as ethnic subculture and social class, as well as the personalities of the individuals involved. Thus the extent to which individuals will internalize social norms and roles varies, although the fact that rewards are normally utilized to some extent helps to ensure substantial success for the process.

Human interaction is crucial to the process of personality development. A newborn infant has no concept of self. By the time a child enters school, it has begun to develop a fairly coherent picture of who it is and what the appropriate behaviors are for that identity. The process of developing this picture is probably never-ending, but by adulthood it is usually subject to relatively less change than it was earlier.

The classical explanation for how an individual's identity emerges is that offered by the symbolic interactionists, dating back a half century or more to George Herbert Mead (1934) and Charles H. Cooley (1909), among others. Through interaction with "significant others," primarily parents and, later, peer groups, children come to form an idea of self consisting of "three principal elements: the imagination of our appearance to the other person; the imagination of his judgment of that appearance, and some sort of self-feeling such as pride or mortification" (Cooley, 1909, p. 152). Cooley called this the "looking glass self." In developing this approach further, Mead emphasized the key role of language in the interaction process. He believed children first develop a sense of "I," namely, a basic awareness of self as actor and organism. Later the "me" develops; this consists of an understanding and internalization of how others perceive the child. The "me" is the social component of the personality; it entails the internalization of roles, norms, and values presented by society and is in many ways similar to Freud's superego. It is learned by the child through role-playing— taking the role of the other in negotiating human interactions. This is only possible through the manipulation of symbols, that is, language. In this way the child eventually learns the organized attitudes and expectations of larger social groupings, called by Mead "the generalized other." Stated in its simplest form, children learn who they are and internalize what they are expected to be by trying to put themselves in the place of others and experience themselves as others perceive them. This is possible only through the use of symbolic communication.

Two other related concepts are relevant to a discussion of the socialization process. W.I. Thomas's (1923) renowned concept of the "definition of the situation" entails recognition of the fact that if human beings define a situation as real, then, regardless of objective reality, the fact of defining it in that way has real social consequences. If, for instance, a boy is told that "boys are athletic," regardless of the truth of this assertion it will have a real impact on that child's behavior and expectations of himself. Robert K. Merton (1957) was essentially noting the same phenomenon when he developed the notion of the "self-fulfilling (or defeating) prophecy." Merton's concept applies to those cases where the act of predicting something helps to ensure that the phenomenon in question will (or will not) occur. Thus, for instance, the girl who is told she will never be strong (because girls aren't) will probably take no steps by which she could become strong. When later she lacks strength, a self-fulfilling prophecy will have been realized.

This chapter will primarily be concerned with the ways in which children and adolescents learn to internalize the gender role stereotypes discussed in Chapter 2 and the control mechanisms employed to reinforce these stereotypes.

The Captive Audience: Childhood

The first crucial question asked by the parents of a newborn baby is "What is it? A boy or a girl?" Only later will they be concerned with any other attribute of the infant, even its physical condition; the first priority is to establish its sex. Indeed, almost immediately, gender identity is permanently stamped on the child by the name it is given. Typically, parents have spent long hours mulling over names for a prospective son or daughter months before the birth. They may even have turned to a name glossary for help: here they would find the message that "Boys' and girls' names are, and should be, different. Boys need important names; girls need pretty ones" (Walum, 1977, p. 39). Laurel Walum explains that

> Male names tend to be short, hard-hitting, and explosive, e.g., Bret, Lance, Mark, Craig, Bruce, etc. Even when the given name is multisyllabic (e.g., Benjamin, Joshua, William, Thomas, etc.), the nickname tends to imply hardness and energy (e.g., Ben, Josh, Bill, Tom, etc.). Female names, on the other hand, are longer, more melodic, and softer (e.g., Deborah, Caroline, Jessica, Christina) and easily succumb to the diminuitive *ie*-ending form (e.g., Debbie, Cary, Jessie, Christy). And although the feminization of male names (e.g., Fredericka, Roberta, Alexandra) is not uncommon, the inverse rarely occurs (p. 39).

When the proud new father lifts his infant he might jostle it just a little if it's a boy; he will pet and cuddle it if it is a girl. In the months that follow mother will speak to the infant more if it happens to be female—and later everyone will wonder why it is that young girls show greater linguistic skills than boys (Lewis, 1972, p. 54). Father will continue to play a bit rough with the infant if the child is male (see Maccoby & Jacklin, 1974, p. 307). Both parents will discourage a male toddler from "clinging"—but not his sister. Research shows that up to six months of age male infants receive more physical contact from their mothers than do female babies (probably because the male child is valued more), while after that males are more quickly and totally discouraged from such contact (Lewis, 1972, p. 56).

In one study of 30 new parents it was found that, despite the fact that the boy and girl babies did not differ in physical traits (other than sex), neurological characteristics, or even size, the parents of the girl babies rated them as softer, more finely featured, smaller, and more inattentive than did the parents of boy babies. In general, research shows that parents are more apprehensive about the physical safety of their daughters than their sons (Pederson & Robson, 1969; Minton et al., 1971). Moreover, parents devote comparatively more attention to teaching their daughters how to smile (Lake, 1975, p. 24). And parents soon begin telling little Dick that "big boys don't cry," but the same does not apply to little Jane.

From the beginning of life, the objects that surround an infant, including the clothes in which it is dressed, reflect its sex. Walum (1977,

p. 42) points out that "there are different styles and colors for male and female babies in such basics as cribs, potty seats, comforters, changing tables, diaper pins, and toys." A trip through any infant and children's store shows that not merely are the colors different, but so are the styles. Often the same basic piece of apparel is designed in two ways: "The male variant snaps from right to left, has a pointed collar and a football motif; the female snaps left to right, has a peter pan collar with lace trim and embroidered butterflies" (Walum, 1977, p. 42). A little later in life, parents will devote hours to combing *her* hair and putting decorations in it and will bedeck *her* with jewelry, but they will look with horror on *his* games with mother's lipstick or clothes. Jane will often be attired in dresses and told not to get dirty and not to do anything that will let her "underpants show"; Dick will be in trousers with no such restrictions—and later everyone will say that girls are innately less well physically coordinated and weaker than boys. And so begins the life and training of these new human beings.

The description of the early treatment of infants can provide useful insights in terms of the concepts developed above. First, from birth the nature of the interaction between parents and children differs markedly according to the sex of the child. If, indeed, the interaction process is crucial to the development of self-images, it is clear that those of males and females will eventually be quite different. The parents of the little girl relate to her as a breakable object to be carefully tended, protected, and beautified; the little boy's parents treat him as self-reliant, physically active, even "tough," and not very emotionally expressive. These images are undoubtedly learned by the children. In addition, children are verbally instructed and sanctioned for doing or refraining from certain things according to sex. Finally, these restrictions and encouragements serve to "define reality" for children in self-fulfilling ways. If little Jane is assumed to be weak, in need of protection, and an ornamental thing, she will be clothed in apparel reflecting these attributes and informed not to do anything out of keeping with her attire. Unable to swing on the jungle gym and still live up to her parents' image of her and the strictures they impose, she will most certainly fail to develop her muscles; ultimately, she will indeed be weak, in need of protection, and engrossed in her own appearance.

In taking a closer look at the process by which young children are thought to internalize their gender roles, David Lynn's excellent short text *Parental and Sex Role Identification* (1969) is useful. A vast quantity of child development literature is reviewed, and 38 propositions are developed to summarize the relevant theory and research. Lynn's approach to the subject is only one of many, but it is more sociologically relevant than most. For a somewhat more technical and detailed discussion, see Eleanor Maccoby's fine collection of articles entitled *The Development of Sex Differences* (1966) and also her more recent work with Carol Jacklin, *The Psychology of Sex Differences* (1974).

Lynn begins by asserting that both male and female infants usually establish their initial and principal identification with the mother, an identification that neither sex ever loses entirely (1969, pp. 21-23). This is predicated on the assumption, true in the majority of cases in this society, that the mother functions as the infant's chief caretaker. It is important to note that any change of that norm would invalidate this proposition. At any rate, having established this identity, the female child can continue it and, in so doing, learn the "appropriate" gender role behavior. To the extent that "identification" strongly entails imitation, young Jane need only copy her mother to be rewarded. In this way she quickly begins to internalize the feminine role behavior expected of her.

Little Dick, however, faces a serious problem. Given the relative absence of male figures during his waking hours, the male toddler is hard pressed to find out what he is supposed to do. Early in life his mother begins to sanction him negatively for imitating many of her ways. In this society the father is absent so often the child cannot imitate him, and when he is present, he joins the mother in punishing the boy for being "too feminine." Indeed, he usually surpasses the mother in this, perhaps because of his own gender role insecurities and a resulting fear of homosexuality. The result is that where Jane identifies easily with her mother, Dick must identify with a cultural definition of masculinity that he pieces together from peers, media, a series of don'ts from his parents and so on (Lynn, 1969, pp. 23-26). In fact, according to Lynn, peers are more important in shaping the identity of males than females (p. 92). The boy finds out that "boys don't cry," "boys don't cling," and so on, but often on the basis of negative sanctions from parents and peers. Given the lesser efficacy of punishments compared to rewards in the socialization process, it is not surprising that males have greater difficulty establishing their gender role identities than females do. They also fail in this endeavor more frequently, are more anxious about it throughout their lives, and are more hostile toward the other sex (Lynn, pp. 57-64). It is also interesting to note that when they become parents, males appear to be more strongly influenced in their behavior and attitudes by the sex of their offspring than do females (Block, 1973, p. 69). This might also reflect insecurity concerning their own gender identity.

The ramifications of this duality are everywhere. Male fear of and hostility toward homosexuality finds little parallel among females, nor does the hang-up of "proving one's masculinity." Girls are far less concerned about the label "tomboy" (and, in fact, often wear it with pride) than boys are about "sissy." Undoubtedly, too, there is a relationship between this phenomenon and the kinds of problems presented by school-aged boys, some of which were mentioned in Chapter 2 (see Sexton, 1969).

There are other implications of the two rather radically different methods of early gender role learning. Jane, it will be recalled, learns by imitation and positive reinforcement. Dick, on the other hand, has to make a mental effort to comprehend what he is supposed to be, and he more frequently receives negative sanctions. One result, according to Lynn, is that throughout their lives females rely more on affection, or demonstrate a "greater need for affiliation," than males. Males develop greater problem-solving abilities because of this early mental exercise. Moreover, they become more concerned with internalized moral standards than females, who rely more on the opinions of others (Lynn, 1969, chap. 4).

It is important to bear in mind that this duality is predicated on the relatively constant presence of the mother and, conversely, the relative absence of the father. This is certainly the typical (although hardly necessary) American pattern. If this pattern were reversed, all of the traits discussed as common to one or the other sex would need to be reversed as well. In examining the relationship of family structure to gender role learning, Lynn offers a series of other arguments (Lynn, chap. 5). The "normal" family is assumed to consist of a close mother and *moderately* distant father. A moderately distant father is close enough to provide some model for the young boy, as well as the motivation to use that model, but sufficiently remote to require the mental effort on the part of the boy that was discussed above. Boys with either very close or very distant fathers will not develop analytical skills superior to those of the average girl. In the first case, the boy will directly imitate the father, much as the girl does the mother. In the second, the intellectual effort (and lack of motivation) may be just too great to cope with. Conversely, girls with more distant mothers and/or fathers as caretakers will develop analytical skills commensurate with those of the average male. Lois Hoffman (1972) has even suggested that girls may "need a little maternal rejection if they are to become independently competent and self-confident." Certainly, the assumption made by many that the best way to bring up any child, regardless of sex, is with a constantly present mother must be open to serious question.

In our society males have considerably more prestige, power, and freedom than females. Little children are not oblivious to this fact. Thus, again according to Lynn (1969, pp. 65-78), although boys experience initially much greater gender role identity problems than girls, as time goes on they become more firmly identified with the masculine role. Females, however, do not do so with reference to the feminine role. Indeed, more girls show preference for the high-prestige and powerful masculine role than boys do for the feminine role, as witnessed by the relative numbers of "tomboys" and "sissies." Pushing this logic a step further, it is likely that given the higher prestige of the masculine role, homosexuality and sissiness may appear as a kind of betrayal, while lesbianism and tomboyishness may appear as more or less understandable imitations of a superior status role. This would help to explain the far greater social antipathy to the former than the latter (see Pogrebin, 1972). Similarly, feminine fashions often "ape" masculine ones, but the opposite rarely occurs. The whole notion of transvestism basically applies to males only; no one blinks an eye at a female in jeans, a shirt, and boots or sneakers, much less suggests that she is a transvestite, but a male in a skirt (unless he is Scotch or an ancient Roman) is a different matter.

It is clear that parents play a major role in the process of socialization in general and the communication of gender role identity and behavior in particular. Moreover, it is clear that children have established a firm notion of their gender role by about age 3, if not earlier. By this age, little Dick is already objecting to certain things because they are for girls, and Jane is happily imitating mother with her dolls and tea parties.

However, a view of human development that claims that any identities or behavior patterns are irrevocably set for life by that age seems to me to be myopic. Life for most humans *is* change, to a greater or lesser degree. If such changes are slow relative to those occurring in the first years of life, they nonetheless exist and, cumulatively, may sometimes acquire substantial dimensions. Any such changes away from patterns established by parents must logically be initiated from some source outside the home environment. If society at large provides strong, even coercive supports for identities and behaviors learned early in life from parents, they will be further reinforced rather than changed. This seems, by and large, to be the case with reference to gender roles, inasmuch as most parents reflect stereotypical gender role definitions.

The following sections will consider some of these reinforcing and control mechanisms as they act on the child. A fitting prelude to this discussion would be Lois Gould's "X: A Fabulous Child's Story" (1972). This is a short story describing what happens to one young child (Baby X) who is reared without the traditional gender role identity as part of a "secret scientific Xperiment known as Project Baby X." The author whimsically relates the adventures and frustrations experienced by the family, which refuses to divulge the sex of their child.

Communication

During infancy and early childhood people learn the characteristic modes of communication of their culture and subculture. Both verbal and nonverbal forms of communication are involved. Most American children learn English, beginning in early infancy. In addition, most children learn a series of gender-appropriate ways to use the language and to use their bodies to communicate. Both the language itself and the different usages associated with each sex reflect and reinforce stereotypical gender roles. A detailed discussion of communication and gender roles can be found in Robin Lakoff's excellent book *Language and Woman's Place* (1975). Other good summaries of existing research on this topic are Henley and Thorne (1977), Walum (1977), and Deaux (1976).

For the English-speaking population as well as for many others, sex is an overwhelmingly important fact of language. While most if not all languages probably have words to distinguish the sexes, English makes it almost impossible *not to* so distinguish in discussing humans. This is true even if the sex involved is not known or is irrelevant to the topic. We do not have a sex-free singular pronoun to refer to a human; "it" is not generally used for this purpose. Thus, when speaking of another person, at least in the singular, we either use the name (which is sex linked) or "he" or "she." I have conspicuously tried to avoid assigning sex when it is not called for in this book and have found it a difficult task requiring constant attention (and rewriting). Moreover, it could involve incorrect grammar, because the only non-sex-linked pronoun is plural ("they"). If I begin a sentence with reference to "a child" and then need to refer back to it with a pronoun, I should use the singular "he" or "she," but I am tempted to use "they." One means of avoiding irrelevant uses of a sex-specific pronoun is to avoid using the singular altogether. Kate Millett and Casey Swift (1972) have suggested the institution of a new singular "common gender" to overcome this problem. It would consist of "tey" (he or she), "ter" (his or her), and "tem" (him or her).

On the surface it may seem trivial to be concerned that the pronoun "he" is commonly used generically, to refer to all people. However, the fact that such usage reinforces, at least subconsciously, an impression that humanity is male becomes clear when we note the exception. As Nancy Henley and Barrie Thorne (1977, p. 203) point out, "many people who claim they are referring to both males and females when they use the word *he* switch to the feminine pronoun when they begin to speak of someone in a traditionally female occupation, such as homemaker or schoolteacher or nurse."

Many other words, particularly adjectives, are sex-linked. We rarely speak of "beautiful" males and "handsome" females, and when we do, the male is very young and the female somewhat old; in short, both are desexed. To call a woman "ambitious" or "aggressive" is an insult, but to say either of a man is a compliment. The opposite is the case with such words as "sensitive" and "intuitive." Even many objects and animals are generally associated with one of the sexes. Ships are feminine, as are hurricanes; cats are feminine, rats and dogs masculine (except if we insult a female by calling her a "bitch").

Sex is everywhere evident in occupational names: salesman/ saleswoman, waiter/ waitress, poet/poetess, not to mention titles such as king/queen, duke/duchess, Mr./Mrs., Miss, Ms. Where we lack a feminine equivalent for an occupational title we typically add "lady" or "woman" to the title, thus conveying that we normally presume the occupation is masculine. Thus, for instance, we hear about "lady doctors" and "women lawyers" but never of "gentlemen" or "men" doctors or lawyers. Presumably, in the latter case it would sound redundant. Carol Tarvis and Carole Offir (1977, p. 184, footnote 7) report the following case as illustrative of the confusion arising out of occupational titles. The British were faced with a linguistic crisis when Elizabeth Lane became their first female High Court Justice. They did not want to call her "My Lord," yet "Mrs. Justice" did not seem appropriate either. The decision rendered by the Lord Chancellor's office converted Mrs. Lane into Mr. Justice Lane, who was thus to be called "My Lord." This also entitled "His Lordship" to a bachelor knighthood. The Chancellor actually justified this as the "least absurd decision"!

Such identification, however, does not merely separate the sexes; our language makes the male the basic reality and, in Simone de Beauvoir's (1953) words, the female the "other." Where I have talked about "humans," "people," and "Homo sapiens," most people in our culture would use the equally correct term "men." Indeed, *homo* means precisely that; the root of "human" is "man." Even the root of "female" is found in "male," and the root of "woman" in "man." The problem discussed above with reference to the singular pronoun is not solved by approximately equal reference to "him" and "her" when sex is unknown or irrelevant; the masculine form is uniformly used. We have *his*tory to learn; in anthropology classes we study Peking *man* and Neanderthal *man;* in other social science courses, economic *man* and political *man.* Economists speak of *man*power; organizations have chair*men;* police go on *man*hunts; and utilities are found in *man*holes. We even pronounce couples man (not husband) and wife (not woman)!

In her marvelous chapter in *Adam's Rib* entitled "Society Writes Biology," Ruth Herschberger (1954; also see Stannard, 1972) demonstrates how the language used by medical science "under the guise of objective fact" consistently "animates" the male part in the reproductive cycle and "deanimates" the female. Thus, for instance, the identical process is called an "erection" for males and "congestion" for females. Similarly, the terms "impotence" and "frigidity," both of which represent the same basic physiological phenomenon, convey very different images. In the first case there is a lack of power or activity; in the second, merely an unpleasant environmental factor.

Over time words change their meanings. It is interesting to note that in English, a wide variety of words referring to women have been deprecated over the ages, although the reverse has not happened to their masculine counterparts. Henley and Thorne (1977, p. 204) point out that "words such as *king, prince, lord, father* have all maintained their stately meanings," compared to "the similar words *queen, madam,* and *dame. . . ."* According to Walum (1977, p. 21) "nymph" once meant "beautiful young female," rather than "a sexually loose woman." We even derogate males by using female words such as "pussy" or "sissy" (diminutive of sister), or by impugning the dignity of a man's mother with labels such as "bastard" or "son of a bitch." Another example of a word changing its meaning and, in the process, derogating females, is the term "gossip." Originally, the word simply referred to close relationships. Only in the 19th century did it begin to take on the meaning of idle talk, but as it did so, it became specifically associated with females. Today, a male who engages in the behavior that would earn a female the title "gossip" is called "an old woman" (Rysman, 1977).

It should be clear that our language itself does two things in relation to gender roles: it constantly focuses attention on sex, and it does so in such a way as to imply that females are less than fully human, or at least that the model of humanity is male. The manner in which we learn to use our language further encourages both of these phenomena. As pointed out above, many adjectives mean one thing when applied to males and another when applied to females. In addition, we do not use counterpart words to refer to the two sexes. An adult male is a "man"; to call him a "boy" is an insult, and that word is used only to refer to those of very low status. Rarely do we use the term "gentleman." An adult female is usually a "lady" or a "girl," but rarely a "woman." "Lady" effectively desexes females, while "girl" denotes immaturity as well as a lack of sexuality, thus conveying an inferior status. The impact of these differences is often quite powerful. Imagine for a moment referring to the members of a professional football team as boys or gentlemen! Consider what you mean when you say "He's a real gentleman" versus "He's a real man." Then think of "Ladies' Liberation Movement" versus "Women's Liberation Movement" (Walum, 1977, p. 17). Or consider the words "bachelor" and "spinster" and compare the sentences "Mary hopes to meet an eligible bachelor" to "Fred hopes to meet an eligible spinster" (Lakoff, 1975, p. 32).

Females are taught not to use slang or curse words; they aren't "ladylike." The result is that females' speech lacks forcefulness. Consider the difference between "Oh dear! I stubbed my toe" and "Oh shit! I stubbed my toe." Females tend to use euphemisms ("powder room"), diminutives ("hanky," "meanie"), extravagant adjectives ("heavenly," "divine"), and intensifiers ("awfully," "quite"). All of these practices rob women's language of force and trivialize their thoughts (see Lakoff, 1975; Henley & Thorne, 1977). Compare "What a terrific steel mill" to "What a lovely steel mill" (Lakoff, 1975, p. 13).

The vocabulary available to men and women differs too. Women have many more words to express their emotions, feelings, and such things as colors (ever hear a man say "mauve" to describe the color of an object?). Men have more words available to use in conversing about physical objects (other than color), sports, mechanical objects, and so on.

Men also use a more forceful inflection in speaking than women do. In addition, the difference in pitch between the way women and men speak is far greater than that dictated by biological differences in vocal cords. Even before puberty, when no biological differences in vocal cords exist, boys speak in a lower pitch than girls. Moreover, females tend to convey a "polite, cheerful pattern" with a marked upswing in pitch at the end of their sentences (Deaux, 1976, p. 59). All of these traits detract from the authoritativeness of speech for women. This is further exacerbated by women's tendency to use what Lakoff calls the tag question in what would otherwise be a command or statement. For instance, suppose Jane is cooking dinner; she knows perfectly well when it will be ready. Instead of saying to husband Dick, "Dinner will be ready at 6:00" she might say "Dinner will be ready around 6:00?" Or consider the difference between the following statements, the first two of which are most typically male:

> Close the door.
> Please close the door.
> Will you close the door?
> Will you please close the door?
> Won't you close the door? (Lakoff, 1975, p. 18)

Women are not used to commanding, and especially not used to commanding men. By converting their statements to questions they soften the command, lose forcefulness, and convey an inferior status.

Myth to the contrary, women speak less than men, especially in mixed-sex situations. Men more frequently initiate topics and interrupt speakers. Men also less frequently respond to topics initiated by women than vice versa. Women are more likely to react to the comments of others in a supportive fashion, conveying interest with sounds such as "mmm." Because they are more frequently interrupted and less frequently supported in conversation by males, females tend to become passive recipients of conversations. Women also ask questions more frequently than men and use attention-getting devices such as prefacing a statement with "This is interesting" (Brantley, 1977). The result is that women's ideas are often not expressed and, when expressed, are often ignored.

Finally, males and females differ in their nonverbal styles of communicating. Women smile much more than men. Indeed, some women almost constantly wear smiles. This may be interpreted as "the equivalent of the Uncle Tom shuffle—a gesture made to indicate submissiveness in the face of a superior" (Deaux, 1976, p. 63). Women also spend more time looking directly at their conversational partners than do men, which enables them to be more sensitive to nonverbal communication. In fact, Kay Deaux suggests (p. 64) that the much-touted "women's intuition" is, in actuality, a matter of women reading nonverbal communication (which may contradict the verbal message) because of more eye contact. Males tend to allow their bodies to take up more space during conversation by the way they stand and the way they gesture. This adds a presence and a flamboyance to their communication (Henley & Thorne, 1977, p. 213). Another way in which nonverbal communication demonstrates gender role inequality is in touching. Many students of this topic point out that superiors initiate touching; it is a sign of dominance. Cuddling in response to the touch is a gesture of submissiveness (see Deaux, 1976; Henley & Thorne, 1977). Bosses touch employees, but not vice versa; the same with teachers and students and, in this context, males and females. Whether or not the intent is even remotely sexual, males initiate touching and females often respond by cuddling. In fact, if a female initiates touching with a male, it is immediately assumed that a sexual overture is being made. The same is not the case if a male casually touches a female.

Young children are constantly surrounded by people communicating, verbally and nonverbally. Given the way our language treats the two sexes as separate and unequal, the way the sexes use the language to convey that phenomenon, and the ways in which our body language further reinforces the message, it can be assumed that in communication powerful, subconscious reinforcement of traditional gender roles occurs.

Toys and Sports

The importance of play in teaching children the roles and values of society has been stressed by George Mead (1934), as well as by the famous Swiss child psychologist Jean Piaget (1932). As children move from solitary play, which usually consists of imitative role-playing (mother, fire fighter, truck driver), to organized games with other children, they gradually come to understand that society is based on a system of rules and interlocking roles; in Mead's terminology, they learn about "the generalized other." The play and games characteristic of a society contribute rather substantially to socializing children into their particular sociocultural milieu.

Past a relatively early age, children are usually segregated by sex in their play groups, which function almost as little "subcultures" with their own norms and roles. Nonetheless, these groups strongly reflect the broader culture and serve, by and large, to reinforce gender role stereotyping. From an early age boys' groups engage in more competitive team games with more elaborate rules than girls' groups do.

Young girls alone play "house"; this is probably also one of their most frequent activities together. They also play games that are relatively uncomplex and have few rules, like jump rope and hopscotch. Neither of these consists of any team effort, and both are only minimally competitive. Girls frequently "practice" twirling and cheerleading as they get a bit older, or they might engage in arts and crafts or dancing, activities which are not competitive and do not have elaborate rules. Sports considered appropriate for females include swimming, skating, and horseback riding, all of which have few rules and often no competition. Also considered appropriate are golf and tennis, both of which have less elaborate rules than popular male sports do and usually do not entail team effort. A more complete discussion of sports which females participate in is to be found in Ellen Gerber et al., *The American Woman in Sport* (1974).

Meanwhile, their brothers have organized or been organized to play baseball, football, soccer, and basketball, all quite elaborate games emphasizing the strong need for intrateam cooperation, strategy development, and interteam competition. Popular also is some form of "guns" (cowboys and Indians, cops 'n robbers), again usually a competitive team effort.

In a study of predominantly white, middle-class, fifth-graders, Janet Lever (1976) documented a number of ways in which the play of boys and girls was found to differ. Boys played outdoors more frequently than girls, and they also played more often in larger groups. Boys played in more age-heterogeneous groups than did girls. The reason for this is that boys' games, unlike those played by girls, often require that someone—anyone—play a given position (e.g., outfielder). If no older boy was available, they would accept a younger one rather than leave the position unfilled. Lever also found that girls were more prominent in boys' games than boys were in girls' games. This reflects the less negative reactions to a "tomboy" than to a "sissy." Boys played more competitive games than did girls. In fact, boys "gamed" more, while girls "played" more, and the games required more skill than the play. Boys' games also lasted longer than girls' did. Lever argues that the girls hadn't developed sufficient motor skills to make their games challenging and exciting. And boys were able to resolve disputes better; in girls' games, arguments often resulted in break-up of the game. In short, girls were not learning how to deal with direct competition, the judicial process of conflict resolution, cooperation with teammates, or the execution of complex game plans. Lever concludes by suggesting that boys, but not girls, learn skills needed later for business and professional careers in their childhood play. Alan Booth (1972) reaches essentially similar conclusions about the importance of games for boys: "Team competition fosters and provides social conditions favorable to friendship formation. . . . Furthermore, in team activities a boy learns group procedures and practices which he can later apply to role performance. . . . Thus, . . . team activities develop social initiative in males" (p. 184; see also Walum, 1977, pp. 62-63).

Until very recently, girls were systematically barred from most team sports. This occurred both in the informal context of the neighborhood and, more importantly, in such increasingly organized contexts as school and Little League competition. Indeed, only a few years ago some states forbade interscholastic athletic competition for females (Booth, 1972, p. 184). Despite recent federal regulations prohibiting different treatment of boys' and girls' athletics in schools, it remains the case that much more money flows to boys' athletic programs than to those for girls. The facilities, coaching, and training for girls continue to be inferior, despite some recent gains. Research cited by Walum (1977, pp. 64-65) demonstrates that there are few actual differences in strength, endurance, or body composition (ratio of fat to lean) between girl and boy athletes; their performance differences are primarily due to differences in training programs.

The division of play by sex is strongly supported by toy and game manufacturers, who undoubtedly sell more if sister Jane needs an entirely different set of toys from brother Dick's. How else can one explain the existence of "boy's" and "girl's" bikes? The bar on a boy's bicycle is dangerous for both boys and girls, but the average boy would sooner walk than risk being seen on a girl's bike and labeled "sissy"! To say the least, this constitutes a very profitable situation for bicycle manufacturers and retail stores.

In a study observing purchasing patterns of children's toys at Christmas time, Louis Goodman and Janet Lever (1974) found that up to about the age of 3, children of both sexes receive many of the same toys. The older the child, the greater the differentiation between the toys purchased for boys and for girls. Most adults purchasing toys bought those traditionally associated with the sex of the recipient. Boys received a wider range of toys than did girls, and, although both received about the same number of gifts, boys' gifts were more often toys. Adults spent more time in selecting toys for boys than for girls. Not a single scientific toy was bought for a girl. Goodman and Lever also examined toy catalogs of nine major department stores and found 102 categories of items illustrated exclusively with pictures of boys, compared to 73 showing only a girl.

Walum (1977, p. 49) made a similar study of Sears's Christmas "Wish Book" (toy catalog). Illustrations of those toys that are preparatory for spousehood and parenthood pictured only girls in 84 percent, and none pictured only boys. For manipulatory toys (e.g., construction sets) 75 percent of the illustrations showed only boys, and 8 percent only girls. For toys which are preparatory for occupational roles, 25 percent of the illustrations showed boys only, 8 percent girls only; the other 67 percent pictured both. While almost all the pictures associated with cultural and educational toys included both sexes, even here boys-only pictures constituted 9 percent compared to only 2 percent showing girls only.

Several students in a 1971 course on the sociology of sex roles did content analyses on toy catalogs from Sears, Montgomery Ward's, Creative Playthings, and a few local department stores. They found a strong emphasis on gender role stereotyping. Another perusal of a Creative Playthings catalog found that while this company conspicuously avoided sex typing the toys in the written descriptions, the pictures were another matter altogether. In the bulk of cases the boys pictured were quite actively playing with the toy; girls pictured were usually watching a boy play or, at best, were seated at a table using only their hands. These impressions are only somewhat borne out by the findings reported in Table 3.1 from a study by students Diana Black and Betsy Mellus of three catalogs, including Creative Playthings. Boys were indeed pictured more frequently as physically active and mechanical, and girls as more physically passive, but the differences were quite small. The outstanding fact to be noted in this table is that altogether boys were pictured more than twice as frequently as girls.

TABLE 3.1

GENDER ROLE CHARACTERISTICS AS PICTURED IN THREE TOY CATALOGS

| | Percent of Children Pictured with Characteristics | |
Characteristic	Male Children	Female Children
Physically active	18%	14%
Physically passive	17	23
Mechanical or manipulative	23	17
Competitive	6	5
Vocational	8	6
Emotionally expressive	27	34
Number of children pictured	132	64

A study of Christmas toy catalogs from Sears and Ward's by students Janna Wilder and Deborah Scott found marked sex-related differences, beginning with the division into "boys'" and "girls'" sections. The girls' sections were full of dolls of every description, particularly baby dolls. Full sets of household goods, from dishes to toy vacuum cleaners and ovens, were also displayed. In the costume section little Jane was shown she could be a nurse, a bride, a fairy princess, a ballerina, a majorette, or a cowgirl in a skirt. Other pages showed makeup kits, manicure sets, and other "beauty aids." The boys' sections were full of athletic gear, technological toys (tractors, building materials, etc.), toy soldiers, guns, and cars. Boys' dolls depicted Joe Namath, G. I. Joe, and an astronaut. A boy doctor was pictured with a girl nurse; boys were pictured being served "tea" by girls. Boys' costumes included a marine, Superman, an astronaut, a race car driver, a policeman, and a football player.

Altogether, there were 356 female dolls and only 68 male; 4 girls playing the organ or piano compared to no boys; 6 boys playing guitars or drums and no girls; 13 boys but only 1 girl riding a toy; 29 boys but no girls operating a model vehicle (train, car, tractor, etc.); 29 boys and only 2 girls operating construction toys; and so on. To the extent that such toys prepare their users for adult roles, it is clear that they do so in a most stereotypical fashion. Girls are being trained to be mothers, helpmates, and homemakers, or for one of a very limited number of "feminine" occupations. They are also encouraged to care for their appearance, although not particularly for the development of their muscles. Boys are patently not being trained for a major role most will eventually play: fatherhood. They are encouraged to consider a myriad of occupational possibilities and to develop their bodily strength and coordination, but not particularly to care for their appearance.

In another analysis of toy catalogs, students George Bronson and Ben Herring studied the types of toys and games advertised for the two sexes according to age. They found that those designed for toddlers (under 3) were not particularly differentiated for boys and girls. Beginning in the preschool category (ages 3—6) and reaching virtually 100 percent by elementary school age, toys and games were found to be stereotypically sex linked. However, games oriented to adults (over 20) again showed relatively very little sex differentiation. In short, during the age when gender role learning is most salient, toys and games are oriented toward reinforcing stereotypical notions of masculinity and femininity, but not before or after that period.

Given such differences in advertising and in purchasing patterns of toys for boys and girls, it is little wonder that research concerning the contents of boys' and girls' rooms shows that they differ substantially (Weitz, 1977). In a study of middle-class homes, Shirley Weitz found that the rooms of boys contained more animal-related furnishings, more educational art materials, more spatial-temporal toys, more sports equipment, and more toy animals. Girls' rooms contained more dolls, more floral furnishings, and more ruffles. In 48 boys' rooms there were 375 vehicles; in 48 girls' rooms, 17. Baby dolls were found in 26 of the girls' rooms, compared to only 3 of the boys'.

Communications Media

The studies of communications media reviewed in Chapter 2 found that for adults, the media reflect stereotypical notions of gender roles. For children, the TV programs they watch and the books they read can further serve to *teach* or *reinforce* learned gender roles which may be of a stereotypical nature. Because children have a less well-developed capacity than adults to judge what they see and hear and to reject some or all of it, whatever is presented to them by various media may be taken seriously as "truth." Thus, though such stereotypes in adult media might affect grown people's behaviors and self-images, similar material oriented to children will have a vastly greater impact on young Dick and Jane.

Research concerning children's television, books, and school texts consistently supports the conclusion that media aimed at children strongly reinforce gender role stereotypes. In research conducted by Helen Streicher (1974) on Saturday and Sunday morning televised cartoons and accompanying commercials, it was found that females were pictured less often than males, had fewer lines, played fewer lead roles, were less active, occupied many fewer positions of responsibility, and were more preponderantly juvenile. Mothers worked only in the home, and males did not participate in housework. Where females were depicted in an activity displaying skill (e.g., cheerleading), their performance was often duplicated by an animal. The only major lead part played by a female was Maid Marian, Robin Hoodnick's girl friend, and she was depicted as constantly nagging, complaining, wanting, and talking until she was shut up (by someone putting a bag over her head). In the commercials, boys outnumbered girls 3 to 1 as actors; the announcers were all male. Girls did not appear at all in ads for action toys but were overrepresented in doll and appliance commercials.

In a study by Muriel Cantor (1977) of six series of children's programs aired on public television, the percentage of female characters was found to range from 22 to 47 and the range of occupations was greater for male than for female characters. Sarah Sternglanz and Lisa Serbin (1974) also studied popular children's television programs and reported that

> . . . males came out as aggressive, constructive, and helpful, and they were most likely to be rewarded for their actions. Females were deferential and passive more often than males, and sometimes they were punished for being too active. Females did not have as much impact as males on the course of events, except when they used magic. Indeed, four of five female title-role stars were witches of some sort.

The same general findings are also reported in Levinson (1975).

An examination of books for children—preschool and school texts—shows about the same results as were found for television content. The following was discovered in a survey of elementary school readers by a group affiliated with the National Organization for Women (NOW) called Women on Words and Images (1972); a heavy preponderance (5 to 2 ratio) of boys' stories; younger sister-girl "ninny" syndrome; older and taller boys outnumbering girls in most illustrations; smarter boys with greater initiative and achievement; fathers who work and play creatively with children; aproned mothers in supportive and passive roles; men depicted in a wide variety of roles and activities; women almost exclusively depicted as mothers and teachers. These same types of stereotypes were found in an intensive examination of award-winning picture books for preschoolers (Weitzman et al., 1972). A study of coloring books by Susan Rachlin and Glenda Vogt (1974) found that the activities in which boys were pictured included fishing, building, and camping, while girls were shown playing in the sand, swinging, and jumping rope. Boys were pictured out-of-doors almost twice as often as girls. Girls were frequently pictured playing with dolls, while boys were almost never pictured in any domestic or parental roles. Concern for appearance was obviously displayed by girls but not by boys. Not only were males depicted more often than females in occupational roles, by a ratio of 3.5 to 1, but four times more occupational roles were displayed for males. These same general findings are repeated in Elizabeth Fisher's (1974) study of children's books. Few females were pictured relative to males, and when they were the females were most often shown as passive, with their roles limited in number and heavily oriented to homemaker activities. A later study, Hillman (1976), again replicates the same general findings.

Even in topic-specific texts, such as math and history, gender role stereotypes abound. In her study of math texts, Marsha Federbush (1974) found girls being depicted in domestic and passive roles and boys shown in constant activity. Moreover, girls were depicted as lacking mathematical competence, with statements such as: "Susan could not figure out how to," "Jim showed her how," "I guess girls are just no good in math," and so forth. In her review of over a dozen of the most popular U.S. history texts, Janice Trecker (1974) concluded that they omit many women of importance, while simultaneously minimizing the legal, social, and cultural disabilities women have faced. In a study of high school history books and a second-year Spanish text, students Diana Phillips and Pat Steed found clear evidence that females were portrayed as domestics and caretakers of children, males as workers of all types; females were pictured as frequently passive, males as generally active. Most striking, 98 percent of the people discussed in one history book were male; such an illustrious woman as Madame Curie was found only in the context of a sentence in which Monsieur Curie was said to have been "assisted by his wife." In another history book, in which females comprised only 3 percent of the entries, famous females like Amelia Earhart, Catherine the Great, and Queen Victoria were absent. Where Boy Scouts and the YMCA were discussed, their female counterparts were not mentioned. The author of *Frankenstein,* Mary Wollstonecraft Shelley, was introduced as the poet Shelley's wife, and, again, Madame Curie was presented as her husband's helpmate.

One recurring finding in these studies of children's media is that many more males are portrayed than females. This could be a reflection of the fact that both males and females in our society find males much more interesting characters, capable of doing a wider variety of things and doing them well. An alternative explanation relating to the gender role learning process, as discussed by Lynn (1969) and reviewed above, is also possible. Recall that little boys need to piece together their concept of masculinity from a variety of sources, whereas young girls need only imitate a model readily available to achieve femininity. TV, books, and toy catalogs can all be viewed as instruments representing a model of masculinity to the growing boy for his emulation. It is patently clear that such a model is highly stereotyped.

School

If Dick and Jane have "normal" parents, that is, parents functioning more or less within their stereotyped gender roles, and if they play with peers, look at TV, and are read the typical preschool books, they will arrive at school pretty firmly entrenched in their respective stereotyped gender roles. When they get there, as we have seen, their books will reinforce this further; so, generally, will their teachers, counselors, and administrators (Andreas, 1971, chap. 2; Guttentag & Bray, 1977).

The manner in which the school system is staffed in itself may reinforce children's notions that the masculine role is identified with more power and prestige than the feminine role is. Succinctly put, women work in an educational system run by men. Men comprise the overwhelming proportion of school administrators, including principals and policy-makers such as members of the school board. Women comprise the overwhelming proportion of grade school teachers, although as one moves up in grade level the proportion of male teachers increases (Guttentag & Bray, 1977). Indeed, although nearly 90 percent of grade school teachers are female, nearly 90 percent of their principals are male (Walum, 1977, p. 57).

Until the last few years, in many schools girls were not permitted by school administrators to wear slacks or pants of any variety. Attired in dresses, little girls were obviously less willing to engage in a variety of play activities designed to develop strength, stamina, and coordination. On many a school playground they could be observed using the jump ropes provided by their teachers or the swings, while the little boys were climbing the jungle gym or beginning to play baseball and football. Even where girls were engaged in some sort of ball game (usually segregated from the boys), they found it hard to devote themselves to it wholeheartedly. Picture Jane sliding into second base on her bare legs, skirt flying! While Jane was finding it difficult to play such games, Dick was discovering that if he couldn't play them well, his friends and even teachers would make life rough for him. This situation was exacerbated by the fact that having matured earlier, little Janes are likely to be stronger, taller, and better coordinated than little Dicks, who nevertheless have learned to consider themselves physically superior to girls. According to Marcia Guttentag and Helen Bray (1977, p. 397) teachers have reported that recent changes in dress codes which now allow girls to wear pants "are the most important factors in erasing distinctions in activities, since the elementary school girls can now climb and run as fast as the boys without hindrance of a skirt."

Boys and girls are separated and treated somewhat differently in a variety of other ways during grammar school. They are often lined up separately for assemblies, play, and such, separated in seating arrangements, and placed on opposing teams for spelling bees and other competitions. Such separation supports the desires for exclusiveness of little boys, who generally already understand their superior social status. Girls serve the cookies and punch during school parties, while boys move the furniture and carry the books (Pogrebin, 1972, p. 27). Boys are permitted to engage in considerably more physical activity and make more noise in the classroom (Howe, 1971, p. 81). The sexes are probably most frequently separated throughout the school years for discussions of hygiene and sex education, a procedure designed to ensure poor communication between them later on the subject of sex. When boys "put girls down," as they often do at that age, teachers (female usually) frequently say and do nothing to correct them (Baumrind, 1972, p. 166), thus tacitly encouraging their notion of superiority. According to studies cited by Florence Howe (1971, p. 81), teachers assume that girls "are likely to 'love' reading and to 'hate' mathematics and sciences," and the opposite is expected of boys. Here are some self-fulfilling prophecies on the way to becoming realities.

As Dick and Jane progress through school, she will learn figure-watching exercises in gym while he is climbing the ropes; she may, at least in the past, play a variety of basketball requiring little movement or contact while he risks a broken nose to prove how good and brave an athlete he is in contact sports; she will giggle when she strikes out at softball and her pals will hardly care (nor will her teacher), while he will be ostracized if his coordination is lacking. After school, while Dick is trying out for school teams in football, baseball, track, or basketball, Jane is learning such ancillary activities as cheerleading, twirling, and "dancing" with a large group of her friends.

Past grammar school the curriculum itself becomes somewhat "sexregated." Although the formal rules by which different curricula were offered and/or required of males and females have largely been abolished in the past few years, custom still dictates a strong sex-segregated curriculum in certain areas. At many schools girls were required to take cooking and sewing and occasionally typing; woodworking and machine shop were required of boys. Frequently school administrators did not permit students of one sex to take a course designed for the other one, and certainly they were not encouraged to do so by peers or teachers. Very recently, however, girls seem to be enrolling in such "boys' courses" as woodshop and auto mechanics, though boys have been more reluctant to enroll in "girls' courses." Often when boys show an interest in the subject matter of the traditional "girls' courses," new courses are instituted for them. For instance, boys who want to learn to cook may be offered "bachelor living," and those who wish to acquire clerical skills may be given a course in "office management" (Walum, 1977, p. 56).

By junior high, too, school counselors are strongly encouraging males and females in different career directions. It was not too many years ago that black and brown youngsters were systematically discouraged by their "counselors" from seeking a college education or setting their sights on white-collar jobs. By and large such racist practices have now ceased, but their sexist counterparts have not. College-bound girls are still frequently counseled into considering "typically feminine" curricula such as nursing, teaching, and home economics, and avoiding "masculine" fields like engineering, medicine, or business. Conversely, boys are urged to consider engineering, business, medicine, and so forth, and to eschew the fine arts, grammar school teaching, and other "feminine" fields. A good science student will be urged into high school science teaching if female; if male, into engineering, "pure" science, or medicine. Non-college-bound girls are pushed into typing courses to prepare them for secretarial futures, while their brothers are encouraged to become mechanics. The possibility of a male secretary or a female mechanic never seems to occur to counselors. Indeed, when there is doubt as to whether or not youngsters should pursue a college education, counselors frequently encourage males and discourage females.

In their guidance activities, school counselors employ standardized preference and aptitude tests, which often are stereotyped in terms of gender role and the interpretations given to identical scores. If they gave the same answers, a boy and a girl would be presented with different sets of occupations to which they would be advised to aspire. For instance, a female who scored high in interest in the health professions would be advised to become a dietician, nurse, physical therapist, or dental hygienist; her male counterpart would be directed to careers in medicine, pharmacy, or dentistry (Walum, 1977, p. 56).

Counselors defend such practices on the basis of what youngsters may "realistically" expect to face in the future: for females, marriage, child care, and lack of opportunity in a number of career fields; for males, the need to support a family at the highest income and status levels possible. "Realism," however, has always been an excuse for maintaining the status quo, and it is no different in the case of gender role stereotypes. If, for instance, females do not prepare to enter previously masculine fields, such fields will remain male dominated, and another generation of counselors can then assure girls that females can't work in them. In addition, it is questionable whether counselors' notions of "reality" in fact keep pace with reality. There is undoubtedly a lag between expanding opportunities and changing gender role definitions on the one hand, and counselors' awareness of these phenomena on the other.

The behavior of teachers also reinforces gender role stereotypes, which is scarcely surprising since they were raised in the same culture as their students. Despite the fact that in very recent years most teachers have expressed a socially acceptable equalitarian attitude toward the sexes (see the research cited by Guttentag & Bray, 1977, p. 398), their behavior and other attitudes continue to reflect different expectations of male and female students. Guttentag and Bray report that teachers see their role as meeting student needs, and they perceive that males and females have very different needs. The idea of shaping these needs is not considered valid. Further, these perceived student needs are highly stereotyped. In one study (Walum, 1977, p. 580), "good female students" were described by such adjectives as "calm," "cooperative," "dependable," "obliging," "thorough," and "mannerly," while "good male students" were described as "active," "aggressive," "assertive," "independent," and "curious." In another study, observations of first-grade classes led to the following description: "Boys were questioned more, criticized more, and had more ideas accepted and rejected. Girls volunteered significantly more often but were not called on" (Guttentag & Bray, 1977, p. 399). Boys are perceived by teachers as greater behavioral problems than girls, and, as a result, they receive far more attention. Although much of the attention boys receive is negative, the fact remains that girls are rewarded for their passivity and "goodness" and largely ignored most of the time, thus reinforcing female "invisibility."

Children spend approximately 1,000 hours a year in school (Walum, 1977, p. 57). It is very clear that the structure of the school, its "hidden curriculum," and even its actual curriculum serve to reinforce gender role stereotypes.

Adolescence: A Time for "Adjustment"

In any consideration of adolescents, two related concepts appear repeatedly: "identity crisis" and "anxiety." From puberty until they complete school and enter their adult statuses both males and females in contemporary American society are thought to undergo more or less severe emotional crises centered around questions of who they are and what they will become. Questions concerning gender role identities contribute mightily to such problems, although they are broader than this alone. It is during the years following the onset of puberty that both males and females are faced with making major decisions that will usually influence the manner in which they live the rest of their lives. Such decisions are most often made within the boundaries of gender role ˉtereotypes. Boys are generally urged into courses of action preparatory to some occupational commitment, girls into behaviors designed ultimately to attract a suitable mate (see Rosenberg & Simmons, 1975).

The impact of peers on behavior and thought is probably never greater than at this period of life when, as young adults, they strive to establish their independence by breaking ties with their parents (Weitz, 1977, pp. 88-89). The strong sex segregation characteristic of younger peer groups begins to break down somewhat during adolescence, with dating. However, all-male and all-female friendship groups or cliques persist, as indeed they do in adulthood. Moreover, peer groups become relatively more important in influencing the behaviors and attitudes of young adults. They also play a major role in determining the chances of their members for success with the other sex.

As a general rule, all-male groups determine the relative status and prestige of the various individual males within them. Such prestige is a function of how well the adolescent boy fulfills the norms of the group. Thus, in middle-class peer groups, boys are often expected to be good (but not *too* good) students and active in a number of extracurricular activities, which function as modes of preparation for college and high-status career. They are also expected to maintain athletic competence and to achieve considerable independence from their families. Working-

and lower-class peer groups usually place heaviest emphasis on independence, physical courage, and adventuresomeness, sometimes as tested in illegal ventures. These groups generally deemphasize and even denigrate school success. Regardless of social class, athletic skill plays a central role, one that is "disproportionate to its role in adult life" (Coleman, 1961), in establishing the popularity and prestige of adolescent males.

Those who manage to achieve high status within all-male groups attract more of the most attractive females from among class and ethnic equals. In turn, status within all-female groups is largely contingent upon the status of the males the girl is able to attract as dates or "steadies." In other words, female peer groups at this stage of the life cycle (and probably thereafter) base their internal prestige structure on their members' relative abilities to do best what society commands: to attract (potential) outstanding mates.

Note that in the case of female groups there are no differences by socioeconomic class (see Flora, 1971, for a related argument). Male groups also base their internal structure on that which society suggests is appropriate to the sex, but class variations do exist. Females of all classes are enjoined to find mates as their primary responsibility. Males of all classes are enjoined to be physically coordinated and aggressive, and to acquire an occupation. However, the occupational roles anticipated by working- and lower-class youths are generally not of a nature where school performance is very relevant. In these peer groups, other aspects of the stereotype become overwhelmingly dominant. Middle-class males, for whom school performance is relevant to future occupational expectations, develop norms by which these other characteristics share importance with academic success.

In examining the pressures exerted on adolescents and the ways in which they contribute to "anxieties" arising from "identity crises," it should be noted that whether or not the female has conformed previously to stereotypical notions of femininity (and substantial numbers of "tomboys" have not), the pressure by peers and parents to do so in adolescence becomes substantial (Freeman, 1970, pp. 38-39). At this point in her life, preparation for the search for a "mate" and the search itself begin in earnest, and that is presumably the one crucial fact of her entire future existence and identity. Thus, at this stage girls turn their attention to interpersonal success, to being "well liked," while boys' attention remains riveted on "doing well" or instrumental success (Rosenberg & Simmons, 1975).

Girls perform substantially better than boys in the earlier years of school, probably out of a "feminine" desire to please the teacher. Suddenly in high school and, especially, college their performance declines noticeably, while that of males, particularly those in the middle class, improves markedly in preparation for a career. Adolescent girls are enjoined to "play dumb and weak" in order to "boost male egos" and thereby attract and hold a suitable mate, whose identity they can then assume. In a now-famous series of experiments conducted among female college students, Matina Horner (1969) demonstrated that females fear achievement and success (also see Gornick, 1972; Tarvis & Offir, 1977, pp. 190-93). While subsequent research in the area of fear of success has been more ambiguous in its results, it is probably still safe to say that there is pressure on adolescent females to dampen or minimize their achievement strivings in areas other than popularity. The bright, dynamic, adolescent Jane, the one who is planning a career or the good athlete, either "plays dumb and weak" and lives a frustrating lie, or she pursues her interests as a relative outcast, dateless and low in prestige among her peers, wondering bitterly and anxiously why she isn't more "feminine." This will continue and increase in college, in graduate school, and even throughout life. Many finally conclude that they cannot have both a fulfilling life in terms of their own interests and aspirations and a satisfactory relationship with a male. Whichever goes by the wayside, life will be less rich as a result of the phony choice offered by society, beginning most noticeably in adolescence.

Nor is the girl who opts for "femininity" at the expense of her individual needs and inclinations any better off later, as the material cited in Chapter 2 demonstrates. In their quest for identity through an attachment to a male, many adolescent females find themselves pressured into sexual relationships in an attempt to attract, please, or "hold" boyfriends. This may be particularly true for less attractive girls. Such relationships often result in out-of-wedlock pregnancies, "shotgun" marriages, adjudication as "delinquent," or serious emotional problems for those who have been trained to consider sex outside of marriage as "evil" or "sinful." In any case, such sexual experiences, *when engaged in for those kinds of reasons,* often develop into unpleasant situations, fraught with problems of every variety and hardly beneficial to the development of a positive identity. In this context I am not considering all premarital sexual relations but only those engaged in out of a desire on the part of the female to please the male, regardless of her own personal needs and feelings at the time. In their quest for identity through attachment to a male, all too many young women leave themselves open to crass sexual exploitation and, as we shall see, most males are pressured into taking advantage of such situations. The recent rise in teenage pregnancies, during an era of rapidly declining birth rates, undoubtedly attests to this phenomenon. For many young women, female liberation may amount to little more than freedom to engage in premarital sex, without the psychic wherewithal to withstand male pressure to do so.

Dick, too, is facing his share of problems at this stage. Where Jane at least has the option, however unpleasant the consequences may eventually become, of taking a future mate's identity as her own with no further ado, Dick must work out his own in an increasingly complex and incomprehensible world. First and foremost, especially if Dick is middle class, that identity will be in terms of his occupation, and beginning in high school he must seriously begin to decide what he "wants to be when he grows up." The decision to become a minister rather than a professional soldier, for instance, is based on rather different notions about oneself and the world, and these must first be sorted out. In addition, if his potential occupational talents and personal predilections run in certain tabooed directions, such as art, literature, or music, he will face ridicule from his peers for being something less than "masculine"; in many cases, the same is true if he takes his studies "too seriously."

While engaged in these decisions, he must nonetheless maintain some demonstration of his "physical prowess" and "bravery." That may not present too much of a problem if he happens to be 6 feet tall, 180 pounds, and coordinated, but what of all those who are 5 feet, 6 inches and 115 pounds? Those who, in the old Charles Atlas ads, got sand kicked in their faces, the sensitive souls who cannot bear to inflict pain on others, the boys who lack coordination, are all subject to severe doubts about their masculine identity. Such "shortcomings" can be particularly anxiety-producing for working- and lower-class youth, although they will obviously affect the middle-class male as well.

Equally important to adolescent boys is the need for independence, sometimes financial and almost always in terms of freedom from adult supervision. However, in a society where, increasingly, males remain in school under adult supervision and out of the labor force well into their twenties, such independence becomes problematic. Told to "act like a man" but often constrained to "beg" his parents for money, use of the car, and other "necessities," adolescent males sometimes find it difficult to live up to the social prescriptions and so begin to doubt their very "masculinity." Dick finds himself in need of emotional support from people who accept him as he is, with all his weaknesses, shortcomings, and insecurities. Yet he is trying to break away from emotional dependence on his family, about the only people who might accept him unconditionally. The world of adolescent males has little mercy for the boy who never managed to make the break from a too-close identification with and attachment to mother.

Left with residual doubts about his masculinity from childhood (if we accept Lynn's analysis), faced with making important career decisions, encouraged to be independent and physically and emotionally strong while also constrained from these things by his inexperience, student status, and need for emotional support, the adolescent male faces a tough time in developing a sense of himself. Finally, while he is not pressured into seeking a mate at this point (except by adolescent females), he is expected by his peers to "prove his masculinity" by revealing his "prowess" with the girls. As they brag to one another about their sexual exploits, some unfortunate lads actually believe what they hear (or say). A vicious cycle of anxiety and lies is often the result. The inexperienced (namely, most boys) lie about their conquests to cover their felt inferiority, listen to others do the same, believe them, and feel yet more anxiety about their masculinity. At its worst, this eventuates in sexual exploitation of girls who allow themselves to be used in an attempt to establish their own feminine identity.

This brings us to the subject of the nature of the relationship between adolescent males and females. It is, first and foremost, broadly sexual in nature and based on "dating." For the boy or girl who is not interested in this or who matures late physically, relationships with the other sex are almost nonexistent, and prestige with the same sex is low. We are all quite familiar with the pattern: the female more or less passively awaits an invitation from a male, after taking the greatest pains to appear "attractive" by whatever are the standards of the day; the boy will usually try to "get as much" as he can from her sexually; she, as the repository of "sexual morality," is responsible for not allowing sexual play to "get out of hand." She has been fed (and believes) a diet of "romantic" notions about love and sex which puts her at a disadvantage in relationship to boys, who are usually substantially less devoted to the ideal of romance. While she bases her existence on his attentions, he has a variety of other, often more important, matters to attend to. The game that ensues makes honest communication and affection between two human beings difficult, if not impossible. Moreover, in many ways this process comprises the worst possible preparation for a satisfactory marriage for either. Indeed, as Margaret Mead (1970, chap. 14) first pointed out nearly three decades ago, dating is really oriented toward gaining prestige among the peers of one's own sex, and it is thus quite impersonal. More recently the process has been viewed as a failure "because it does not assist couples in learning how to develop and maintain vital and meaningful relationships" (Olson, 1972, p. 16).

Juvenile Delinquency

Given the stresses inherent in adolescence in our society, it is little wonder that rates of juvenile delinquency are high and rising rapidly. As in other areas, gender roles impact delinquency rates for boys compared to girls and the types of offenses for which members of each sex are found delinquent. Boys are adjudicated delinquent at a ratio of about 5 to 1, compared to girls (Sexton, 1969, p. 7). This does not necessarily mean that they commit that many more offenses, only that they are arrested and found guilty more often. It is probably impossible to say what the ratio of offenses is between the sexes, since it is likely that both the police and the courts treat boys more harshly than girls. However, as society has increasingly begun to redefine the feminine role, rates of female delinquency have gone up much more rapidly than rates of male delinquency. Thus, between 1960 and 1972 there was a 240 percent increase in the number of females declared delinquent, compared to a 104 percent rise for males (Haskell & Yablonsky, 1974, p. 68). This may or may not reflect a rise in actual delinquent acts among girls; just as likely, it reflects changes in attitudes among police and judges when confronted by a girl who has committed a delinquent act.

Juveniles are not found guilty of crimes; they are adjudicated delinquent irrespective of the act of which they are guilty. Some of the offenses for which a youth may be adjudicated delinquent are not crimes; that is, if the same behavior were displayed by an adult the law would not be broken. Such acts include running away, truancy, and being "ungovernable" (which often means sexually active for girls, but not boys). In a 1965 study of 19 cities, it was found that over half (52 percent) of the delinquent girls were "guilty" of offenses that are only applicable to youth ("status offenses"), compared to 20 percent of the boys (Haskell & Yablonsky, 1974). The only other offenses which had been committed by more than 5 percent of the delinquent girls were larceny/theft (10 percent) and sex offenses (7 percent). In contrast, the offenses committed most frequently by delinquent boys were burglary (14 percent), petty larceny (11 percent), and auto theft (9 percent).

M. Chesney-Lind (1974) has argued that female juvenile delinquency is sexualized. Delinquent boys, by and large, are arrested for offenses that would be crimes were they adults, while "the system selects for punishment girls who have transgressed sexually or defied parental authority" (p. 45). Females who commit these "crimes" are not only treated more harshly than males who engage in the same behaviors, they are more likely to be detained for trials than girls arrested for activities that would be crimes were they adults. In addition, girls are kept in custody longer than boys before trial and have longer sentences afterward if their offenses are sexual or represent defiance of parental authority (pp. 45-47).

That delinquent boys commit actual "crimes" against property and persons may be interpreted as part of a process by which they are attempting to establish their masculine prowess and independence (Brenton, 1966, pp. 64-66). Girls' transgressions, however, may often be viewed as involving an attempt to gain male attention or affection. At least, it is with these types of offenses that the authorities have been primarily concerned in the case of girls. In both cases, delinquency and reactions to it reflect the gender role stereotypes.

Other Bulwarks of Gender Role Stereotypes

It should be clear by now that in the normal course of events most children rather completely internalize socially defined roles, including gender roles, at a young age. However, no society can affort to rest on the assumption that the socialization process alone, as conducted rather informally by parents, teachers, and peers, will ensure substantial compliance or conformity. Therefore, in every human group there are a variety of "reinforcers" and social control mechanisms constantly at work to more or less subtly pressure individuals into conformity with social expectations. Some of these have already been examined, including the media, Madison Avenue's commercial use of the media (see Andreas, 1971, pp. 87-91), and the schools. The next chapter will consider the ways in which the political, legal, economic, and advanced educational institutions function to support gender role stereotypes. Here two types of idea systems, religion and science, that strongly support the status quo in a variety of ways, including the one in question, will be briefly examined. These two ideological structures constitute potent forces in the thinking of most Americans.

Religion

Virtually all major religions of the world include strong commandments to the two sexes to act in a manner consistent with traditional patriarchal social arrangements (Andreas, 1971, pp. 68-77). Since the United States is overwhelmingly a Judeo-Christian society, the two Testaments can be taken as the religious basis of our society. However, it should be noted that certain tenets of various other faiths, including traditional Hindu practices such as *suttee* (widow suicide by burning) and Confucian injunctions to wives to distrust themselves and obey their husbands, are even more traditional in their treatment of the sexes as separate and unequal than contemporary Judeo-Christian practice and theology is. More detailed discussion of the Judeo-Christian tradition and gender roles can be found in Pagels (1976), Miller and Swift (1977, chap. 5), Reuther (1973), and Bird (1973).

God is a male to most Americans who visualize a deity; so is His son Jesus. We refer to our deity as Lord, Father, King, and Master—all masculine terms (Pagels, 1976). In the version of Genesis best known today, that male God single-handedly created a male human. Then, in further opposition to all the laws of nature, he is said to have had that first male symbolically give birth to a female to function as his helpmate. It seems, in fact, that the mythology of much of the ancient civilized world included a major male deity giving birth to offspring in a manner that makes him in fact a "mother" (Stannard, 1970, pp. 25-26). The concept of "womb envy" discussed in Chapter 1 might help explain such a widespread phenomenon. In a lesser-known version of the creation, however, God created Adam and Lilith simultaneously. When she insisted upon her equality Adam became angry, and Lilith left. Later mythology depicts her as the first demon, the female counterpart of Satan (Rivlin, 1972). Subsequently, God created Eve, who becomes the chief instigator of evil and the human agent responsible for their departure from earthly paradise. As punishment Eve and her female descendants will have to birth future generations painfully and submit to the will of Adam's future male descendants who, in turn, are enjoined to work hard for little return. A good woman, henceforth, is a faithful and submissive one. The stage is set for rationalizing patriarchy.

Various laws and traditions in the Old Testament rather clearly establish male primacy (see Bird, 1973). For instance, only a male could divorce a spouse. A girl who was not a virgin upon marriage could be stoned to death. A man who raped a virgin, however, had merely to pay indemnity to her father and marry her. If a woman made a vow, her father or husband could void it. Polygamy was frequent in the Old Testament, polyandry nonexistent. Females were frequently bought from their parents by men wanting wives, such as the purchase of Rebecca by Isaac. While a few females, such as Deborah, Bathsheba, and Jezebel, had *de facto* political influence, leadership and power were essentially male prerogatives. Only one Old Testament book, Ruth, is devoted specifically to a woman. Males are frequently found making misogynic comments such as that in Ecclesiastes: "And I find more bitter than death the woman, whose heart is snares and nets, and her hands as bands; whoso pleaseth God shall escape from her, but the sinner shall be taken by her." Women worked hard and had important economic functions tending flocks, working wool and flax, planting vineyards, cooking, minding children, and so on. Husbands of such hard-working wives are often pictured sitting around talking with the elders. To this day an Orthodox male Jew begins each day with a prayer thanking God for not making him a woman. Until very recently the Jewish scholar (rabbi) was virtually excused from any economic duties. Since rabbis were always male, these duties fell to their wives. In fact, it was only in May 1972 that the first female rabbi was ordained.

The advent of Jesus was a mixed blessing for females. Sexual intercourse becomes a rather nasty thing in Christianity, presumably because women are somehow "dirty." Jesus was supposedly born without benefit of it, and to this day the Catholic Church grants legitimacy to sexuality only inasmuch as offspring may result. The Virgin Mary is practically deified and has high status in the New Testament and Church dogma. However, this status rests only on the fact that she is the mother of the Savior and not on any real accomplishments of her own; after all, Jesus is the son of a male God, not really Mary. Jesus himself did not seem to make any distinctions between the sexes, although it is curious that all of his disciples were male. He raised the prostitute Mary Magdalene to respectability; Mary of Bethany is portrayed in theological disputes with males; it is females, not even the disciples, who stand by Him at the crucifixion and discover the empty tomb. However, it was the Apostle Paul who chiefly shaped the early church, and his pronouncements included such statements as "The husband is supreme over his wife," "Wives, be obedient to your husbands," and "But woman reflects the glory of man; for man was not created . . . for woman's sake, but woman was created for man's sake." In these statements Paul was reflecting his times and the patriarchal structure of classical Roman and Hebrew society. That he was a product of his sociocultural milieu is also clear in his assertion that "It is a disgraceful thing for a woman to speak in a church meeting." If a female wants to know something, she is enjoined by Paul to ask her husband at home.

In the millenium that followed the death of Jesus, the role of women in Christian doctrine diminished, as emphasis was placed on female sexuality which, in turn, was considered evil. Periodic waves of witchburning occurred in Europe and later in America, and, of course, witches were overwhelmingly female (see Weitz, 1977). A 16th-century treatise on witches argued: "Certainly I remember to have heard of far more cases of women than men: and it is not unreasonable that this scum of humanity should be chiefly drawn from the feminine sex . . . since that sex is the more susceptible to evil counsels" (Weitz, 1977, p. 164). Some observers have noted that the accusation of witchcraft served as a social control mechanism to be used against women who failed to conform to their constricted role. Thus, witch-hunting was a mechanism of female subordination (Weitz, p. 166). The subordinate status of women in orthodox Christianity was evidently not totally obscure to women. Pagels (1976, p. 300) quotes a bishop's complaint that women in particular seemed to be attracted to heretical groups, especially those in which prayers were offered to the Mother and in which women, along with men, became priests.

The subordination of women as a central tenet of Christianity has yet to disappear totally. The Catholic Church still does not have female clergy, and only very recently have various Protestant denominations and sects allowed women to assume that role. Moreover, only recently has "cherish" been substituted for "obey" in the traditional religious marriage vows made by the female.

Science

Although religious affiliations and attendance figures have increased in recent decades, it is probably the case that most Americans are taking traditional theology less seriously than in the past and are relating to their religious institutions in a more secular manner (Herberg, 1960, pp. 1-4). "Science" has become our national theology, although this may be changing somewhat, especially among the young. However, science has not been value-free on the issue of gender roles or, for that matter, any other topic. A few of the gender role biases that have crept into medical science have already been mentioned. Those disciplines that deal more directly with human behavior, especially sociology and psychology, have in recent decades contributed substantially to reinforcement of the gender role stereotypes under the guise of "scientific truth."

From World War II until the late 1960s, sociology was dominated by that theoretical approach known as functionalism, which is associated primarily with Talcott Parsons. Perhaps nowhere was the influence of this orientation greater than in the field of marriage and the family, in which it remained dominant long after the rest of the discipline increasingly questioned it. Marriage and family courses are probably taken by more undergraduate students, including majors from virtually every discipline, than any other sociology courses except the introductory one. It is most frequently taken by college women as a "practical" course preparatory to marriage. It is, therefore, of utmost importance to consider the kinds of things students have been learning in such classes and will very likely attempt to practice someday in their own lives.

A basic criticism of the functional approach is that it tends to confuse description with prescription, or what is with what ought to be. In very simplified terms and at the risk of some distortion, functional sociology may be said to be concerned with those social structures and processes that contribute to the maintenance of "equilibrium." In turn, many modern functionalists tend to equate equilibrium with existing social structures and processes, namely, the status quo. Forces that encourage change in the status quo, including conflict of any variety, are often viewed as "deviant" or "pathological." Given this approach, the implicit if not explicit approach to social arrangements is "if it exists, it is good." Stated otherwise, starting with the (questionable) assumption that our society is in a "state of equilibrium," namely, functioning in a basically satisfactory manner, the various social arrangements characteristic of the society are considered to be mostly functional for maintaining equilibrium. From this theoretical perspective, major changes in social institutions will usually result in "disequilibrium," which is implicitly bad.

In terms of an analysis of marriage and the family, this approach leads to the inevitable conclusion that many aspects of traditional gender role stereotypes are inviolate, but for social, not necessarily biological, reasons. Utilizing Robert Bales's (1950) analysis of "expressive" and "instrumental" role functions in all human groups, functionalists conclude that females do (and implicitly ought to) fulfill the former functions, and males the latter. Since groups, including families, presumably cannot survive without such functions being fulfilled, and since in contemporary American society there exists a division of labor between the sexes in their fulfillment, therefore (so the argument goes), the "normal" family will consist of an expressive female and an instrumental male. Quite simply, students are told in scientific jargon that males accomplish the instrumental goal of working and making money, and females fulfill the expressive function of soothing feelings and caring for husband and offspring. Moreover, to disrupt this pattern is "pathological" and will eventuate in the probable failure of the family to persist. In this scheme the individual carries the burden of adjusting to social reality, that is, the status quo. Until the past few years, most of the popular marriage and family texts utilized this approach. It is exemplified in the following quotes from a typical family text (Martinson, 1970); any number of other books could be used to demonstrate the same thing.

Systems which endure over a period of time are characterized by the fact that roles within the system become differentiated from each other. . . . A major part of the way of life of any family that lasts over a period of years is made up of expectations specifying how each member of the family should behave. . . .

. . . Father and mother in a nuclear family tend to constitute a leadership coalition, but they also enact roles differentiated from each other. . . . The two basic problems of the family system—adapting to other social systems and integrating inside activities—call for different kinds of leadership. . . . The outside activities in large measure determine how the family survives in the community; the inside activities are concerned with integrating the group behavior that arises out of the external system and reacts upon it. . . .

The function of bearing and giving early care to children establishes a strong presumptive primacy for the mother as integrative-emotional leader in the family. She becomes the focus of gratification as the source of security and comfort not only for the newborn but for all members of the family. . . . Her support of her husband becomes a critical condition of the stability of the family. . . .

. . . his primary function in the family is to supply an income (pp. 112-13).

Or again:

In marriage the wife is supportive of the husband's tasks. . . . He carries an instrumental role—that is, he is responsible for the family's standard of living and sets the pace of upward mobility. Ideally, he has the interest, moral support, and appreciation of his wife (pp. 116-17).

Carol Ehrlich's (1971) study of six widely used marriage and family texts demonstrates that this approach is endemic to the field. Moreover, the fact that they strongly reinforce gender role stereotypes has not been lost to feminists. Betty Friedan (1963, chap. 6) and Kate Millett (1970, pp. 220-33) mount scathing attacks on the functional school of sociology (and anthropology). Addressing themselves to such biases, increasing numbers of students and faculty in the early 1970s began demanding less stereotyped academic consideration of the roles of males and females in contemporary society. Such pressure resulted in the creation of new courses entitled "Sex Roles," "The Sociology of Women," and so forth. Subsequently, changing notions of gender role behavior began to be found in courses in "Marriage and Family Life."

Marriage and the family has not been the only area of sociology that has helped to reinforce the traditional gender role stereotypes. Daniels (1975), Lipman-Blumen and Tickameyer (1975), Millman and Kanter (1975), Oakley (1974), and Acker (1973) all offer critiques of the many ways in which the discipline in general has perceived the social world through traditional, masculine blinders. For instance, in the field of social stratification the unit of analysis has traditionally been the family, whose social class is measured with reference to the occupation of the male "head of household." Indeed, the very concept of a "head of household" presupposes that the male is superior unless absent, in which case reference is made specifically to the "female head of household." Moreover, "female-headed households" are typically viewed as pathological. Theories of delinquency and crime have almost totally ignored females, while discussions of fertility have almost totally ignored males.

Functional sociology has drawn rather heavily on neo-Freudian theory, as have many areas of psychology, psychiatry, and social work. Freud's ideas pertaining to psychosexual development were discussed briefly in Chapter 1. As they have been interpreted and popularized by several generations of his followers, Freud's ideas have become potent bulwarks for traditional notions about gender roles, and they have been thoroughly criticized by feminists (Friedan, 1963, chap. 5; Firestone, 1970, chap. 3; Greer, 1970, pp. 82-91; Millet, 1970, pp. 176-220; Weisstein, 1970). They, too, have long been disseminated as scientific truth in academe, in the offices of the "helping professions" such as clinical psychology, social work, and psychiatry, and through literally thousands of popular "advice" columns, articles, and books. Indeed, Phyllis Chesler (1971, p. 746) views psychotherapy as a "major socially approved institution" for white middle-class women through which they may gain "salvation" with the aid of "an understanding and benevolent (male) authority." The feminist criticisms of psychotherapy have been summarized by Ann Seiden (1976), who points first to the sexual abuse of the therapeutic relationship by some male therapists who engage in sexual relationships with their female patients. Second, she claims that the therapeutic relationship may replicate rather than remedy the "one down" position of women. In so doing, the woman may be further encouraged in a fantasy that an idealized relationship with a more powerful (male) other is a better solution to her problems than taking autonomous action. Seiden also argues that many therapeutic theories reinforce gender role stereotypes and hold different standards of mental health for men and women. Finally, she claims that psychotherapists have failed to appraise the occupational hazards of the housewife role realistically.

Many psychotherapeutic theories have been based on Freud's formulations, and thus even more than functional sociology, neo-Freudian notions of masculinity and femininity have shaped our concepts of "mental health" and "normal" behavior. Those who fail to conform are not merely considered "deviant"; they are labeled "sick," "neurotic," and so forth. Moreover, objections to this theoretical framework are usually taken by its proponents as further evidence of just how "sick" the objector is. This type of approach constitutes a truly potent social control mechanism.

Material critical of Freudian and neo-Freudian theory is widely available (for a summary see Weitz, 1977, pp. 67-76). The phrase often used to summarize this school of thought is "Biology is destiny." Freud himself may have been at least somewhat more sensitive than many of his later followers to the crucial impact of society, via the inputs of parents, on psychosexual development. Even granted this, however, it is clear in many of his writings that he thought that females are by nature designed to rear as well as bear children and not to compete in the world of work; that they are passive and masochistic; and that to be otherwise is "neurotic." Conversely, he viewed the male as an active agent, creative in all areas of endeavor save childbirth and child rearing and equipped with a well-developed conscience (superego). Females emerge in his writing as defective males missing that most crucial of all appendages, the penis. Males appear as perpetually frightened lest they lose that presumably glorious tool. In short, the two sexes are depicted as distinctly different:

> . . . women are different beings—we will not say lesser, rather the opposite—from men. . . . Nature has determined woman's destiny through beauty, charm and sweetness. Law and custom have much to give women that has been withheld from them, but the position of women will surely be what it is: in youth an adored darling and in mature years a loved wife (Jones, 1961, p. 118).

Freud and his followers saw their neurotic female patients as basically in need of sexual fulfillment. This, in turn, could result only from an acceptance of their passive feminine role (as then defined in Western society) and a rejection of their "masculinity complex." Translated by popularizers and practitioners alike, this came to mean that an ambitious woman who sought independence and career and/or rejected domesticity and child rearing was by definition neurotic and incapable of sexual fulfillment. She had never overcome her childhood "penis envy," which in "normal" females is presumably translated into a desire for babies. Moreover, if she enters the masculine world of work, she is defined as a "castrating female," desexing not merely herself but the males around her. Males, by comparison, are presumed by Freud and his followers to have a substantially greater "libido." It is through the "sublimation" of this, required in working through their "Oedipal complex" and overcoming "castration anxiety," that males gain their vastly superior creative energy upon which civilizations are built. Relatedly, sex differences in libido mean that males are naturally much more aggressive and females passive, even masochistic. In Freud's own words:

> Women represent the interests of the family and the sexual life; the work of civilization has become more and more men's business; it confronts them with ever harder tasks, compels them to sublimations of instinct which women are not easily able to achieve. Since man has not an unlimited amount of mental energy at his disposal, he must accomplish his tasks by distributing his libido to the best advantage. What he employs for cultural purposes he withdraws to a great extent from women and his sexual life; his constant association with men and his dependence on his relations with them even estrange him from his duties as husband and father. Woman finds herself thus forced into the background by the claims of culture, and she adopts an inimical attitude towards it (1930, p. 73).

In the preceding chapter some material was reviewed which suggested sex-based bias in medical diagnoses. Physicians, as products of our culture, are heir to the same stereotypes as others, and these stereotypes affect their judgments concerning illness—both physical and mental. Levinson (1976) argues that physicians tend to treat menstruation, pregnancy, and menopause, all normal conditions for women, as pathological conditions contributing to the frailty of females. Research concerning the content of recent gynecology texts further demonstrates pervasive gender role stereotyping in medicine (Scully & Bart, 1973). Many physicians continue to assume that women are motivated by a maternal instinct rather than by a desire for sexual pleasure (Levinson, 1976). Indeed, contemporary sex manuals, written after medical science had "discovered" females' ability to achieve multiple orgasms, continue to stress the passive role of the female vis-à-vis the male (Gordon & Shankweiler, 1971). Dr. Benjamin Spock has recently rewritten his famous book on *Baby and Child Care,* and in its current guise it is essentially free of gender role stereotypes. However, 28 million copies of the book were sold in two earlier editions which strongly reinforced both stereotypes. He described as normal the use of sex-stereotyped toys, disapproved of mothers employed outside the home, and used the pronoun "he" in reference to all babies (Weitz, 1977, p. 66).

Sociology, psychology, and medical science have, at least until the past few years, been strongly supportive of the gender role status quo. They have offered powerful "reasons" why males must persevere in work even at the expense of their personal lives, and females must confine themselves to home and children regardless of personal inclinations—why the former must be aggressive, the latter passive.

Dick and Jane go to Sunday (or Saturday) school and learn their religious heritage. They go to public school and college and learn the latest that science has "discovered." They look to scientific specialists to solve their personal problems. The notions they have learned more or less informally from parents, peers, the media, and school personnel are constantly being reinforced, explained, justified, and rationalized. Against the combined weight of all these factors, it is difficult to argue.

Postscript

By now readers should be wondering why it is that many if not most people they know do not appear to be nearly as stereotypically "masculine" or "feminine" as the last two chapters depict. I have been concerned to this point with a discussion of the forces that reinforce any social arrangement and predispose systems to maintain the status quo. Socialization and social control are two of the most potent such forces.

Similar effects from a number of other institutional networks will be discussed in the next chapter. However, there are powerful mechanisms at work that are encouraging change in the gender role status quo. Even as I write, changes continue to make my description of current gender roles increasingly obsolete. The nature and roots of changes in gender role stereotypes will be analyzed more fully in the final chapter.

References

Acker, Joan. "Women and Social Stratification: A Case of Intellectual Sexism." *American Journal of Sociology* 78 (January 1973): 936-45.

Andreas, Carol. *Sex and Caste in America.* Englewood Cliffs, N.J.: Prentice-Hall, 1971.

Baumrind, Diana. "From Each According to Her Ability." *School Review* 80 (February 1972): 161-95.

Bales, Robert F. *Interaction Process Analysis.* Reading, Mass.: Addison-Wesley Publishing Co., 1950.

Bird, Phyllis. "Images of Women in the Old Testament." In Rosemary Reuther (ed.), *Religion and Sexism: Images of Woman in the Jewish and Christian Traditions.* New York: Simon & Schuster, 1973.

Block, Jeanne. "Conceptions of Sex Role: Some Cross-Cultural and Longitudinal Perspectives." *American Psychologist* 28 (1973): 512-26.

Booth, Alan. "Sex and Social Participation." *American Sociological Review* 37 (April 1972): 183-93.

Brantley, Robin. "Men Dominate Conversations with Women, Study Shows." *Houston Chronicle,* May 1, 1977.

Brenton, Myron. *The American Male.* Greenwich, Conn.: Fawcett Publishers, 1966.

Cantor, Muriel. "Women and Public Broadcasting." *Journal of Communications* 27 (1977): 14-19.

Chesler, Phyllis. "Women as Psychiatric and Psychotherapeutic Patients." *Journal of Marriage and the Family* 33 (November 1971): 746-59.

Chesney-Lind, M. "Juvenile Delinquency: The Sexualization of Female Crime." *Psychology Today* (July 1974): 43-46.

Coleman, James. "Athletics in High School." *Annals of the American Academy of Political and Social Science* (November 1961): 338.

Cooley, Charles H. *Social Organization.* New York: Scribners, 1909.

Daniels, Arlene. "Feminist Perspectives in Sociological Research." In Marcia Millman and Rosabeth Kanter (eds.), *Another Voice: Feminist Perspectives on Social Life and Social Science,* pp. 340-80. Garden City, N.Y.: Anchor Books, 1975.

Deaux, Kay. *The Behavior of Women and Men.* Monterey, Calif.: Brooks/Cole Publishing Co., 1976.

De Beauvoir, Simone. *The Second Sex.* Translated by H.M. Parshey. New York: Alfred A. Knopf, 1953.

Ehrlich, Carol. "The Male Sociologists' Burden: The Place of Women in Marriage and Family Texts." *Journal of Marriage and the Family* 33 (August 1971): 431-30.

Federbush, Marsha. "The Sex Problems of School Math Books." In Judith Stacey, Susan Béreaud, and Joan Daniels (eds.), *And Jill Came Tumbling After: Sexism in American Education,* pp. 178-84. New York: Dell Publishing Co., 1974.

Firestone, Shulamith. *The Dialectic of Sex.* New York: Bantam Books, 1970.

Fisher, Elizabeth. "The Second Sex, Junior Division." In Judith Stacey, Susan Béreaud, and Joan Daniels (eds.), *And Jill Came Tumbling After: Sexism in American Education.* New York: Dell Publishing Co., 1974.

Flora, Cornelia Butler. "The Passive Female: Her Comparative Image by Class and Culture in Women's Magazine Fiction." *Journal of Marriage and the Family* 33 (August 1971): 435-44.

Freeman, Jo. "Growing Up Girlish," *Trans-Action* 8 (November-December 1970), pp. 36-43.

Friedan, Betty. *The Feminine Mystique.* New York: Dell Publishing Co., 1963.

Freud, Sigmund. *Civilization and Its Discontents.* London: Hogarth Press, 1930.

Gerber, Ellen; Felshin, Jan; Berlin, Pearl; and Wyrick, Waneen. *The American Woman in Sport.* Reading, Mass.: Addison-Wesley Publishing Co., 1974.

Goodman, Louis, and Lever, Janet. "A Report on Children's Toys." In Judith Stacey, Susan Bereaud, and Joan Daniels (eds.), *And Jill Came Tumbling After: Sexism in American Education,* pp. 123-25. New York: Dell Publishing Co., 1974.

Gordon, Michael, and Shankweiler, Penelope J. "Different Equals Less: Female Sexuality in Recent Marriage Manuals." *Journal of Marriage and the Family* 33 (August 1971): 459-66.

Gornick, Vivian. "Why Women Fear Success." *Ms.,* Spring 1972, pp. 50-53.

Gould, Lois. "X: A Fabulous Child's Story." *Ms.,* December 1972, pp. 321-30.

Greer, Germaine. *The Female Eunuch.* New York: McGraw-Hill Book Co., 1970.

Guttentag, Marcia, and Bray, Helen. "Teachers as Mediators of Sex-Role

Standards." In Alice Sargent (ed.), *Beyond Sex Roles,* pp. 395-411. St. Paul, Minn.: West Publishing Co., 1977.

Haskell, M., and Yablonsky, L. *Juvenile Delinquency.* Chicago: Rand McNally & Co., 1974.

Henley, Nancy, and Thorne, Barrie. "Womanspeak and Manspeak: Sex Differences and Sexism in Communication, Verbal and Nonverbal." In Alice Sargent (ed.), *Beyond Sex Roles,* pp. 201-18. St. Paul, Minn.: West Publishing Co., 1977.

Herberg, Will. *Protestant, Catholic, Jew.* Garden City, N.Y.: Anchor Books, 1960.

Herschberger, Ruth. *Adam's Rib.* New York: Harper & Row, 1954.

Hillman, Judith. "Occupational Roles in Children's Literature." *Elementary School Journal* 77 (September 1976): 1-4.

Hoffman, Lois. "Early Childhood Experiences and Women's Achievement Motives." *Journal of Social Issues* 28 (1972): 129-55.

Horner, Matina. "Fail: Bright Women." *Psychology Today,* 1969, p. 36.

Howe, Florence. "Sexual Stereotypes Start Early." *Saturday Review,* October 16, 1971.

Jones, Ernest. *The Life and Work of Sigmund Freud.* Abridged by Lionel Trilling and Steven Marcus. New York: Basic Books, 1961.

Lake, Alice. "Are We Born Into Our Sex Roles or Programmed Into Them?" *Woman's Day,* January 1975, pp. 24-25.

Lakoff, Robin. *Language and Woman's Place.* New York: Harper & Row, 1975.

Lever, Janet. "Sex Differences in the Games Children Play." *Social Problems* 23 (1976): 478-87.

Levinson, Richard. "From Olive Oyl to Sweet Polly Purebread: Sex Role Stereotypes and Televised Cartoons." *Journal of Popular Culture* 9 (1975): 561-72.

Levinson, Richard. "Sexism in Medicine." *American Journal of Nursing,* March 1976, pp. 426-31.

Lewis, Michael. "Culture and Gender Roles: There's No Unisex in the Nursery." *Psychology Today,* May 1972, pp. 54-57.

Lipman-Blumen, Jean, and Tickameyer, A. "Sex Roles in Transition: A Ten Year Perspective." In Alex Inkeles (ed.), *Annual Review of Sociology* (Vol. 1), pp. 297-337. Palo Alto, Calif.: Annual Reviews, 1975.

Lynn, David B. *Parental and Sex Role Identification: A Theoretical Formulation.* Berkeley, Calif.: McCutchan Publishing Corp., 1969.

Maccoby, Eleanor (ed.). *The Development of Sex Differences.* Stanford, Calif.: Stanford University Press, 1966.

Maccoby, Eleanor, and Jacklin, Carol. *The Psychology of Sex Differences.* Stanford, Calif.: Stanford University Press, 1974.

Martinson, Floyd Mansfield. *Family in Society.* New York: Dodd, Mead & Co., 1970.

Mead, George Herbert. *Mind, Self, and Society.* Chicago: University of Chicago Press, 1934.

Mead, Margaret. *Male and Female: A Study of the Sexes in a Changing World.* New York: Dell Publishing Co., 1970; first published 1949.

Merton, Robert K. *Social Theory and Social Structure.* 2nd ed. Glencoe, Ill.: Free Press, 1957.

Miller, Casey, and Swift, Kate. *Words and Women: New Language in New Times.* New York: Anchor Books, 1977.

Millett, Kate. *Sexual Politics.* Garden City, N.Y.: Doubleday & Co., 1970.

Millett, Kate, and Swift, Casey. "De-sexing the English Language," *Ms.,* Spring 1972, p. 7.

Millman, Marcia, and Kanter, Rosabeth. *Another Voice: Feminist Perspectives on Social Life and Social Science.* Garden City, N.Y.: Anchor Books, 1975.

Minton, Cheryl; Kagan, Jerome; and Levine, Janet. "Maternal Control and Obedience in the Two Year Old." *Child Development* 42 (1971): 1873-94.

Oakley, Ann. *The Sociology of Housework.* New York: Pantheon Books, 1974.

Olson, David. "Marriage of the Future: Revolutionary or Evolutionary Change?" In Marion Sussman (ed.), *Non-Traditional Family Forms in the 1970's,* pp. 15-25. Minneapolis, Minn.: National Council on Family Relations, 1972.

Pagels, Elaine. "What Became of God the Mother? Conflicting Images of God in Early Christianity." *Signs* 2 (1976): 293-315.

Pederson, F. A., and Robson, K. S. "Father Participation in Infancy." *American Journal of Orthopsychiatry* 39 (1969): 466-72.

Piaget, Jean. *The Moral Judgement of the Child.* Translated by Marjorie Gabain. New York: Harcourt, Brace, 1932.

Pogrebin, Letty Cottin. "Down with Sexist Upbringing." *Ms.,* Spring 1972, pp. 18, 20, 25-30.

Rachlin, Susan, and Vogt, Glenda. "Sex Roles as Presented to Children by Coloring Books." *Journal of Popular Culture* 8 (1974): 549-56.

Reuther, Rosemary. *Religion and Sexism: Images of Woman in the Jewish and Christian Traditions.* New York: Simon & Schuster, 1973.

Rivlin, Lilly. "Lilith." *Ms.,* December 1972, pp. 92-97 and 114-15.

Rosenberg, Florence, and Simmons, Roberta. "Sex Differences in the Self-Concept in Adolescence." *Sex Roles* 1 (1975): 147-59.

Rysman, Alexander. "How the 'Gossip' Became a Woman." *Journal of Communications* 27 (1977): 176-80.

Scully, Diana, and Bart, Pauline. "A Funny Thing Happened on the Way to the Orifice: Women in Gynecology Textbooks." *American Journal of Sociology* 78 (January 1973): 1045-50.

Seiden, Ann. "Overview: Research on the Psychology of Women, II: Women in Families, Work and Psychotherapy." *American Journal of Psychiatry* (October 1976): 1111-123.

Sexton, Patricia Cayo. *The Feminized Male.* New York: Vintage Books, 1969.

Stannard, Una. "Adam's Rib, or the Woman Within." *Trans-Action* 8 (November-December, 1970): 24-35.

Sternglanz, Sarah, and Serbin, Lisa. "Sex Role Stereotyping in Children's Television Programs." *Developmental Psychology* 10 (1974): 710-15.

Streicher, Helen. "The Girls in the Cartoons." *Journal of Communications* 24 (Spring 1974): 125-29.

Tarvis, Carol and Offir, Carole. *The Longest War: Sex Differences in Perspective.* New York: Harcourt, Brace, Jovanovich, 1977.

Thomas, W. I. *The Unadjusted Girl.* Boston: Little, Brown & Co., 1923.

Trecker, Janice. "Women in U.S. History High School Textbooks." In Judith Stacey, Susan Béreaud and Joan Daniels (eds.), *And Jill Came Tumbling After: Sexism in American Education,* pp. 249-68. New York: Dell Publishing Co., 1974.

Walum, Laurel. *The Dynamics of Sex and Gender: A Sociological Perspective.* Chicago: Rand McNally & Co., 1977.

Weisstein, Naomi. "'Kinder, Kuche, Kirche' as Scientific Law: Psychology Constructs the Female." In Robin Morgan (ed.), *Sisterhood is Powerful,* pp. 205-20. New York: Vintage Books, 1970.

Weitz, Shirley. *Sex Roles: Biological, Psychological and Social Foundations.* New York: Oxford University Press, 1977.

Weitzman, Lenore J.; Eifles, Deborah; Hokada, Elizabeth; and Ross, Catherine. "Sex Role Socialization in Picture Books for Preschool Children." *American Journal of Sociology* 72 (May 1972): 1125-50.

Women on Words and Images. *Dick and Jane as Victims: Sex Stereotyping in Children's Readers.* Princeton, N.J., 1972.

Chapter 4

The Bringing Down of Jane

In our society, as well as in most others, the sexes are not only different but unequal. This has become so obvious that some students of gender role phenomena (Andreas, 1971; Hacker, 1951; Hochschild, 1973; Lipman-Blumen, 1975; Engels, 1902) view the relationship between males and females in terms of the stratification concept of caste. In all known human societies, people rank one another hierarchically on a continuum from "superior" to "inferior." Individuals or groups are generally ranked according to how well they embody key societal values. Since such values differ, the nature of ranking or stratification systems varies from one society to another.

Among the many types of variations in the way people rank one another, one is particularly important in the sociology of gender roles: stratification levels may be more or less permeable. This variable relates to the degree to which movement up or down the hierarchy is possible for individuals. One of the attributes of a caste society is that groups of people are assigned superior or inferior positions in the stratification hierarchy on the basis of some common ascribed characteristic. Because the basis of that assignment is ascriptive (an unchangeable, often physically identifiable characteristic with which individuals are born), there is virtually no vertical mobility between castes; they are, for all practical purposes, impermeable. The classic caste society was India, but the concept has been widely used with considerable justification to refer to the stratification of races in American society.

Another attribute of a caste society is that intermarriage and other forms of intimate social interaction between castes do not occur. In order to conceptualize the sexes as constituting castes, however, we must ignore this component of the definition. We will do this because fruitful insights into the status of women may be gained by conceptualizing the sexes as castes, based on the impermeability of the line between males and females and the inequality of their statuses as collectivities.

Given this more limited definition of caste, we can say that patriarchy is caste. It implies the superiority of one group of individuals—males—over another—females. Moreover, sex is an ascribed and, except for very few individuals, unchangeable characteristic. Patriarchy is probably the oldest form of exploitation and subjugation of one part of a population by another. It probably has also served as the model for all other forms of relegation, be they on the basis of race, ethnicity, religion, or class. Once such a system is established, those in high-caste positions, in this case males, develop a vested interest in the maintenance of the basic structure and their own advantaged status. Moreover, caste considerations pervade the major (and even minor) institutions of a society, so that they also have a vested interest in the maintenance of the caste status quo (see Hartmann, 1976). Thus the short-run interests of males as males and, perhaps more importantly, as leaders of political, legal, economic, and cultural institutions are best served by maintaining and reinforcing traditional gender roles. It is the task of this chapter to document this assertion.

The Female Caste

The discussion in the first three chapters of this book has often shown that the sexes are not merely different but, in many ways, unequal in contemporary society. The review of gender role stereotypes made it obvious that many more negative attributes are attached to the feminine role than to the masculine one. Similarly, in the discussion of language, males emerged as the basic norm, females as "the other." Science and religion were noted as being strongly supportive of male dominance over females. In short, prejudgment (or stereotyping), as defined in Chapter 2, is, in fact, antifeminine prejudice. The question to be considered now is whether antifeminine prejudice is operationally translated into discrimination in our society.

A few words of clarification are needed at this point. The statement that males comprise a higher caste than females and that it is in their direct self-interest to maintain the gender role status quo is subject to certain qualifications:

1. Very real "costs" are involved in the masculine role, as has already been shown.
2. Many *individual* males will favor basic changes in the gender role status quo and perceive that their own *long-range* interests are, in fact, better served through such changes.
3. There is no implication that all females are of an equal status to one another, or all are lower than all males. As Jessie Bernard (1971, chap. 1) cogently points out, the differences among females are often as great as those between males and females.

Stratification hierarchies, be they in the form of a caste or any other type, are based on specifiable attributes prized by society. In industrial societies, the single most important such trait is generally occupational prestige, although such considerations as amount of income and education, life-style or consumption level and habits, and power are also relevant. These usually correlate highly with one another, especially with occupational prestige. The difficulty in conceptualizing the sexes as being in a castelike relationship arises from two related facts. First, until recently most females were not gainfully employed (that is, employed for wages outside of the household), and even today at any given time about half of all adult American females are not. Thus, as traditionally defined, occupational prestige is difficult to assign to many females. Second, largely because of this, the status of an adult female is assumed both by society and by those who study stratification phenomena to be that of her husband (and the status of children of both sexes is that of their father). This is reflected in the fact that the U.S. government, social scientists, and society at large all automatically designate the adult male as "head of household," and only in the absence of an adult male can a female be so designated. Thus, typically, studies of social stratification are studies of male samples. Of course, this very difficulty may be a function of the fact that students of social stratification have been overwhelmingly male. Whatever the reason, the fact is that the available conceptual apparatus does not easily lend itself to an attempt to look at females as well as males in terms of a unitary stratification hierarchy (Acker, 1973).

To accomplish this the first step would involve ruling out any consideration of status accruing to an adult female solely on the basis of her relationship to a male. This approach would be generally unacceptable to women who function as homemakers for high-status husbands. Be that as it may, it appears that it is possible to measure the prestige accruing directly to the homemaker role, irrespective of husband's occupation. Using a standard technique to measure the prestige of various paid jobs, Rosalind Dworkin (n.d.) demonstrated that the housewife role falls in the middle of the occupational prestige scale, on about the same level as sales clerk and nurse. A different research technique employed by Bose (1976) reached the same conclusion. Thus, the half or so of all adult women who are not members of the labor force fall at the median of prestige, and, as will be demonstrated below, most women who are gainfully employed fare no better, and often worse, in terms of occupational prestige. The upper half of the prestige hierarchy is left overwhelmingly to males.

Occupation: Homemaker

More people work as homemakers than in any other single job in our society, yet very few people, including social scientists, conceptualize this work as a job or occupation. Only recently have some sociologists begun to examine this work role in the same kind of terms typically employed to study paid employment roles (Oakley, 1974, 1975; Lopata, 1971; Glazer, 1976). There is no doubt that people, normally women, who are homemakers do indeed *work*. The job can be analyzed in terms of its prestige (see above), the extent to which "employees" are satisfied with their jobs, the range of tasks involved (cooking, dusting, laundry, chauffeuring, etc.), the extent of supervision, the norms concerning adequate performance, and so on. Research has barely begun in terms of studying these phenomena as they apply to unpaid household work.

However, a few things are relatively clear.

First of all, homemakers are paid nothing for their work. Any money the housewife receives is granted for "expenses," or out of "kindness" as an "allowance"; it is not considered *rightful* remuneration for her activities. Whether her spouse receives $40,000 or $15,000, is generous or stingy, she will do the same basic work. In short, whatever funds she receives are not pegged to *her* toil. Moreover, the society deems the performance of homemaking tasks as having essentially no market value, since they are not computed in the gross national product. When paid employees perform household work they are paid wages that rank among the lowest in the society.

A homemaker's work will, however, be influenced by the equipment she has available, and her husband's income will help to determine what appliances she will be able to own. Thus, the nature of many tasks will vary in arduousness depending on husband's income, with the lower-class homemaker generally being faced with more strenuous work. In the extreme, a wealthy husband may provide the wherewithal for the housewife to hire someone (or service companies) to do much of the work.

Unlike most paid jobs in our society, in homemaking the tasks involved are very varied, free from direct supervision, and timed by the worker herself. In short, when compared to many white-collar jobs and most blue-collar jobs, the homemaker has more opportunity to be her own boss in every sense and to change tasks frequently when she gets bored. Some of the tasks, especially those involved in child care and interior design, may allow considerable creativity, an attribute missing in many, if not most, paid jobs. These attributes of the homemaker's role make it more pleasant as a form of work than most paid jobs in our economy.

On the other side, there are problems inherent in this work role besides the lack of pay. First, homemakers receive no employee benefits, such as social security in their own right, nor do they ever actually retire. Most of the tasks involved are no sooner ended than they must be started again. Furniture only stays dusted, floors mopped or vacuumed, laundry done and put away for a few short hours before dirt reappears. Moreover, in the relatively few cases where a finished product, such as a meal, is the result of the work, it is immediately consumed. Thus, the homemaker can rarely look with pride upon a permanent product she has produced. However, in many paid jobs there are similar problems. Unlike most jobs in the labor force, homemaking lacks clearly specified performance norms. Extreme mess or layers of dirt clearly identify a woman as inadequately fulfilling the role, but short of that extreme, expectations are unclear. This makes it difficult for homemakers to take much pride in their work, since they cannot readily assess it in terms of some set of expectations. Each homemaker is left, in effect, to set her own norms, which may result in excessively high standards. The "compulsive" housekeeper who launders, dusts, and mops daily, cooks gourmet dinners, and so on is not unheard of. She is probably responding in this fashion to the normlessness involved in the role. Another disadvantage this work role has more than most paid work roles do is that despite the freedom to set their own work tasks, homemakers, especially those with children, are often interrupted by the demands of others. Thus, no matter what she is doing, the homemaker may have to stop abruptly to chauffeur a child to an appointment, to respond to the needs of a baby or toddler, or to accommodate a change of plans made by her husband. Most paid jobs also do not have another drawback of the homemaker role: in our society, as in most industrial societies, the homemaker performs her work in relative isolation from other adults. Few people enjoy working alone for most if not all of the day, and indeed, it seems to be the case that many women enter the paid work force in part to seek adult interaction.

It should be clear by now that the homemaking role is amenable to the same type of analysis as other work roles to which it can be compared. Relative to many jobs it seems to be advantageous, despite the lack of pay and benefits associated with it. Many women, faced with the alternative of a low-paying, low-prestige, boring job in the labor force, are undoubtedly better off remaining home if they can afford to do so financially. The working or lower-class wife may in fact be accorded higher prestige by remaining home than she would by taking the kinds of paid jobs available to her. It is her better educated, middle-class sister who loses prestige by staying out of the labor force. Such women are increasingly choosing to stay in or to reenter the world of employment, joining the divorced, single, and widowed women and lower-class wives who must work in the labor force for economic reasons.

It is still the case, however, that many homemakers fail to perceive the relatively low social prestige attached to their role. At some psychological level many do recognize it, as evidenced by the not infrequent statement that "I'm *only* (just) a housewife." However, the general society has taken great pains to hide from women its fairly low opinion of the role. Every institution in American society is geared toward defining the wife in terms of her husband's identity, as we have noted. Particularly for those males in the upper reaches of the stratification hierarchy, but also for all those who can conceivably afford it, wives, along with children and household goods, have provided displays of what Thorstein Veblen labeled three quarters of a century ago "conspicuous consumption" and "conspicuous leisure" (Veblen, 1899/1953). To the degree that the male's dependents appear pampered, surrounded by goods and services, and relieved of the necessity of being "productive" (i.e., gainfully employed), his personal status is enhanced. Moreover, although American housewives work very hard, from any perspective other than middle-class America's many are surrounded by an incredible luxury of goods and services. Auspicious and noncompulsive use of these goods and services can potentially result in rather large quantities of leisure, although as often as not they are not used to accomplish this purpose. All of this is hardly geared to create in the housewife an awareness of her own *personal* low-caste position. Just as the liveried servants (and even many slaves) of the 19th-century "gentlemen" vicariously basked in the reflected glory of their masters, so too does today's housewife. They are all examples of what Karl Marx labeled "false class consciousness" (see Amundsen, 1971, p. 21).

Patriarchy, or the sexual caste system, has been with us at least since the dawn of civilized society. It predates current institutional arrangements, be they capitalism or socialism in the economic sphere, democracy or totalitarianism in the political arena, and so forth. The key institutions in current society thus arose after a well-established system of super-subordinate relationships between the sexes had been established, and they can be expected to rather fully reflect this fact. Stated otherwise, the institutional arrangements of society support the sexual caste system, or what contemporary feminists label sexism, and that system, in turn, feeds back and supports current institutional arrangements. In the remainder of this chapter, several key American institutional networks will be examined from this perspective.

The Economy

So much has been written recently on the position of females in the economy that a thorough analysis would comprise several volumes. The facts, figures, and anecdotes of job, pay, and promotion discrimination in contemporary America are widely available and will only be mentioned here as needed. For more detailed analyses, see Chapman (1976); Kreps (1976); Glazer and Waehrer (1977); Epstein (1970); Knudsen (1969); and Mead and Kaplan (1965).

In the past, most females participated to a large extent in the production activities of their societies. From at least the inception of settled agrarian communities until a mere century or less ago, women and even children worked beside men in the fields, in the barn, and in the household, producing almost all the goods and services needed to sustain their lives. Since about 90 percent of all families in preindustrial societies were agrarian, it is clear that the overwhelming proportion of humans spent the bulk of their lives in active production activities (see Blau, 1975).

As the household economy gave way to factory-centered production with the advent of the Industrial Revolution, this pattern began to alter. At first the wives and children of the poor continued to engage in production, side by side with males, although they were hideously exploited as "cheap labor" until laws at the close of the 19th century came somewhat to their rescue. The secular trend during the past half century or more has been toward an ever-increasing standard of living which has permitted more and more wives to choose to absent themselves from production activities. Homemaking, like virtually all other tasks, has become a specialized activity. It is important to realize, however, that the phenomenon of a large proportion of women devoting many years or all of their adult existence to child rearing, housekeeping, and consumption is new in history. While many more females are "employed" in official terms today than in the past, most of those who were not technically "working" in earlier times were probably in fact functioning as producers. Until a half century or so ago only a tiny minority of the wealthy and the aristocratic had the luxury of orienting their lives to nonproductive activities.

Two other related economic phenomena have been occurring in what is increasingly being labeled "postindustrial" societies. Expanding production techniques brought an undreamed opulence of goods and a general prosperity to most workers. As an increasing number of women were relieved of engaging in productive work in order to acquire family necessities, the economy *as structured* was coming to rely more and more heavily on very high levels of consumption to maintain growth and prosperity. Moreover, production of goods was becoming less labor intensive, and a relatively smaller proportion of the population was needed to run the machines (although the labor force has grown through the increase of service industries). What better support for a postindustrial, particularly a capitalistic, economy could there be than a definition of gender roles that bound males to continued efforts to produce and most females, at least in the middle classes, to continued efforts to stay home and consume for much of their lives, if not the entirety? Such a circumstance would ensure, if nothing else, good profits for industry. In addition, the more babies middle-class women, in particular, could be induced to have, the more consumption would be increased in the present as well as the indefinite future. Only in the past few years, as inflation has become a fact of our daily lives, have we witnessed the serious reversal of this trend. Now young middle-class women, along with their sisters in the lower socioeconomic strata are beginning to assume that they will work in the labor force for the majority of their adult lives in order to maintain their accustomed life-styles, if for no other reason.

Women, especially married women, have comprised a reserve labor force to be manipulated as the economy needs them. They are truly the last hired and the first fired. If and when the labor market is in need of more people, the conditions and definitions are altered enough to bring married women back into the labor force, a phenomenon most evident in wartime. After the emergency they can be sent home again, as was done after World War II, when the number of women in the labor force declined by more than two million between 1944 and 1946, despite the fact that polls revealed most women in the wartime economy wanted to continue employment after the end of hostilities (Trey, 1972). Males, too, have been manipulated, in this case into an overwhelming devotion to productive labor (the "Protestant work ethic"). Only now, as our productive capacity is beginning to outstrip even the female's ability to consume, is the male being enjoined by the media to add consumption to his definition of "masculinity." Males are now informed that all kinds of cosmetics, hair products, deodorants and so on will add stature to their masculine image.

Males in Postindustrial Economies

Regardless of personal preference, males are enjoined from childhood to plan on working in the economy for virtually their entire adult existence. The upper caste creates its own trap. However, as we saw when discussing the economic relevance of gender role stereotypes in Chapter 2 and again in Chapter 3, relative to females males are generally well equipped from youth with the personality attributes and social skills that contribute to success in the occupational realm. This is particularly true if their family origin is middle class.

Essentially, one of two things can happen in the occupational lives of males. Most do not become what Americans would call very "successful" on the job. The majority are manual workers or low-level white-collar employees earning modest to poor wages. Many spend the bulk of their waking hours five days a week doing mindless, alienating, and sometimes backbreaking work. As Arthur Shostak puts it, "Blue collarites . . . may find the meaning of work as often as not a negation rather than an affirmation of a basic sense of worthiness" (1976, p. 101). In return, they are only capable of supporting their families in what, by American standards (and by contrast with the "ideal" exemplified in the media), is a more or less minimal fashion. Such men often suffer feelings of inadequacy and may even desert their families to avoid such feelings (see the analysis of poor black males in Liebow, 1967; also see Grønseth, 1971-72). Countless others feel inadequate as males because their wives go to work to supplement their meager incomes. Some men take second jobs, thereby sacrificing virtually all other activities.

What of the substantial numbers of males, particularly those in nonmanual occupations, who are "successful" in career terms? In an excellent analysis of the modern work environment, Myron Brenton (1966, chap. 1) argues that the nature of jobs today is such that most males will be frustrated regardless of how high they may rise in the prestige hierarchy. Having learned the stereotypical notions of masculine prowess, activity, aggressiveness, and competitiveness, the increasingly bureaucratic setting of most work creates for males the problem of

> . . . how to reconcile the sedentary, overrefined present, which is marked by an extreme lack of physical challenges, with the age-old image of the male as hunter, builder, hewer of wood, and drawer of water—a male who, in short, establishes a primitive contact between himself and his surroundings (Brenton, 1966, p. 18).

Since William H. Whyte's analysis of the "organization man" nearly two decades ago, the modern middle-class male has frequently been viewed as primarily seeking security and orderly progression up the bureaucratic ladder. To accomplish this when numerous others are seeking the same goals means competition, but not the overt, "invigorating" competition that spurs "a man to give the very best he has . . ." (Brenton, 1966, p. 35). Rather, confined by the "social ethic" (Whyte, 1956, p. 13), modern man engages in a "frantic, paralyzing kind" of competition, always under pressure to "succeed" (Brenton, p. 35). The result of this struggle can be summarized as follows:

> Organizational disciplines and symbols came to pervade the life of the manager. Automobiles, homes, and tastes conformed to the requirements or organizational role and status. . . . The manner and content of greeting other men, engaging in small talk, and joking became ritualized and differentiated at and between different levels of organization. (Shepard, 1977, p. 390)

Shepard also points out that "most managers still feel guilty if they leave the office early; . . . most managers are still seeking money and status in the shadow of the fear of failure rather than seeking beauty in life and work" (p. 394).

It should also be noted that, while males do not face discrimination barring them from various fields of employment, there are a number of jobs which are considered "unmanly" and in which male incumbents are made to suffer in a variety of ways. Nursing, secretarial work, elementary school teaching, and library positions are such jobs. Fein (1977) points out that "Men entering fields seen as traditionally female are not infrequently questioned about their masculinity" (p. 196).

Regardless of these costs, males in our society have been encouraged to view themselves as active, responsible people endowed with both brains and brawn superior to those of females, which most certainly entitles them to better jobs with better pay. In addition, the male generally has a wife, and this is no minor consideration in occupational achievement (Papanek, 1973). An article by Judy Syfers (1972) depicts the advantages of having a wife (simply substitute "job" for "school" and "work" for "study"):

> I would like to go back to school so that I can become economically independent, support myself, and, if need be, support those dependent upon me. I want a wife who will work and send me to school. . . . I want a wife who takes care of the children when they are sick, a wife who arranges to be around when the children need special care, because, of course, I cannot miss classes at school. . . .
>
> I want a wife who will care for *my* physical needs. I want a wife who will keep my house clean. A wife who will pick up after me. . . . I want a wife who cooks the meals, . . . a wife who will plan the menus, do the necessary shopping, prepare the meals, serve them pleasantly, and then do the cleaning up while I do my studying. . . . I want a wife to go along when our family takes a vacation so that someone can continue to care for me and my children when I need a rest and change of scene.
>
> . . . I want a wife who will listen to me explain a rather difficult point I have come across in my course of studies. . . .
>
> I want a wife who will take care of the details of my social life. . . . When I meet people at school that I like and want to entertain, I want a wife who will have the house clean, will prepare a special meal, serve it to me and my friends, and not interrupt when I talk about the things that interest me and my friends.

Wives allow husbands to concentrate their major attention on their work and not clutter their minds with the myriad details of daily living. Moreover, husbands and fathers suffer little loss of prestige if they perform these roles poorly; not much is socially expected of males in terms of family commitments. For the male competing to move up the organizational structure, what could be more convenient? Females trying to make that same move have no "wives" to help them. Indeed, they usually *are* also wives; as such, they are held responsible by society for being "good wives and mothers," regardless of other commitments.

Females in the World of Work

Most females in our society marry at some time in their lives. Most also work in the labor force at some point. In 1975 37 million, or 46 percent, of all adult females were employed; women comprised 40 percent of the total work force (U.S. Bureau of the Census, 1976, p. 355). This percentage was higher for black women, nearly 49 percent of whom were employed, but lower for Spanish-surnamed women, 42 percent of whom were in the labor market. The fact that women can expect to marry and to work has effects on their job opportunities which cannot be overstated. One of the most important is the problem of role conflict. The term "role conflict" refers to two phenomena: a conflict of expectations arising from two or more roles that an individual holds simultaneously, and a conflict of expectations built into a single role. Employed females, especially but not solely if they are married and have children, are subject to both.

It has been noted that the mere fact that males have wives is important in helping to advance the husbands' own career aspirations. More than two thirds of all American wives are employed outside the home at some time in their married lives. In 1975, over 44 percent of all married women with husbands present were working; moreover, nearly 37 percent of mothers with children under the age of six and with husbands present were in the labor force that year (U.S. Bureau of the Census, 1976, p. 358). Such women are trying to fulfill two separate roles, each of which makes strong (and often conflicting) demands on time, energy, and attention. Wives and mothers who work outside their homes are not excused by society, nor do they excuse themselves (Paloma & Garland, 1971) from the many time-consuming activities involved in these family roles. When daughter Jane has the flu, Mother is somehow expected to arrange her workday to get daughter to the doctor. The ironing and vacuuming get done at night or on Saturday, but they are expected to be done by the wife (few employed wives can afford the services of even part-time household help). An "understanding" husband-father may, out of "the goodness of his heart," "help" his wife by drying the dishes; he may even "babysit" while his wife attends an important evening or Saturday meeting (but have you ever heard of a mother "babysitting" for her own children while father is out?). However, he is always a "helpmate," and the responsibility remains hers. A variety of studies all seem to point in the same direction: married women with full-time jobs work an additional 30 to 35 hours on household tasks (see Barrett, 1976; Kahne, 1976). Moreover, this is true of other industrialized societies. Males average four or five hours a week of household labor when their spouses are employed full time.

The employed wife ends up working at two full-time jobs, and the time and energy commitments of these necessarily conflict as well as exhaust her. Since the husband and father roles specify so little by way of actual, expected tasks at home, few such conflicts are apt to arise for the male. In short, most work roles are currently structured for people whose main, indeed sole, important task is that of "provider" and who have little else to divert their attention. Wives and mothers are simply not, by social and personal definition, in that situation.

Thus roles in the labor force are structured in our economy for males (which is perhaps the real meaning of "sexism"). It is hardly likely that research scientists, lawyers, artists, administrators, or anyone else can compete for excellence in their chosen fields, and enjoy the promotions and raises that result, if they are diverted constantly by worries about what to defrost for dinner, running noses, dry cleaning, the plumbing, and so forth. This is especially the case if the competitors are freed from such concerns. In addition, many women lose valuable years of work and experience on the dubious assumption, reinforced, as we have seen, by the media and "scientific" experts, that newborns need the constant presence and attention of their mothers. This, too, puts them at a competitive disadvantage. Indeed, a number of organizations which in the past routinely granted leaves to males for the discharge of military obligations, guaranteeing their jobs on return, have had no parallel policy for pregnancy leave. This virtually forces females to quit work when pregnant, only to have to begin again from the bottom when they return to the labor market. Pregnancy leaves have, however, become more commonplace in the past few years.

The problems faced by women who are both wives and employees exemplify one kind of role conflict, namely, interrole conflict. Females are also handicapped by the other type: intrarole conflict. This second type of conflict exists for female workers regardless of marital status and may even be somewhat worse for the unmarried. The modern work environment in postindustrial societies is heavily bureaucratic and administrative. A premium is placed on brains rather than brawn, since few jobs today require a degree of physical strength greater than that probably possessed by all healthy adults. Thus females should be in an infinitely better position to compete in the economy than they were previously, when physical strength was a more important component of most work. The fact that this is not the case results from the values instilled in females by the kind of upbringing documented in the preceding chapter and strongly reinforced by male-dominated media, science, and religion.

Females are trained to be sensitive, emotional, intuitive, passive, unaggressive, and so forth, but the modern work environment increasingly requires rational, logical, aggressive, ambitious, competitive, and mechanical traits. It has, in fact, a "masculine" orientation. On the one hand "feminine" females lose out in the job market because they lack the requisite mental habits to function in any but the most menial jobs. On the other, females who enter the world of work at higher levels, unlike males, are forced to behave in one way on the job and another with dates and families. Moreover, if they exhibit too strongly those "masculine" traits that enable success, they are labeled "bitches" or "castrating females" and shunned by male colleagues, to their personal and professional detriment (Rossi, 1970). Females in more responsible positions are thus faced with a "catch 22." They must maneuver on a narrow balance beam between the contradictory traits that on the one side would win them admiration as females and on the other would enable them to function professionally. The psychic costs and waste of valuable energy are immeasurable, and the result again is a strong competitive disadvantage with males. However, it should be noted that many women who may look, objectively, as if they experience one or both types of role conflicts do not *feel* as if they do. For these women, juggling a variety of roles may be exhilarating rather than debilitating.

Several other considerations work to the detriment of women in the world of work. Faced with psychologically distressing and physically exhausting role conflicts, females who compete for good jobs find their male "peers" expect little of them—after all, they're "only" females. If she performs as well as a mediocre male a woman will often find herself loudly praised, and when she does poorly it may be dismissed with "Well, what did you expect of a woman?" These kinds of responses come to constitute self-fulfilling prophecies and hardly comprise the kind of spur that promotes excellence (Epstein, 1970, p. 131).

When a woman finds herself discouraged at work, as everyone, regardless of sex, does from time to time, she will know that she can quit without suffering social criticism. Indeed, she will often be praised for leaving career behind and devoting herself full time to home and family. She must, therefore, constantly recommit herself to work. By comparison, males are rarely free to leave the world of work and are thus, ironically, freed from the psychological stress entailed in worrying about whether or not to remain employed. From youth females have been encouraged by schools, parents, and peers to view work in terms of "contingency plans" in case they "have to work," and they have been told to leave enough options open to avoid conflict with the career needs of whatever males they may marry (Husbands, 1972). As a result, many females find themselves in fields they dislike but have chosen because they can practice them anywhere their husbands might go. They only too eagerly give their jobs up when it is possible to do so, or at least they approach them with something less than enthusiasm.

Finally, a "victimized" person (whether a racial or ethnic minority member or a female) tends to suffer from a lack of self-confidence, or an inferiority complex. The feminine stereotype explicitly encourages such a self-concept in regard to males, and males are taught from an early age that they are indeed "superior" to females. These attitudes will hardly benefit a female in pressing for the acceptance of her ideas or in any aspect of job competition with males. Indeed, most employed females have had the experience of finding themselves virtually "invisible" to their male colleagues, their ideas ignored or stolen, and incapable of asserting themselves in response. For a more complete discussion of on-the-job problems unique to women, see Korda (1972) and Kanter (1977).

Job Discrimination Against Women

These competitive disadvantages rooted in the feminine role are strengthened by overt, as well as more subtle, forms of discrimination on the part of employers, who still are overwhelmingly male. Rationalizing on the basis of a series of myths, employers often continue to disregard the law, failing to hire females in more than token numbers for numerous high-status and well-paid positions, failing to promote them, and paying them less than males engaged in the same work. Since the 1964 Civil Rights Act and a number of subsequent laws and executive orders, discrimination on the basis of sex has been illegal. It is noteworthy that this stipulation was originally added by Senator Harry Byrd as a "joke," in an effort to block passage of a law designed chiefly to end racial discrimination.

One of the more subtle forms of discrimination is that, to a large extent, policy is formed, "deals" are closed, contacts are made, and information is exchanged in male-only clubs, bars, and such lofty sites as men's rooms and locker rooms. When feminists picket men's grills or clubs they are not engaged in a trivial exercise. Among other things, they are asking that the key sites for important business dealings be made accessible to females—how else can they hope to achieve anything in the business world, even if they manage to reach positions with grandiose titles? (see Lipman-Blumen, 1976). The "protégé" or apprentice system, especially in academia and other professions, constitutes another subtle form of discrimination (Epstein, 1970, pp. 169-73). Top positions in many fields are filled by an informal process in which the potential employer calls around to his (male) friends and asks whom they recommend. They recommend their protégés, who, given the sponsors' own prejudices, are rarely female. Only open advertising of all openings can avoid this type of discrimination, and this is a major demand of many professional women's groups. There is, finally, what Cynthia Epstein (1970, pp. 87-90) refers to as "status-set typing." This "occurs when a class of persons shares statuses (that is, certain statuses tend to cluster) *and when it is considered appropriate that they do so"* (p. 87). For instance, most top-level administrators of large corporations also share other statuses in common, namely, they are white, Protestant, and male. Although these other statuses are theoretically irrelevant to their functioning as corporate administrators, people who do not share the cluster make the others "uncomfortable"; something doesn't seem to "fit." The irrelevant statuses then become the most salient ones to the individual as well as to colleagues, in the process obscuring the chief status, which in this case is that of corporate administrator. Under these circumstances the individual will find it difficult to function effectively. Virtually all economic positions of much prestige have as part of their status set the attribute of maleness.

Discrimination is hardly limited to these subtleties. The myths and half-truths employers have used to justify discrimination against females are still believed by many, and although few present-day employers would openly defend their right to preferentially hire, pay, and promote males, many do discriminate in more subtle fashion because of them. Nine of these myths are examined here. For a discussion of a different, but related, set of myths concerning females and employment, see Judith Long Laws's interesting article entitled "Work Aspirations of Women" (1976).

Myth 1:   Females are only working for "pin money." The idea behind this myth is that since they probably have husbands who are supporting them, females do not need as much income as males. The single group of women which made the largest gain in proportion employed between 1940 and 1970 was married women with husbands present (Vatter, 1976, p. 211). Nonetheless, about 40 percent of all employed women are not married, and for these women employment is clearly a financial necessity. In 1975 24 percent, or 17.6 million families, were "headed" by females. Their average annual household income was $7,201, compared to nearly $16,000 for male-headed households (U.S. Bureau of the Census, 1976, p. 412). In 1972, 43 percent of all poverty families were female-headed (Ross, 1976, p. 137). As the divorce rate continues to rise, no female can assume any longer that she will be supported for the rest of her life. Over 50 percent of divorced women receive neither alimony nor child support, and for the other 50 percent the median total payment is $1,300 per year, scarcely enough for one person, let alone a woman and her children, to live on (Griffiths, 1976, p. 8).

But what about working wives with husbands present and employed? The truth is that the bulk of employed wives are married to men who do not earn very much, and it is often their wages that maintain the family above the poverty line (Suelzle, 1970, pp. 55-56). In 1972, nearly a third of all married women in the labor force had husbands whose income was less than $5,000 (Cordell & McHale, 1975, p. 38). In short, women who work are generally either the sole support of self, and frequently family, or they provide much-needed income to maintain life above the poverty line. Salaries are scarcely pin money to these millions.

Despite the fact that the income of most employed women covers more than incidentals, females do not *receive* as much pay as males, even those in the same jobs. In 1974 full-time employed females earned 57 percent of males' average income; the median female income was $6,772 compared to $11,835 for males (U.S. Bureau of the Census, 1976, p. 413). In 1975, when 45 percent of all employed males earned in excess of $10,000, the corresponding percentage for females was 10.3. The median wages of white females are considerably below those of black males, and the doubly discriminated-against black females are at the very bottom of the salary scale (Bird, 1968, p. 3; Hart, 1977; Amundsen, 1971, p. 32). Chicanos fare about the same as black women (Burciaga, Gonzales, & Hepburn, 1977). Moreover, college-educated women earn about the equivalent of a male with some high school but no diploma (U.S. Bureau of the Census, 1976, p. 413). Females in sales positions earn only 41 percent of the salaries of males in sales; those in the census category "professional, technical and kindred," about 64 percent of males' salaries; craftsmen and foremen, 56 percent; clerical personnel, 59 percent; and so on (U.S. Bureau of the Census, 1976, p. 383). Females have an unemployment rate double that of white males (Amundsen, 1971, p. 44; Griffiths, 1976). Salary discrepancies are also not irrelevant to business. A 1972 report published in the *Houston Chronicle* estimated that if females were paid at the same rate as males, the annual national payroll would have to be increased by $59 billion! Exploitation is only too profitable.

Myth 2: The wealth of our nation is mainly in the hands of females. Females comprise about 40 percent of the top wealthholders in this country and about half of the adult, individual stockholders (U.S. Bureau of the Census, 1976, p. 425). Moreover, they acquire their wealth at a much later age than males, primarily through widowhood. Of the women who rank among the top wealthholders, 58 percent are over 50 and 18 percent are over 70. The comparable male figures are 46 and 10 percent (U.S. Bureau of the Census, 1976, p. 425). Much of the wealth of the younger women in this group is largely a matter of assets assigned them in name only by husbands and fathers for tax purposes. In any case, de facto control of wealth usually remains in male hands, be it father, husband, or a trustee in the form of a lawyer, banker, or broker (Amundsen, 1971, pp. 52, 93-95). Kristen Amundsen concludes that "The implications of these findings are quite clear: Women wealthholders are not likely to have the expertise, the experience, or the opportunity for putting their resources to use in an attempt to influence the trend and shape of the economy" (p. 94).

Myth 3: Women aren't worth hiring where any training or investment is involved, since they just get married or pregnant and quit. Females do indeed quit jobs more often than males, and frequently they give family-related reasons. However, when occupational level and income are held constant, males and females do not differ significantly in turnover rates (Mead & Kaplan, 1965, p. 52). What does this mean? Females are more frequently hired for menial, routinized, duller jobs than males. Moreover, they are often "overeducated" for them. The college-educated female working as a receptionist or clerk-typist (while supposedly "proving" she is worthy of more serious consideration) is no rarity. Among all such jobs turnover rates are very high; the overwhelmingly male, but dull, routinized auto-assembly industry is plagued with the highest job turnover rate of any. Where females and males in the *same* job and income categories are compared, little difference is found.

It is because of their differential distribution within the occupational structure that females have a higher turnover rate (see Barron & Norris, 1976, p. 50). For instance in 1975 14 percent of all male workers but only 5 percent of females were in proprietary or managerial positions; the corresponding figures for craftsmen were 20 and 1. These are relatively interesting and well-paid jobs. In the more routinized, poorly paid occupations, 42 percent of the employed females were clerks or sales workers (mainly retailing the less expensive items for poor wages), compared to 13 percent of the males (mainly wholesaling industrial products or retailing expensive items on commission); 6 percent of the females and less than 1 percent of the males were household workers (servants); and the corresponding percentages for service workers were 22 and 9 (U.S. Bureau of the Census, 1976, p. 372).

It should also be noted that in 1975 males between the ages of 18 and 65 (i.e., the age range that comprises the bulk of the labor force) had a death rate twice that of females. This fact has implications for the length of time men and women can potentially contribute to the labor force. Unlike marriage and pregnancy, death represents a permanent loss to the labor force. In 1975, U.S. males lost 5.5 million potential person-years in the labor force due to death; females lost 2.8 million potential years, or about half the male loss. These greater male deaths have a direct impact on the return employers receive for their training investment, a fact rarely mentioned and never considered in personnel decisions (data computed by Maradee Davis from U.S. Bureau of the Census, 1976, p. 23).

Myth 4: Women are weak and frequently sick, and thus they miss too many days of work. This is seen as a justification for not giving females much responsibility. The facts are that females miss more days due to acute health conditions than males, but males miss more days due to chronic conditions. In 1974 females averaged 5.1 sick days in the course of the year and males averaged 4.8 such days (U.S. Bureau of the Census, 1976, p. 88).

Myth 5: No one wants a woman boss.   This is really not a myth; most employees of both sexes seem to resent the idea of a female superior (Kanter, 1977, pp. 373-76). Rosabeth Kanter (1976) analyzed some of the major reasons why females suffer this disadvantage, other than plain prejudice. She argues that high status in the external world (i.e., the world outside the workplace) contributes to the power and influence of an organizational leader. Subordinates are more likely to inhibit aggression and negative attitudes toward someone who is seen as having generally higher status; relative to men, women of course have low status outside their work organizations. High-status supervisors tend to have close contact with those higher up on the organizational ladder, which enables them to acquire more information and to extract more benefits for their subordinates. Women, by and large, lack these contacts because of their lower social status, and thus they may be less effective vis-à-vis their subordinates. Also, leaders who are themselves on the rise may gain the loyalty of subordinates who anticipate rising with them; women frequently suffer blocked mobility and are not permitted to rise. Finally, given their own vulnerability and insecurity arising from low status and blocked mobility, women supervisors (like any supervisor who shares these problems) are likely to be authoritarian and restrictive toward their subordinates. Thus, the low status suffered by women handicaps them in their efforts to perform well in supervisory capacities, and this, in turn, reinforces women's low status.

Myth 6: Women don't want the responsibility entailed in many high-status jobs.   Given the upbringing of most females, again it might be a shock to find any women who do want this responsibility, but there are in fact many. And again, to assume that a particular Jane does not want responsibility because most females do not want it is nothing less than discrimination. At any rate, it is clear that females are not to be found in substantial numbers in decision-making positions. For instance, in the federal Civil Service, where discrimination is supposedly nonexistent, only 4 percent of the top-level bureaucrats are female. In the predominantly female field of social work, where almost all workers have about the same educational accomplishments, 58 percent of the males but only 43 percent of the females function in any kind of administrative capacity. Moreover, the very top positions in social work agencies and departments are almost all filled by males (Stamm, 1969, pp. 41-42; also see Chafetz, 1972). A similar phenomenon is evident in two other "female" fields: nursing and public school teaching. In 1966 46 percent of all male nurses but only 32 percent of the females were functioning in an administrative capacity (Grimm & Stern, 1972). Indeed, despite the fact that women constitute 75 percent of the health care labor force, they fill less than 10 percent of the managerial positions in this industry (Grant, 1977). It is also clear that males are disproportionately promoted to principalships and school district administrative positions. Thus, whereas 90 percent of the elementary school teachers are female, less than 50 percent of the principals of elementary schools are, and women's proportion of the latter roles has been declining (Lewis, 1968, p. 134).

As virtually all semiprofessional and professional fields become more bureaucratic and "scientific," the few "havens" for ambitious women that existed in such traditionally female occupations as library science, social work, nursing, and public school teaching are being taken over at the top levels by males. The converse has not happened, in other than token members, in traditionally male fields. The female professions in the past represented something of an extension of traditional female duties within the home. It was considered "legitimate" and "feminine" to be employed teaching children, nursing the sick, and caring for the needy—all activities females normally do for free as homemakers. Because it was "only" females who were engaged in such activities, salaries and prestige were uniformly low in the "feminine professions" (Chafetz, 1972). As they changed somewhat in character, males entered them and salaries gradually increased (although which came first is unclear). The result is that the female social worker or teacher who might readily have worked her way into an administrative role years ago has less chance today, since the newly entering males are preferred for such jobs.

Myth 7: Females lack the physical strength for many highly skilled and well-paid manual jobs, especially in the crafts. Unions have often been guilty of perpetuating this myth. Given current machinery, most such jobs rarely entail more physical exertion that that involved in carrying a 60-pound child or transporting a desk typewriter from one office to another—both tasks done frequently by a large number of the "weaker sex." In any event, recalling the discussion of overlapping normal curves in Chapter 2, it is clear that some males are physically weaker than most females, while some females are stronger than most males.

Myth 8: Well, anyway, a woman who is really ambitious and qualified can get ahead and acquire an interesting, responsible job. True. If she has somehow managed to avoid the tremendous pressure to conform to stereotypical "femininity"; and if she has put up with many years of drudgery, poor pay, and discouragement from everyone; and if she still has energy, creativity, and ambition left, *then,* when she reaches middle age, she may be in a position commensurate with that of a male 15 years her junior who has less experience, ability, and frequently less by way of formal credentials. Almost every researcher who has examined female employment has concluded that women are discriminated against; that is, for the same effort, position, educational attainment, and so on, they receive fewer rewards financially and are promoted more slowly, if at all. (For a review of this research see Almquist, 1977.) The research evidence also supports the assertion that the level at which women enter the labor force is below that of men with similar qualifications, and they are shunted into jobs with less career mobility built into the position (Almquist, 1977; see also Treiman & Ferrell, 1975).

Personal "horror stories" abound among working women to document this also. Typically, Jane was graduated from college and headed for the "big city." There, at office after office, she was administered a typing test while classmate Dick took an aptitude test. Finally, she settled for a secretarial job at $100 a week on the promise that "if things work out" she would be promoted to research, editing, copywriting, administration, or whatever. Meanwhile, Dick was hired at $10,000 as a management trainee. Jane worked overtime and Saturdays (without extra pay) and gradually took over many of the duties assigned to her $30,000-per-year boss. If she was lucky, five or so years later her boss was promoted or quit, and she moved up to his job (which she had been doing all along)—for less than half his pay and a new, less official-sounding title. The bigger the company, the more apt this scenario is to be played. Even with all this, her advancement opportunities were not infrequently tied to sexual favors granted to various levels of bosses, or at least the willingness to play flattering "alter ego." For an excellent discussion of how this process works in the publishing industry, see Michael Korda's *Male Chauvinism* (1972).

Myth 9: "I don't know what American women today are complaining about; they are much better off than ever before." (You know, "You've come a long way, baby.") Those who espouse this myth also maintain that American women are much better off than their sisters in other nations and that it takes time to change things, but "we're getting there." Nothing could be more incorrect than these assertions. In a now-classic article written in 1969, Dean Knudsen documented the declining status of females in American society from 1940 to 1966. He concluded that:

> . . . women have experienced a gradual but persistent decline in status as measured by occupation, income, and education. The sources of the lowered status include diminished efforts by women and institutionalized discrimination, both of which derive from a normative definition of sex roles based upon functionalist assumptions and presuppositions about the nature of society and reality. Thus, given the conviction that women should not pursue occupations in competition with men, women and employers together develop a self-fulfilling prophecy (p. 192).

Nearly a decade later, and more than a decade after it became illegal to discriminate against women in the labor market, Almquist (1977) reached similar conclusions.

The statistics indicate few improvements in pay, job status, or unemployment rates. In fact, relative to men, women continue to become progressively worse off, working more and getting paid less. Despite the fact that women's wages, like those of nonwhites, have increased steadily since 1970, those of white men have increased faster, leaving women and minorities *relatively* worse off each year. Where in 1940 41.6 percent of those in professional and technical jobs were female, by 1966 this figure had declined to 37.9 percent; the 1940 level was not regained until 1975. In routine jobs like clerical positions the proportion of females rose sharply, from 53.9 percent to 71.3 percent between 1940 and 1966, and then made a further gain to 77.8 percent by 1975. The proportion of private household workers who are female increased from 94.4 to 98 percent from 1940 to 1966 and has remained above the 1940 level. Perhaps the largest change has been in the low-paying area of service workers, where 38.4 percent were female in 1940,

55.0 percent in 1966, and 62.3 percent in 1975 (Knudsen, 1969, p. 186; U.S. Bureau of the Census, 1976, p. 372).

More specifically, and with reference to selected professional occupations, the proportion of females in college teaching and administration dropped from 32 percent in 1930 to 19 percent in 1960; by 1975 it had nearly, but not quite, regained the 1930 level. In the field of dentistry, females comprised 3.2 percent of dentists in 1920, 2.1 percent in 1960, and 3.4 percent by 1975. In the sciences, at least, there have been some recent gains for women. After declining from 11.4 to 9.9 percent between 1950 and 1960, the proportion of women professionals in the life, physical, and social sciences reached 15.2 percent in 1975 (Epstein, 1970, p. 7; U.S. Bureau of the Census, 1976, pp. 373-376). In short, even as the share of women in the job market grew from the fifties on, it was not until the midseventies that they regained their pre-World War II proportions in high-status fields. They were, and to a large extent still are, entering the labor market at the lowest levels and remaining there.

The income gap between men and women, too, has widened in many cases. In 1939 female managers and proprietors earned 57.3 percent of the income of similarly employed males; in 1966, only 54 percent; and in 1974, 55 percent. Between 1939 and 1966 females in clerical jobs went from 78.5 percent of the income of their male counterparts to 66.5 percent, and that figure declined further, to 59 percent, in 1974. In sales, this percentage dropped from 51.3 in 1939 to 41.0 in 1974. Female craftsmen and supervisors earned 63.7 percent of the average male salary in 1939, 60.4 percent in 1966, and 56 percent in 1974. The salaries of female service workers declined from 59.6 percent of similar male salaries in 1939 to 55.4 percent in 1966, and they went back up, to 58 percent, only in 1974. In no case has the male-female income gap between 1939 and the midseventies decreased (Knudsen, 1969, p. 187; U.S. Bureau of the Census, 1976, p. 383; Sullerot, 1971, p. 122).

One reason women may fare so poorly in the labor market is because, relative to men, they are not unionized. In 1972 only 12.5 percent of employed women were union members, and they were mostly concentrated in a small number of unions. Half of all unionized females belonged to 1 of 12 unions. Men are unionized at nearly double that rate and belong to a much wider range of unions. In addition, from the mid-1960s to the mid-1970s the proportion of female labor force participants who were unionized declined, from 13.8 percent to 12.5 (Roby, 1976; Wertheimer, 1976).

Females in our society are no better off than in many other places in the world and are in a worse relative position than women in some nations. Females in the United States comprise 8 percent of the medical doctors, whereas in Sweden they represent 13 percent; India and Japan, 9 percent; France, 22 percent; Great Britain, 25 percent; and the U.S.S.R., 76 percent (Epstein, 1970, p. 12; Sullerot, 1971, p. 151). In 1960 over 40 percent of the medical students in China were female (Cohen, 1970, p. 417). Of all the U.S. lawyers 3.5 percent are female, a figure considerably below that for France, Denmark, Sweden, Germany, Poland, and the Soviet Union, where females comprise 38 percent of the lawyers (Epstein, 1970, p. 11; Sullerot, 1971, p. 152). Comparative figures reveal similar findings with reference to engineering, science, university-level education, judgeships, and so forth. Clearly, many European societies are somewhat ahead of the United States in opening the professions to women, and the Soviet Union is very far ahead. It is true that some of these professions are less prestigeful and less well paid abroad than here, especially medicine (which in the U.S.S.R. is considered a "woman's occupation," as grammar school teaching or social work is here), but the fact remains that interesting, responsible positions are more open to women in numerous other nations than in America. In many nations, especially those in the Third World, the status of the *average* women is considerably lower than here, but the small minority of *elite* females who achieve high levels of education face less discrimination and fewer job-related problems than their well-educated American sisters.

When relative income is considered, females in this country seem to fare about the same as their counterparts abroad. Women in France earn about 70 percent of males' income, somewhat better than in this country, but in Great Britain the figure is about 50 percent, or somewhat below ours. In no case does it seem to approach real equality (Sullerot, 1971, pp. 125-27). However, in a number of nations, including Austria, Denmark, France, Germany, Italy, Spain, Sweden, and Yugoslavia, postnatal maternity leave varying from four to ten weeks is a right granted by law, and in many instances such leave is either with partial pay or accompanied by governmental allowances (Sullerot, p. 241).

In addition to these common myths, two other factors have a strong bearing on the job prospects of females—age and "looks." Quite bluntly, male employers often look at female employees as sex objects, and "good looks" are for women an important consideration in acquiring many jobs; the unattractive female, regardless of qualifications, is seriously handicapped. This is compounded by the fact that our society generally has as its model of feminine pulchritude the looks of an attractive 20-year-old. In contrast, good looks are far less important for males in the labor market. The model of an attractive male is also taken to be the successful, middle-aged man, graying slightly at the temples, and having "character" in his face (those "unsightly lines" in females). A quick check of advertising in television or magazines will verify this difference. A female is thus considered "old" about the time a male is considered to be in his "prime" (Bell, 1970; Moss, 1970; Whitehurst, 1977, p. 7).

The implications of this emphasis on looks and age are very important for women. Females are most frequently in the labor market at two times in their life cycle: for a few years before marriage and childbearing, and for a much greater number of years after age 35. Most females have had their last child by about age 30, and this child is in school full time by the time the mother is in her middle or late thirties. Since females have a life expectancy of about 75 years, increasing numbers are looking to the job market to provide a functional role for the many years after the main child-rearing tasks have been completed. However, by that age they are already considered "old" and "unattractive," and therefore unsuitable for many jobs. Thus, for instance, in 1965 between 40 and 50 percent of the women in the labor force aged 45 and over were officially unemployed (Bell, 1970, p. 78). In a study of want ads Inge Bell found that 97 percent of all advertisements for females asked for a "girl" or a "gal," compared to a mere 2 out of 2,272 male listings requesting a "boy." When asked what these terms meant, employment agencies explained that employers were seeking females generally under 30, or 35 at the outside. When females over 35 were sought, the term "mature" was used. In addition, ads for females, but almost never for males, frequently employed descriptive adjectives such as "attractive" (Bell, pp. 79-82). It is now illegal to advertise separately for male and female employees, but it is safe to assume that employers' tastes have not changed.

Room at the Top

Some findings from a study by Janet Chafetz and Barbara Polk (1974) of those few females who have "made it to the top" and gained positions that place them in the national "elite" will conclude this section on the economy. In this study, the criterion used for determining "elite" status was a listing in *Who's Who in America* for 1965. A simple random sample of 100 was drawn. Females comprised a mere 4.5 percent of all listings in the 1965 *Who's Who,* down from 8.5 percent in 1925.

The primary bases for elite standing for females differed in some very important ways from those characteristic for males, a sample of 100 of which was also drawn for comparison on this variable alone. These differences can be seen in the data presented in Table 4.1. Females who gained national recognition overwhelmingly did so outside the realm of the private sector of the economy; where only four women were noted for their business role, over one third of the males were. Women were also totally unrepresented in religion and considerably less well represented than males in the professions. The two institutional sectors in which the sexes were similarly represented were education and government service. In those areas that were least dependent on male-dominated, formal institutions, namely, the arts and philanthropic-social action organizations, females strongly outnumbered males. It is

TABLE 4.1

PRIMARY BASES FOR ELITE MEMBERSHIP, BY SEX (1965)

Bases for Elite Membership	Females	Males
Family of birth or marriage	1	0
Activity in philanthropic and/or social action organization	9	0
Religion	0	3
Government service	12	11
Business	4	38
The arts	38	8
Education and education administration	27	24
Professions	12	20
Totals*	103	104

*Totals come to more than 100 because some of the subjects had two primary activities for which they were noted.

also notable that 28 females compared to only 8 males were eminent because of roles that did not require absence from the home—family connections and two of the arts, plastic arts and writing. Over time there has been a considerable change in the proportion of females fulfilling such roles: in a similar 1925 sample substantially more than half of the elite American females functioned in the three roles that did not require their absence from the home.

Considering other characteristics of the 1965 sample, 1 in 3 of all elite females were single and had never married. This is a very high proportion, considering that less than 10 percent of Americans of both sexes fail to marry at some time in their lives, a figure probably more typical of elite males (for similar findings by occupation, see Epstein, 1970, p. 97). The educational level of the single female elites was considerably higher than that of those who had ever been married: 97 percent of the former had university or specialized training, compared to only 73 percent of the latter. This finding suggests the possibility that, on the one hand, marriage and, on the other, substantial education with a resulting profession may to some degree have served as functional alternatives for females of the generation represented in the 1965 sample, namely, those born between 1890 and 1920. Thus, if a female was willing to sacrifice marriage and concentrate her attention on acquiring a superior education, she had a better chance of achieving in socially valued contexts. Such a choice has not, however, been forced on males (Havens, 1973).

Educational Institutions

In postindustrial societies where the economy is dependent on technology and rational administration, education is the key to higher status positions. This is not to say that education guarantees a high-status or well-paid job. It does not. Moreover, it particularly fails to serve as such a guarantee to those who are lower caste, including females and minority members. As noted in the preceding section, females are frequently "overeducated" for their jobs, and they earn the equivalent of males who have substantially less education. However, it is also clear that without the "credentials" supplied by higher education there is little chance for anyone to enter such positions. Therefore, if females in fact comprise a lower caste in our society, this should be reflected in our institutions of higher education which in turn feed into the economic realm.

In public school education, as noted in Chapter 3, school personnel still separate the sexes and treat them differently, urging students to uphold stereotyped notions of masculinity and femininity and to plan their lives accordingly. The substance of many of the courses taught both at that level and in the universities supports the gender role status quo. The concern now centers on the extent of discrimination in higher education, which is being increasingly well-documented by female academics in a wide variety of fields.

When the relative proportions of male and female students are examined, the rule for educational attainment has long been "the higher the fewer" women (Harris, 1970, p. 284). Until the early 1970s more females than males completed high school, and the proportions are about the same now. In fact, back at the turn of the century 60 percent of high school graduates were female (Epstein, 1970, p. 57). But fewer females than males enroll in college; in 1974 45 percent of those enrolled were female (U.S. Bureau of the Census, 1976, p. 143). The principle is again evident in the awarding of higher degrees: in 1973 42 percent of the bachelor's and master's degrees and only 18 percent of the doctorates were awarded to females. Just as females lost status in the labor force between World War II and the 1960s, so did they in terms of degrees earned. In 1940 females earned 41, 37, and 14 percent of the bachelor's, master's, and doctoral degrees, respectively. In 1960 these figures dropped to 35 percent of bachelor's, 32 percent of master's, and 10 percent of doctoral degrees for women (U.S. Bureau of the Census, 1976, p. 146).

Females also tend to specialize more in the "soft" areas which are less directly relevant to the job market than in preparation for high-status jobs. For instance, in 1974 females constituted 34 percent of the social science bachelor's degree students (and 57 percent of those in sociology), but only 10 percent of the students in agriculture, 14 percent of those in architecture, 13 percent of those in business, 2 percent of those in engineering, and 16 percent of those in computer science. The same relative distribution characterizes master's and doctoral students, although the percentages for women are considerably lower. Although the proportion of females in the professional schools has been increasing since the 1960s, in 1973 only 8.9 percent of medical, 1.4 percent of dental, and 8.7 percent of law students were female (U.S. Bureau of the Census, 1976, p. 146).

How much of this is due to overt, antifemale discrimination and how much to a lack of interest in higher education on the part of those socialized to be "feminine"? Both factors are undoubtedly influential, and no figures are available to demonstrate the relative effects of one or the other. However, it has not been difficult to document overt discrimination in the recent past. Several institutions had admissions quotas as recently as the early 1970s: Stanford required a 60 percent male class, Princeton wanted three males for every female, and Harvard allowed only 25 percent female students. Females generally needed much higher grades to get into college. They also received substantially less in scholarship money: $518 per annum was the 1972 average for women, $760 for men (*Time,* March 20, 1972, p. 91). This fact is especially important when we consider that parents are more willing to make financial sacrifices to send their sons than their daughters to college (Roby, 1972, p. 123). In a recent study, McClendon (1976) demonstrated that women obtain less education than would be expected on the basis of their socioeconomic background, in part because families of modest means send their sons rather than their daughters off to college and graduate school.

Prejudice and discrimination against female graduate students has been even more severe. In one year 34 percent of the females entering graduate school at the University of Chicago had at least an A minus average, compared to only 27 percent of the males. Conversely, 41 percent of the males had a B average or below, compared to only 30 percent of the females (Harris, 1970, p. 287). Some medical schools had even established a combined quota for "minorities," that is, females, blacks, and browns, thus setting them in direct competiton with one another without hindering the opportunities for white males to gain entrance (Harris, p. 288). Moreover, the more prestigious the school, the more it has discriminated at all levels. In short females have had to be better qualified than males to get into less prestigious schools (Roby, 1972, pp. 122-23; Bienen, Ostriker, & Ostriker, 1977).

Faculty and administration prejudice against females is rampant. Ann Harris quotes a number of statements "garnered from various institutions" during the 1960s, including such gems as the following:

> I know you're competent and your thesis advisor knows you're competent. The question in our minds is are you *really serious* about what you're doing.
>
> The admissions committee didn't do their job. There is not one good-looking girl in the entering class.
>
> A pretty girl like you will certainly get married: why don't you stop with an M.A.?
>
> You're so cute. I can't see you as a professor of anything.
>
> [Professor to student looking for a job] You've no business looking for work with a child that age.
>
> We expect women who come here to be competent, good students, but we don't expect them to be brilliant or original.
>
> Why don't you find a rich husband and give all this up?
>
> [From Bryn Mawr, a woman's university] Our general admissions policy has been, if the body is warm and male, take it; if it's female, make sure it's an A—.
>
> Somehow I can never take women in this field seriously (1970, p. 285).

During the Vietnam War, the president of Harvard, Nathan Pusey, was quoted as saying, with regard to the effects of the draft on applications to graduate school, "We shall be left with the blind, the lame, and the women" (Harris, 1970, p. 283). Upon assuming the presidency of Sarah Lawrence, a woman's college, Charles de Carlo said "feminine instincts are characterized by caring qualities, concern for beauty and form, reverence for life, empathy in human relations, and a demand that men be better than they are" (Harris, p. 284). In the past few years, since academic institutions began to be included under the laws prohibiting discrimination, fewer such overt comments have been heard. In addition, women are taking to the courts to fight academic discrimination, especially sexual exploitation of female graduate students by their professors (see *Time* magazine, August 8, 1977, pp. 52-53).

Despite some recent gains by females, male academics still cling to a series of myths about women in essence no different from those believed about women in the labor force. These myths involve the idea that women are less "dedicated" than men, more apt to drop out, and less capable. The truth of the matter is that 90 percent of female PhDs are still employed ten years after their degrees have been completed, a figure comparable to that for males (Harris, 1970, p. 284). Moreover, female PhDs are as productive in publishing research papers and books as their male counterparts (Bienen et al., 1977, p. 375). Despite these facts, females, and especially those who are married, have difficulty receiving the scholarships, fellowships, and assistantships that allow people to attend graduate school. This, coupled with faculty members' presuppositions about the seriousness and ability of female graduate students, helps to create self-fulfilling prophecies, since females face an uphill battle merely to gain their professional credentials.

Academia's own record of employment practices is also dismal. The 1964 Civil Rights Act did not cover universities; until the bill was expanded in the fall of 1972, it was not *illegal* for institutions of higher learning to practice job discrimination. However, since virtually all colleges and universities are dependent on monies from the federal Department of Health, Education, and Welfare, and since by earlier executive order federal monies could not go to discriminatory institutions, academic females have long been active in attempting to force their institutions to end discrimination under the threat of these funds being withdrawn. In the process, their research has unveiled solid facts and figures, discipline by discipline, school by school, to document discrimination. It is in no way dissimilar to the job situation outside of universities: females are hired less frequently and by less prestigious institutions, they are not promoted, and they are paid substantially less than their male colleagues (Roby, 1972, pp. 123-30; see also Bernard, 1964; Rossi, 1974).

Until the early 1970s most universities had nepotism rules which prohibited two members of a family from being employed at the same institution. In practice, this served to keep many qualified females who were wives of faculty members unemployed, exploited as part-time instructors, or in positions far below the level for which they were trained. The results of this practice, and outright discrimination, can be seen by examining the proportions of women in different types of academic institutions and at various ranks. In 1973 women comprised 22.3 percent of all faculty members in institutions of higher education. However, they were overrepresented at two-year colleges and underrepresented at the higher prestige universities. In public institutions, 32.3 percent of teachers at two-year schools were females, compared to only 17.1 percent of university faculty members. At private schools, the discrepancy was even more drastic; 45.4 percent of the faculty in two-year schools, and 14.5 percent in universities, were women. Women accounted for 40 percent of all instructors, the lowest academic rank. The higher the rank, from assistant, to associate, to full professor, the lower the proportion of women, from 23.8 to 16.3 to 9.8 percent, respectively (Bienen et al., 1977, p. 373). The bottom two ranks, instructor and assistant professor, are traditionally untenured, and that is where most women find themselves. To make matters worse, the academic marketplace has shrunk considerably in the past few years and will shrink further as we move into the 1980s, due to declining birth rates. The untenured are the first fired when faculties must be cut back. Clearly, the future for women, just recently entering academia in substantial numbers, is relatively bleak.

As in other areas of the labor force, females are not merely denied promotion, they are paid less than males. In 1973, nearly 6 percent of female college faculty earned less than $6,500, compared to 2 percent of male members. Twice as many male as female faculty earned in excess of $24,600 (10.8 and 5.4 percent, respectively). In fact, slightly over half of all male faculty earned in excess of $15,500, compared to slightly less than a quarter of female faculty (U.S. Bureau of the Census, 1976, p. 142).

The importance of discrimination against females in higher education is probably somewhat greater than similar discrimination in other areas of the economy. As we saw in the preceding chapter, young women are usually discouraged from thinking in terms of a career commitment. In addition, many children of both sexes rarely see females in any but a small number of roles outside the home. By the time they reach college, some female students have never known a female engaged in any occupation other than teacher in a public school, librarian, nurse, secretary, saleswomen, or totally menial types of jobs. In more technical terms, they have had few, if any, role models for other than stereotypically feminine positions. Speaking from personal experience, a female professor can, simply by existing, be a formidable influence on a female student. By occupying a position in a "man's field," she sets an example that says "it can be done." Conversely, the absence or paucity of such role models implies the opposite, and to a large extent that is the situation at most American colleges and universities in all but a few "feminine" fields, such as home economics, library science, education, nursing, and such.

To sum up, females are denied truly equal access to educational opportunities and discouraged systematically from using those that are available. This denial is based on the assumption that they will not adequately utilize their expensive educations in the work world and, therefore, scarce resources are better spent on males—even less qualified ones. This prophecy becomes self-fulfilling, since ill-equipped workers, as well as qualified ones who are assumed to lack dedication, will find only dull, poorly paid jobs which they will readily quit. Just in case a few stubborn women stick it out, male-dominated media, science, religion, and so on will be there to further encourage them to depart the "masculine world" of work and competition. Males *as a group* profit much by a situation that relieves them from having to worry about competition from fully half the human race.

Law and Public Policy

So females are kept down in the economy and in our educational institutions. But, some say, this is surely the result of a tradition which our laws are changing. The fact is that sexual caste and stereotypical notions of both gender roles are strongly reflected in and supported by our present legal system and in public policy in a myriad of ways.

It is virtually impossible to review the entire legal system of our society, consisting as it does of laws on the federal, state, and lesser political levels, as well as judicial precedents on a number of different levels. This section is therefore designed only to suggest some of the most salient ways in which laws reflect and reinforce tradition in this area. Leo Kanowitz's book on the subject, *Women and the Law* (1969), is an excellent reference, as are the more recent works of Eastwood (1975), Whitehurst (1977), De Crow (1974), Gates (1976), Kinsley (1977), Krauskopf (1977), Kamerman (1977), and Galvin and Mendelsohn (1976).

Before reviewing some of the relevant laws, it is necessary to provide a note of qualification. At this writing, the Equal Rights Amendment to the Constitution of the United States is still in the hands of state legislatures for ratification. At that level it has faced increasing opposition, and its future has become very problematic. The amendment was introduced in every congressional session since 1923 and was finally passed by both houses in March 1972. It was passed without the various crippling amendments that had been suggested by many; if ratified, it makes virtually all laws that arbitrarily differentiate between the sexes unconstitutional. In short, it would accomplish for the sexes what the 14th Amendment theoretically did for the races 100 years ago. However, even if it is ratified, decades of court battles would undoubtedly be needed to wipe the vast array of discriminatory laws off the books.

Why is such an amendment needed? The 5th and 14th Amendments, which supposedly extend "equal protection of the law" to "all," have repeatedly (and even recently) been held by the Supreme Court to be inapplicable to females (Kanowitz, 1969, chap. 6). The only *right* females are explicitly guaranteed is the right to vote, won in 1920. Because of this the vast number of criminal and civil laws that treat the sexes in different and unequal ways could only be removed by legislative action on all the various political levels. As we shall see in the next section, males, who usually profit most by such laws, comprise almost the entirety of all the various legislative branches. Under the circumstances, legislative action which would radically undercut the legislators' own caste position is unlikely. However, many states have, in the past half dozen years, passed equal rights amendments to their own constitutions.

Family Law and Policy

With the exception of eight states (Arizona, California, Idaho, Louisiana, Nevada, New Mexico, Texas, and Washington), the legal system of our society is based directly on English common law. The other eight are called community property states and their legal system derives from Continental Europe; in practice, although not in theory, their laws pertaining to the family are quite similar in effect to those of the other 42 states.

Originally, under common law, on marriage a female ceased to be a person in the eyes of the law. Under this doctrine of "coverture," she and her husband became one entity legally. This was meant quite literally; the "one," of course, was the male. The female lost all her property on marriage, as well as her name, her right to select a domicile, to enter contracts, to keep any income earned during the marriage, and so forth (Kanowitz, 1969, chap. 3). During the 19th century, in a series of acts known collectively as the Married Women's Property Acts, the British gradually granted many of these rights to females. There is no direct parallel in this country, however; the changes that have been made have occurred piecemeal and vary widely from state to state.

Until a couple of years ago some states still required that on marriage a woman had to assume her husband's name. She had to petition the courts if she wished to keep her birth name, otherwise known by that curious term "maiden name." In such cases, the husband's permission was often required. As recently as the summer of 1972 a Maryland woman had her driver's license revoked because she had not used her married name in acquiring it. For females who have, for instance, built a professional reputation before marriage, the required name change can be costly. Upon attempting to regain the use of her birth name after 10 years of marriage, a woman was told by a Houston, Texas, judge in 1976 that it would "appear immoral" for her to do so. She was advised to use an assumed name for business purposes and her married name for social purposes.

It is interesting to note also that although married females in many states cannot change their names without their husbands' permission, males are bound by no such restriction. Moreover, in some states a divorced woman must keep her former husband's name if she is the defendant ("guilty party") in divorce proceedings (Kanowitz, 1969, pp. 43-44). In most states a married woman's legal domicile is that of her husband, regardless of where she actually resides. This can pose real problems for women who might be employed somewhere other than where their husbands live (and there are an increasing number of them). They must vote, pay taxes, and conduct all other legal business on the basis of their husbands' residence (Kanowitz, p. 47). On this legal basis, at many state universities if a female student who is a resident of that state marries a nonresident, she must subsequently pay nonresident tuition. The same does not apply where the student is male and the nonresident spouse is female. In some states if a wife dies intestate the husband inherits the entire estate; if the husband leaves no will, the widow receives only half of his estate. For women who would start a business, in at least some states there are legal restrictions on the right of a married female to enter contracts; in many cases her husband must be a co-signer (Kanowitz, p. 52 ff.). In some states married women have been altogether restricted in their rights to engage in a separate business enterprise; in some their independent right to sue is limited; in some they cannot serve in positions of legal trust, and so on and on and on.

These legal restrictions on married women are based on the presupposition that husbands and wives have completely different obligations to their spouses. By law in most states a husband is entitled to his wife's services as "a companion and household servant" (Krauskopf, 1977, p. 95). Thus, for instance, if she is injured, the husband can sue the party who was responsible for the injury for the value of the household services lost. However, despite her responsibility to render household services, the wife is not legally entitled to any share of the family's assets as recompense for that service (Krauskopf, p. 95). By law, as we have seen, the husband is defined as the head of the household, which entails the legal obligation to support the family financially. However, unless the marriage is dissolved, that obligation is essentially unenforceable in the courts. In short, as long as she remains married, a woman must depend on the charity of her husband; upon divorce she may receive support, but as statistics show, she also may not (Krauskopf, pp. 96-97). In addition, on divorce the wife may find that the accumulated assets of the family belong to her husband; the courts do not consider household services rendered as contributing to the accumulation of such assets, except in the community property states (Krauskopf, pp. 96-97).

Until the last few years, in most states the husband alone was held legally responsible to creditors. Thus law as well as tradition led most creditors, including banks, credit card companies, and retail stores, to deny credit in their own name to married women, even those who were employed. Recent federal legislation has made it illegal to discriminate against married women in credit considerations, a practice which often had disastrous consequences for divorced women. Since all credit information was in their husbands' names, divorced women had no credit rating.

Several other features that have been built into law have directly affected the family and have reflected different treatment for males than for females. In the recent past, medical examinations for venereal disease in some states were required of males only upon application for a marriage license, reflecting the double standard by which females only were assumed to be virgins. Until the past few years, too, most states allowed females to marry at a younger age than males, with or without parental permission; a few states still have this provision. The implications of this differentiation are particularly interesting because women have been denied the right to consent to any number of things that have been allowed for men. This stipulation seems curious, therefore, at least until we consider the assumptions involved:

> Recognizing that early marriage impedes preparation for meaningful extrafamily activities, society has decreed that males should not be permitted this digression from life's important business at too early an age. Since women's participation in meaningful activities outside the home was until recently socially inconceivable, no great harm was seen in permitting females to follow their biological inclination and to marry earlier than males (Kanowitz, 1969, p. 11).

Our legal system also helps to legitimate physical violence between spouses, which usually means wife-beating. Straus (1977) has analyzed the cultural and legal underpinnings of this widespread phenomenon which is only beginning to receive public recognition. He points out that not only are the police reluctant to arrest a husband who is physically assaulting his wife, even when her physical safety may be in serious jeopardy, but at every step of the way the legal system attempts to dissuade wives from prosecuting their husbands. In most states the husband is legally immune from prosecution for raping his wife. He is also immune from civil suits brought by his wife, thus preventing that course of action if the criminal courts will not prosecute. In short, the legal system supports our cultural view that husbands have the "right" to chastise their wives—even when that chastisement would constitute assault if the target were any other person. Indeed, the so-called "unwritten law" defense, which was at one time actually written in New Mexico, Utah, and Texas, allows that a husband who kills a wife found in the act of adulterous intercourse has committed justifiable homicide and is guilty of no crime. The wife who perfoms in the same manner is guilty of murder. The law again strongly supports the sexual double standard and holds that it is "proper, if not inevitable, for husbands to be more outraged by the adultery of their wives than wives are expected to be in the reverse situation" (Kanowitz, 1969, p. 93).

A number of public policies also reinforce the separate and unequal treatment of the sexes within the family (Kamerman, 1977). Income tax laws and social security benefits both place married women at a serious disadvantage. Married couples with both partners employed pay higher income taxes in many cases than couples with only one spouse employed or two single persons earning the same salaries. The effect is to discourage married women from seeking employment, since the net return of the additional income may be minimal after taxes. In addition, the rate at which child-care costs may be deducted is much lower than that for other types of work-related expenses, which makes it less attractive for women with children to work outside the home. Another factor discouraging working wives is the payment to spouses of social security benefits which often equal those they would have received if they had been employed and earning social security funds on their own. However, in the event of divorce a woman has no dependent's claim on her former husband's social security benefits unless they had been married at least 20 years. Thus, a woman who has been a full-time homemaker and is divorced before the 20-year limit finds herself with no protection. This will change on January 1, 1979 when the limit will be reduced to 10 years.

Laws and policies pertaining to welfare also function to reinforce gender role stereotypes (Tillmon, 1972). Of all families receiving Aid to Families with Dependent Children (AFDC), 99 percent are headed by females. This is scarcely surprising, since the law in most states stipulates that a family cannot receive these funds if there is an "ablebodied" male in the household. Thus, fathers are discriminated against by being ineligible for welfare except under certain conditions which do not apply to mothers, and millions of husbands and fathers are virtually forced to desert the families they cannot support. As Johnnie Tillmon, a welfare rights activist, put it: "The truth is that AFDC is like a super-sexist marriage. You trade *a* man for *the* man. But you can't divorce him if he treats you bad. He can divorce you, of course, cut you off anytime he wants. But in that case, *he* keeps the kids, not you" (Tillmon, 1972, p. 111; see also Glassman, 1970).

Welfare departments are notorious for their humiliating regulations, which often involve serious invasion of privacy. In essence, the system provides absolutely minimum sustenance to females who, even if they could find employment and were provided with child-care facilities, would scarcely be able to earn enough to support their families. In return, it asks these women to forego a sexual life, accept a myriad of restrictions on their lives, and bow meekly in the face of humiliations heaped upon them by society and politicians. In remaining home to care for their children, indeed in having children, they are doing nothing more or less than that which our society so heartily and repetitiously recommends for all females. It is only their poverty that sets them apart for abuse. Given the high divorce rate, the inequities of our economic and educational institutions, and the law itself, Tillmon is perfectly correct when she warns all females: "Inform yourself on welfare. You may have to live on it sooner or later. Because you're a woman."

Males, too, are discriminated against by policies pertaining to the family. While most laws do not automatically grant custody of children to the mother in case of divorce, it is the policy of most courts to do so unless she is shown to be morally unfit. By law and, in its absence, by court policy, child support payments are made by males, rarely by females, and if alimony is awarded it is paid by males, not females, regardless of ability to pay. As we have seen, fathers are rarely eligible to receive welfare and must often leave their families so that the families can get this support.

Thus our family laws and policies lock husbands firmly into the stereotyped gender role requirement to support the family. Conversely, they seriously limit the ability of wives, many of whom will be unmarried again some day, to compete in the economy. Over and above the actual obstacles placed in their way there are the more subtle, psychological effects of a legal system that defines wives in terms of their husbands, thus reinforcing the cultural stereotype of femininity.

Criminal Law

Most people arrested and convicted of criminal offenses, whether they be crimes against persons, crimes against property (including white-collar crimes), or victimless crimes, are male. As with female juveniles, the rate at which adult women are being arrested and convicted has been increasing faster than the male rate. For a detailed discussion of women and crime, see Adler (1975) or Simon (1975).

There are several ways in which the law has treated male and female offenders differently and, in some cases, continues to do so. At least until recently, it is likely that female offenders were arrested and prosecuted less frequently. Stereotypes concerning females probably prevented them from becoming suspects at times, and notions of chivalry probably worked to limit their prosecution. Married women were further protected because, in some states, they could not be tried for conspiracy with their husbands. The rationale for this was called the doctrine of "presumed coercion," by which the wife is released from responsibility for crimes committed in her husband's presence (Kanowitz, 1969, p. 88 ff.). The implication is that the wife is not a responsible, independent human being; only the husband is. Because women were not assumed to be fully adult and responsible, however, in some states they have been given indefinite sentences to "reforming" institutions called something other than prisons. Such terms can turn out to be far longer than formal jail sentences given males for the same types of crime (Kanowitz, p. 167 ff.). However, in general men tend to receive more harsh sentences than women—or, tellingly, than juveniles (Walum, 1977, p. 114).

Many crimes are specifically defined in terms of only one sex. Prostitution is often defined in such a way that it is legally impossible for a male to be a prostitute. Many states have no provision for punishing the client of a prostitute, without whom there would be no prostitution, yet almost all states have laws against prostitution (Kanowitz, 1969, p. 16). Conversely, statutory rape, or consensual sexual intercourse with someone deemed too young legally, is defined in such a way that only a male can commit the crime. According to the law, there is no such thing as a male too young for sex, or no possibility that an older female might "seduce" a juvenile male. In either case the sexual double standard is assumed.

When it comes to forcible rape, however, a very different image of women has emerged. Before the past few years, when feminists began to publicize and seek changes in the treatment of rape victims, raped women were often treated by the police and in court as if *they* had committed the crime. The presupposition was that the victim probably "asked for it," and thus her sexual history became a salient issue in the case, along with her attire, whether or not she fought the attack (at whatever risk to her life), and so on. Even in 1977 a Wisconsin judge placed an adolescent male on probation for raping a girl student, justifying the lack of penalty by saying the boy was reacting "normally" to the sexual stimuli in his environment. The judge specifically cited the manner in which girls dressed. It is interesting to note, however, that the judge's decision so outraged the community that a recall election was called and he was removed from office. There are places where laws make it illegal for males (only) to use "vulgar," "obscene," or "abusive" language in the presence of children and females (Kanowitz, p. 175 ff.).

Until a Supreme Court decision in January 1973, abortion was a crime in most states; it was also about the only specific medical treatment with which the law was concerned. Prior to that time, in most states a woman was legally obliged to bear an unwanted child unless she could show that doing so would seriously jeopardize her life. In the absence of this decision these laws would undoubtedly remain extant, regardless of the fact that it is her body and hers alone that bears the physical burden and consequences of pregnancy or abortion, and in spite of the fact that more women die from childbirth than from abortions done under proper medical auspices. Indeed, until relatively recently some states (e.g., Connecticut) also banned contraceptives, thus totally denying the female the right to control her own reproductivity. Such laws were particularly harmful since, regardless of legalities, women will abort unwanted fetuses (estimates have placed illegal abortions at about one million per year in the years just prior to the Supreme Court decision), and when forced to do so illegally they face grave dangers to their lives. In 1969, 8,000 women died from illegal abortions, and over a quarter of a million required hospitalization. Moreover, such laws discriminated most stringently against the poor, since if a woman had the money to travel she could easily acquire a safe, legal abortion somewhere. The 1977 Supreme Court decision to allow Congress to withhold Medicaid payments for abortions will return us to a situation in which poor women are denied the opportunity to control their reproductivity with this means.

These examples serve to demonstrate that our criminal laws have treated the sexes differently, to the disadvantage of sometimes one, sometimes the other. In many cases they continue to do so. Thus they have further reinforced many of our cultural stereotypes concerning masculinity and femininity

Civil Law

Until very recently, some types of civil laws (other than those already discussed concerning the family) have discriminated on the basis of sex. Though these laws no longer exist, they did until a very few years ago and are thus worth reviewing briefly.

As recently as 1966 three states denied females the right to serve on juries, and they still are granted some kinds of exemptions not available to males in a large number of states. In a few states females had to volunteer if they wished to serve, but males were required to do so unless specifically exempted (Mead & Kaplan, 1965, pp. 67-68; Kanowitz, 1969, pp. 28-31). The implication of second-class citizenship is evident.

Until the draft was abolished in January 1973, males, but not females, were liable to be drafted into the armed services. The implication was that females do not owe society the same obligations as males. The implication of second-class citizenship is also exemplified in this distinction. Furthermore, given the benefits available to veterans, in terms of low-interest mortgages, educational payments, medical services, and bonus points for civil service jobs, the fact that females were not drafted ultimately worked to their disadvantage. In fact, the various branches of the service had quotas on the number of females they would permit to enlist, thus in effect denying all women the opportunity to earn these benefits. Women also were denied access to the armed services institutions of higher education until the past few years.

All kinds of "protective laws" pertaining to the conditions of work have existed at various points throughout the nation and have served, in recent years although perhaps not originally, to "protect" females out of a number of usually well-paid jobs. Laws specifying the maximum hours females (only) could work per day or week (as low as 40 in South Carolina) "protected" women from time-and-a-half overtime pay, as did laws in 12 states specifying that women could not work at night. These regulations also served as excuses for employers not to hire females at all for many jobs. They were particularly obnoxious given the estimate that housewives, who are not paid at all for their work, average over 90 hours of work per week (Scott, 1972, p. 45). Laws specifying the maximum weight females could lift (in one case as little as 10 pounds!) also "protected" them from getting all kinds of especially skilled manual jobs, as did laws specifying that a job must be located within a certain proximity to a "ladies' room." In a number of states specific, often lucrative occupations were legally barred to females, including mining, bartending and the retail sales of liquor, and working around moving machinery. These laws have been declared illegal under the 1964 Civil Rights Act. The courts now require an employer to prove that a job has a "bona fide occupational qualification" on the basis of sex in order to specify sex in hiring (e.g., an actor for a male role).

This review of different types of laws demonstrates two things. First, substantial progress has been made in the past five years or so in reducing the extent to which the law discriminates on the basis of sex. Second, many laws that are based on, and serve to reinforce, traditional stereotypes of masculinity and femininity remain, and these create hardships for both sexes, and especially for women. Their elimination would be expedited by the passage of the Equal Rights Amendment, which would also serve as a symbol that our government no longer officially supports the gender role stereotypes.

Political Institutions

In the final analysis any group of people whose members find themselves in a lower caste position do so because they lack power. Females are virtually excluded from the major power centers of our society, including the most important ones—the political institutions that govern it. (For more details on the relationship of women and politics see Tolchin & Tolchin, 1974, Kirkpatrick, 1974, and Jacquette, 1974.) Political power in America is also integrally tied to control of economic resources (Domhoff, 1967) and, to a somewhat lesser extent, to elite status within such other important institutional realms as the military, universities, labor unions, and so on (Keller, 1968). We have already noted that the wealth of this nation is controlled by males and indicated that they control other institutional realms as well.

Females are generally lacking in those resources that can be "traded in" for political influence. About the only such resource they possess is superior numbers. However, without any consciousness on the part of females that they do indeed comprise a lower caste with common interests that are different from, and often in opposition to, those of males ("caste consciousness"), these numbers are meaningless; they are not translated into politically relevant terms. The national and state Women's Political Caucus organizations formed in the early 1970s represent the beginnings of such a translation of numbers into power, but they obviously have a long way to go to gain broad support and thus power. According to one study (Burrell, 1977), most of those who participate in the Women's Political Caucuses are fairly young, well-educated, liberal in political ideology, and previously active in politics. However, other types of women also belong, including conservative Republican housewives, radical students, and the professionally employed.

Females actively participate in the political processes of this country. They vote, work for candidates, sometimes contribute funds, and occasionally even run for office. They do so, however, primarily within a context defined and controlled by males. The issues that concern them, far from being directed to their own caste interests, are generally those defined by the male leadership of political and other institutions. Indeed, the current Feminist Movement (as well as the one in the 19th century) arose when a few politically active females finally became aware of and fed up with this phenomenon. In the midsixties radical women working in the so-called Civil Rights and Peace Movements began to understand that *as females* they were being "put down," ignored, left with the typing and coffee making and out of the policy making. They began to resent the mentality, widespread in these supposedly "radical" and "humanitarian" movements, that was so aptly expressed by Stokeley Carmichael's quip: "The only position for a woman in this movement is prone." In short, this relatively small number of females began to become politicized to their own caste interests and became a major nucleus of what is now a rapidly growing social movement. We will return to a discussion of this movement in the final chapter. For now, let us briefly examine the manner in which most females today continue to relate to the political power structure of our society.

Females are virtually absent from governmental executive positions in this country. We have never had a female president or vice-president; in all our history only five women have been governors, and three of these were wives or widows of past governors. Ella Grasso was the first woman elected governor in her own right, and that occurred only a few years ago. Females are also drastically underrepresented in the legislative branches of our various governments. On the national level only ten women have ever been senators, and the proportion in the House of Representatives is normally about 3 percent. The 95th Congress had no female senators until Muriel Humphrey's interim appointment following her husband's death, and a mere 19 out of 435 members of the House were women. Indeed, most of the women who have ever been elected to Congress were widows of former members; 41 percent of all congresswomen have been appointed to fill vacancies left by their husbands, and of all the female senators, a mere four were originally elected to their jobs (Bullock & Heys, 1977, pp. 210-11).

Those females who have managed to become members of Congress have been relatively powerless. In a legislative system where the acquisition of power has rested largely on the seniority principle, over a third of the elected females served only one term, and only about a third served four or more terms. Thus, chairs of important committees are almost never held by females (Amundsen, 1971, pp. 69-70). No woman has ever served as Speaker of the House or as a party whip. Moreover, women tend to be assigned to the low-prestige, uninfluential committees (Walum, 1977, p. 196). They fare little better on the state and local levels. No major cities have had female mayors, and only 4 percent of all mayors are female. In 1977 females comprised only 12.7 percent of all city officials, and most of these were in city clerk jobs (International City Management Association, 1977, p. 223). Even on school boards, females comprise only about 10 percent of members (Amundsen, 1971, pp. 79-80). They preside over few governors' mansions and are largely unrepresented in state legislatures, where they generally comprise only about 4 percent.

The probabilities of women incumbents in top-level appointed positions in the government are no better. As of 1976, only 18 women had held the post of ambassador or minister to a foreign state (Walum, 1977, p. 197). Only three women have ever held Cabinet posts. In 1972 women constituted a mere 4 percent of those in civil service grades 13 and above, and only 2 percent in grades 18 and above. These figures had not changed for five years. In fact, in 1976 only 39 of 1,700 positions considered to have key policy-making roles were filled by women (Walum, p. 197). There has never been a female member of the Supreme

Court, and only a few have made it to any of the higher federal courts. About 3 percent of the judges in the entire nation are female.

In general, women are about as well represented in our political institutions as blacks, despite the fact that the former constitute 51 percent of the population and the latter about 15 percent. In fact, females comprise 53.3 percent of the registered voters in the nation. Black women have, however, been relatively more successful than their white sisters. They constitute about 12 percent of all elected black officials and 25 percent of all women in federal office (Bryce & Warrick, 1977, p. 398; Gethens & Prestage, 1977, p. 344).

Further light can be shed on the political status of American women by examining comparable figures on officeholding in some other societies. The United States has one of the worst records for female officeholders, exceeded only by such countries as Guatemala and Thailand (Lynn, 1975). Several nations have had female chief executives, including Israel and nations we often label "backwards," such as India and Argentina. The head of the Conservative Party in Britain is a female, and, if that party gains office, she will likely become Prime Minister. Between 1960 and 1966, 15 percent of the Finnish, 11 percent of the Danish, 9 percent of the Norwegian, and 14 percent of the Rumanian parliaments, as well as 14 percent of the Swedish lower chamber, were females (Haavio-Mannila, 1972, pp. 161-62; Lynn, 1975). France, Britain, Germany, and Italy have far fewer female legislators than the Scandinavian countries, but in all four cases the proportion is at least double ours (Sullerot, 1971, pp. 222-25). Even in China, where women have traditionally been excluded from all aspects of public life, 8 percent of the Communist Party's Central Committee was female in 1969 (Cohen, 1970, p. 416).

Politics: For Men Only?

Why is it that women are so vastly underrepresented in the political arena in this country? The principal reason is that politics is perceived as basically a masculine business, and girls begin to learn this as children. They are therefore less oriented to becoming politicians in the first place, since, like many other professions, politics is not defined as appropriate. The general dearth of role models serves, of course, to reinforce the impression. Bonnie Freeman (1977) summarizes the results of two studies in which female officeholders were queried about the factors they believe discourage women from seeking office. Their reasons included the following: (1) men's attitudes, including those of husbands and men in public life, which express reluctance to accept women in political roles; (2) women's apathy to politics; (3) women's antipathy to what they perceive as political traits, such as conflict, compromise, and misrepresentation; (4) lack of the necessary resources, including money and experience; (5) lack of time because of household and child-care duties; (6) lack of self-confidence. In short, those attributes of personality that are deemed feminine and the lack of access to resources, both of which result from women's caste position, deter women from seeking public office.

Despite the fact that women rarely gain positions of political power, without their participation our political parties could scarcely function. Because of their economic situation, females are not often in a position where they are able to contribute any substantial sums to the party coffers independently of their husbands. Without their extensive *volunteer* services, however, the machinery of politics would fall apart. Females in vast numbers run the typewriters and mimeos, stuff envelopes, and canvass the voters by phone and on foot. In short, they do all the dull, routine tasks that must get done but which males will not bother with because they are too busy doing "important" things (like deciding strategy and policy), and they do most of them for no return in monetary or power terms. Finally, as wives of politicians females do all the laborious tasks involved in campaigning plus their housekeeping and child-rearing tasks, often in the frequent and prolonged absence of their husbands. It is little wonder that the divorce rate among these women is rapidly rising. In the past half-dozen years several members of Congress and state governors have been divorced or separated from their wives, an act almost unheard of before the 1970s.

If women are active in the political process but not generally on behalf of their own caste interests, then what do they support? First, there is no evidence to reenforce the myth that females vote for "sexy" candidates (*Time,* March 20, 1972, p. 33). Women vote in about equal proportions to men, except among the rural population and those with less than an eighth-grade education (Steinem, 1972, p. 48; U.S. Bureau of the Census, 1976, p. 467). Moreover, most research has shown that more than three quarters of all married couples vote the same, although few are willing any more to conclude from this that the wife is voting like her husband rather than vice versa.

There is some debate concerning whether men and women hold different political attitudes. Because of their lack of experience in decision-making roles in general, females tend to feel less politically competent or efficacious than males. There is some research evidence to support the contention that females have been somewhat more liberal in their political attitudes. According to Steinem (1972, pp. 49-50), females have been somewhat less racist; thus they offered less support for George Wallace's bid for the presidency than males did. Females also have been more sensitive to issues of poverty, more opposed to capital punishment, and more in favor of gun control legislation. Ironically, when the Women's Liberation Movement first surfaced, men's attitudes were more supportive of it than women's were, but that has changed in very recent years. On one issue women have consistently differed from men for a long time: war and peace. Women were more opposed to the Vietnam War than men, more opposed to the Korean War, less opposed to Chamberlain's policy of appeasement before World War II, more supportive of the Nuclear Test Ban Treaty in the Kennedy administration. Thus women supported Johnson over Goldwater more than males did, and McGovern over Nixon. More recently, women, more than men, supported the War Powers Resolution passed by Congress (see Ellsberg, 1972; Starr & Cutler, 1972; Steinem, 1972; *Time,* March 20, 1972, p. 33; Gosnell, 1948; Pomper, 1975; Brown, 1964; Gruberg, 1968; Harris, 1972).

Women's liberation advocate Gloria Steinem (1972) concluded from these facts that in most ways women are more "liberal" than men, but *Time* magazine (March 20, 1972), considering the same phenomena, concluded that "women seem to prefer the safe-and-sound candidate, the one least likely to embark on war or some other hazardous undertaking." These two different conclusions point up a phenomenon that results largely from the fact that our key institutions, especially the political ones, are so lopsidedly masculine. To *Time* war is simply a "hazardous undertaking," and those who do not support it are said to be taking a "safe and sound" approach. This is patently a masculine view that grows directly out of that gender role stereotype. That females do often support and condone violence is only too obvious in a number of circumstances; however, they tend to do so primarily when they perceive it as a matter of self-defense. It is much more a masculine phenomenon to condone and participate in violence for the sake of "honor," face saving, or territorial expansion (Steinem, p. 50). When Nixon (and before him Johnson and Kennedy) proclaimed that he would not preside over this nation's first "defeat," or that we would not be "bullied" by other nations, he was the voice of the "masculine mystique." "Peace with honor" is clearly more important than human lives in such a world view. "Real men" can't appear "chicken" (Stone, 1972). I. F. Stone's analysis of both the United States and the Soviet Union during the Cuban Missile Crisis and in Vietnam revolves around precisely this view: "Their calculus of political expediency rests on the existence within each nation's boundaries of a sizable population of small-boy mentalities and primitives who still see war as a test of their virility" (1972, p. 13).

Social-psychological research (Pruitt, 1971) has shown that the decisions people make in a group tend to be either more cautious or more risky than those that would be made if the individuals comprising the group were acting alone. Stated otherwise, there is a tendency for groups to shift their orientations toward one extreme or the other. The direction of those decisions—greater risk or more caution—is a function of the prior values held by group members, especially those who emerge as group leaders. It is evident that the masculine stereotype encourages adventuresomeness or risk taking far more than the feminine. To the extent that political decision-making groups are comprised overwhelmingly of males, the implication is that decisions arising from such groups will tend to be far more risky than might be the case if they were made either by individuals or by groups comprised of more females. Therefore, to the extent that war is a "risky undertaking," it is likely to result more frequently from male-dominated councils than it might otherwise.

Conclusions

Females *qua* females are devalued in this and most other societies. Thus the things females do are devalued, and devalued activities are left for females to do. Wherever you find any type of activity done largely by females, you will find it has low prestige and little or no pay, be it medicine in the Soviet Union, grammar-school teaching or secretarial work in the United States, or child rearing and housekeeping almost everywhere. Every institution in society is more or less geared to maintaining females in a lower-caste position, thus guaranteeing that females will do the less prestigeful and more poorly paid tasks. Thus males *qua* males and as heads of the key institutions benefit enormously. Housewives do $250 billion worth of unpaid work per annum, and this arduous and necessary labor is not even counted as part of the almighty gross national product (Scott, 1972). Billions more are saved by industry by underpaying employed females. The ego-gratifying rewards of power and prestige are also left primarily to males. In short, males need not compete with more than 50 percent of the population in dividing up the scarce, valued rewards of society.

The most insidious aspect of this caste system is the psychological effect it has on most females. For many it serves as a self-fulfilling prophecy, rendering them virtually unfit to assume anything other than the passive, dependent role for which they have been programmed. For countless others it entails anxiety and guilt over what they are and do versus what they "ought to be," according to society.

But some women, especially some of those who "make it" in the males' world, are led by the caste system to assume the values of the upper (male) caste and to denigrate all aspects of femaleness. It is not uncommon to discover in "successful" career women a deep-seated antipathy to females, to the Feminist Movement, and to all things "feminine" (see Decter, 1972, for a good example). Such women are sometimes called "Queen Bees." These are the ones who staunchly argue that females have only themselves to blame for their problems. They maintain that there is really not much discrimination—at least, that since *they* overcame it, everyone who really wants to can do so. Such women regard females, as a rule, as dull people with whom they would rather not associate (ever notice how many women pride themselves on not liking women and how seldom any male is ever heard to make analogous statements about his entire sex?). In short, they believe that with a few "exceptions" (like themselves), males are the superior sex. Such group "self-hatred" is not unusual among lower-caste peoples, but it is surely one of the most hideous results of subjugation. These women, and especially those who are professionals, might function to provide much-needed role models for the young and to question the sexist assumptions in the practices and theories of their own institutions and society in general. Instead, the self-hatred exacted as the price for their success has led them to side with the upper caste in helping to maintain the gender role status quo, and in so doing to keep their sisters down. However, it is my impression that such women are less common as each year goes by. More and more, women who make it are offering their hands to their sisters and participating in groups dedicated to ensuring that the next generation of women will have fewer battles to fight in order to be treated as equal to men in our society.

References

Acker, Joan. "Women and Social Stratification: A Case of Intellectual Sexism." *American Journal of Sociology* 78 (January 1973): 936-45.

Adler, Freda. *Sisters in Crime: The Rise of the New Female Criminal.* New York: McGraw-Hill Book Co., 1975.

Almquist, Elizabeth. "Women in the Labor Force." *Signs* 2 (Summer 1977): 843-53.

Amundsen, Kristen. *The Silenced Majority.* Englewood Cliffs, N.J.: Prentice-Hall, 1971.

Andreas, Carol. *Sex and Caste in America.* Englewood Cliffs, N.J.: Prentice-Hall, 1971.

Barrett, Nancy Smith. "Women in Industrial Society: An International Perspective." In Jane Chapman (ed.), *Economic Independence for Women,* pp. 77-111. Beverly Hills, Calif.: Sage Publications, 1976.

Barron, R. D., and Norris, G. M. "Sexual Divisions and the Dual Labor Market." In Diana Barker and Sheila Allen (eds.), *Dependence and Exploitation in Work and Marriage,* pp. 47-69. London: Longman, 1976.

Bell, Inge Powell. "The Double Standard." *Trans-Action* 8 (November-December 1970): 75-80.

Bernard, Jessie. *Academic Women.* University Park, Pa.: Pennsylvania State University Press, 1964.

Bernard, Jessie. *Women and the Public Interest.* Chicago: Aldine-Atherton, 1971.

Bienen, Leigh; Ostriker, Alicia; and Ostriker, J. P. "Sex Discrimination in Universities." In Nona Glazer and Helen Waehrer (eds.), *Woman in a Man-Made World,* pp. 370-77, 2nd ed. Chicago: Rand McNally & Co., 1977.

Bird, Caroline. *Born Female: The High Cost of Keeping Women Down.* New York: David McKay Co., 1968.

Blau, Francine. "Women in the Labor Force: An Overview." In Jo Freeman (ed.), *Women: A Feminist Perspective,* pp. 211-26. Palo Alto, Calif.: Mayfield Publishing Co., 1975.

Bose, Christine. "Social Status of Homemaker." Paper presented at the annual meeting of the American Sociological Association, August 1976.

Brenton, Myron. *The American Male.* Greenwich, Conn.: Fawcett Publications, 1966.

Brown, Nona B. "Inquiry into the Feminine Mind." *New York Magazine,* April 12, 1964.

Bryce, Herrington, and Warrick, Alan. "Black Women in Electoral Politics." In M. Gethens and Jewel Prestage (eds.), *A Portrait of Marginality: The Political Behavior of American Women,* pp. 395-400. New York: David McKay Co., 1977.

Bullock, Charles, and Heys, Patricia L. F. "Recruitment of Women for Congress: A Research Note." In M. Gethens and Jewel Prestage (eds.), *A Portrait of Marginality: The Political Behavior of American Women,* pp. 210-20. New York: David McKay Co., 1977.

Burciaga, Cecilia; Gonzales, Viola; and Hepburn, Ruth. "The Chicana as Feminist." In Alice Sargent (ed.), *Beyond Sex Roles,* pp. 266-73. St. Paul, Minn.: West Publishing Co., 1977.

Burrell, Barbara. "A New Dimension in Political Participation: The Women's Political Caucus." In M. Gethens and Jewel Prestage (eds.), *A Portrait of Marginality: The Political Behavior of American Women,* pp. 240-257. New York: David McKay Co., 1977.

Chafetz, Janet Saltzman. "Women in Social Work." *Social Work* 17 (September 1972): 12-18.

Chafetz, Janet S., and Polk, Barbara. "Room at the Top: Social Recognition of British and American Females Over Time." *Social Science Quarterly* 54 (March 1974): 843-53.

Chapman, Jane (ed.). *Economic Independence for Women.* Beverly Hills, Calif.: Sage Publications, 1976.

Cohen, Charlotte Bonny. "Women in China." In Robin Morgan (ed.), *Sisterhood Is Powerful,* pp. 385-417. New York: Vintage Books, 1970.

Cordell, Magda, and McHale, John. *Women in World Terms: Facts and Trends.* Albany, N.Y.: State University of New York Press, 1975.

DeCrow, Karen. *Sexist Justice.* New York: Vintage Books, 1974.

Decter, Midge. *The New Chastity and Other Arguments against Women's Liberation.* New York: Coward, McCann & Geoghegan, 1972.

Domhoff, G. William. *Who Rules America?* Englewood Cliffs, N.J.: Prentice-Hall, 1967.

Dworkin, Rosalind. "The Prestige Ranking of the Housewife Occupation."

Unpublished manuscript, University of Houston, n.d.

Eastwood, Mary. "Feminism and the Law." In Jo Freeman (ed.), *Women: A Feminist Perspective,* pp. 325-34. Palo Alto, Calif.: Mayfield Publishing Co., 1975.

Ellsberg, Daniel. "Daniel Ellsberg Talks about Women and War." *Ms.,* Spring 1972, pp. 36-39.

Engels, Frederick. *The Origins of the Family, Private Property and the State.* Chicago: Charles H. Kerr, 1902.

Epstein, Cynthia Fuchs. *Woman's Place.* Berkeley, Calif.: University of California Press, 1970.

Fein, Robert. "Examining the Nature of Masculinity." In Alice Sargent (ed.), *Beyond Sex Roles,* pp. 188-200. St. Paul, Minn.: West Publishing Co., 1977.

Freeman, Bonnie Cook. "Power, Patriarchy and Political Primitives." In Joan Roberts (ed.), *Beyond Intellectual Sexism,* pp. 241-64. New York: David McKay Co., 1977.

Galvin, John, and Mendelsohn, Ethel. "Legal Status of Women." In Council of State Governments, *The Book of the States, 1976-77,* vol. 21, pp. 231-37. Lexington, Ky., 1976.

Gates, Margaret. "Occupational Segregation and the Law." *Signs* 1 (Spring 1976): 61-74.

Gethens, M., and Prestage, Jewel. "Black Women: A Minority within a Minority." In Gethens and Prestage (eds.), *A Portrait of Marginality: The Political Behavior of American Women,* pp. 339-45. New York: David McKay Co., 1977.

Glassman, Carol. "Women and the Welfare System." In Robin Morgan (ed.), *Sisterhood Is Powerful,* pp. 102-15. New York: Vintage Books, 1970.

Glazer, Nona. "Housework: A Review Essay." In Nona Glazer and Helen Y. Waehrer (eds.), *Woman in a Man-Made World,* pp. 360-69, 2nd ed. Chicago: Rand McNally & Co., 1977.

Glazer, Nona, and Waehrer, Helen Y. (eds.). *Woman in a Man-Made World.* 2nd ed. Chicago: Rand McNally & Co., 1977.

Gosnell, Harold. *Democracy: The Threshold of Freedom.* New York: Ronald Press, 1948.

Grant, Christine. *Future Trends in Health Care Management.* Cambridge, Mass.: Radcliffe Programs in Health Care, 1977.

Griffiths, Martha. "Can We Still Afford Occupational Segregation? Some Remarks." *Signs* 1 (Spring 1976): 7-13.

Grimm, James, and Stern, Robert. "Sex Roles and Professional Labor Markets: Intra-Occupational Structuring." Paper delivered at the annual meeting of the Southwestern Social Science Association, San Antonio, Texas, March 30-April 1, 1972.

Grønseth, Erik. "The Husband Provider Role and Its Dysfunctional Consequences." *Sociological Focus* 5 (Winter 1971-72): 10-18.

Gruberg, Martin. *Women in American Politics.* Oshkosh, Wis.: Academic Press, 1968.

Haavio-Mannila, Elina. "Sex Roles in Politics." In Constantina Safilios-Rothschild (ed.), *Toward a Sociology of Women,* pp. 154-72. Lexington, Mass.: Xerox College Publishing Co., 1972.

Hacker, Helen M. "Women as a Minority Group." *Social Forces* 30 (1951): 60-69.

Harris, Ann Sutherland. "The Second Sex in Academe." *AAUP Bulletin,* Fall 1970, pp. 283-96.

Harris, Louis. *Virginia Slims American Women's Opinion Poll,* 1972.

Hart, Donna. "Minority Women's Issues." In Alice Sargent (ed.), *Beyond Sex Roles,* pp. 256-58. St. Paul, Minn.: West Publishing Co., 1977.

Hartman, Heidi. "Capitalism, Patriarchy, and Job Segregation by Sex." *Signs* 1 (Spring 1976): 137-69.

Havens, Elizabeth. "Women, Work and Wedlock: A Note on Female Marital Patterns in the United States." *American Journal of Sociology* 78 (January 1973): 852-72.

Hochschild, Arlie. "A Review of Sex Role Research." *American Journal of Sociology* 78 (1973): pp. 1011-29.

Husbands, Sandra Acker. "Woman's Place in Higher Education?" *School Review* 80 (February 1972): 261-74.

International City Management Association. *The Municipal Yearbook.* Washington, D.C., 1977.

Jacquette, Jane (ed.). *Women in Politics.* New York: John Wiley & Sons, 1974.

Kahne, Hilda. "Women's Roles in the Economy: Economic Investigation and Research Needs." In Jane Chapman (ed.), *Economic Independence for Women,* pp. 39-76. Beverly Hills, Calif.: Sage Publications, 1976.

Kamerman, Sheila. "Public Policy and the Family: A New Strategy for Women as Wives and Mothers." In Jane Chapman and Margaret Gates (eds.), *Women into Wives: The Legal and Economic Impact of Marriage,* pp. 195-214. Beverly Hills, Calif.: Sage Publications, 1977.

Kanowitz, Leo. *Women and the Law: The Unfinished Revolution.* Albuquerque, N.M.: University of New Mexico Press, 1969.

Kanter, Rosabeth Moss. "The Impact of Hierarchical Structures on the Work Behavior of Women and Men." *Social Problems* 23 (April 1976): 415-30.

Kanter, Rosabeth Moss. "Women in Organizations: Sex Roles, Group Dynamics, and Change Strategies." In Alice Sargent (ed.), *Beyond Sex Roles,* pp. 371-86. St. Paul, Minn.: West Publishing Co., 1977.

Keller, Suzanne. *Beyond the Ruling Class.* New York: Random House, 1968.

Kinsley, Susan. "Women's Dependency and Federal Programs." In Jane

Chapman and Margaret Gates (eds.), *Women into Wives: The Legal and Economic Impact of Marriage,* pp. 79-91. Beverly Hills, Calif.: Sage Publications, 1977.

Kirkpatrick, Jeane. *Political Woman.* New York: Basic Books, 1974.

Knudsen, Dean. "The Declining Status of Women: Popular Myths and the Failure of Functionalist Thought." *Social Forces* 48 (December 1969): 183-93.

Korda, Michael. *Male Chauvinism: How It Works.* New York: Random House, 1972.

Krauskopf, Joan. "Partnership Marriage: Legal Reforms Needed." In Jane Chapman and Margaret Gates (eds.), *Women into Wives: The Legal and Economic Impact of Marriage,* pp. 93-122. Beverly Hills, Calif.: Sage Publications, 1977.

Kreps, Juanita. *Women and the American Economy: A Look to the 1980s.* Englewood Cliffs, N.J.: Prentice-Hall, 1976.

Laws, Judith Long. "Work Aspirations of Women: False Leads and New Starts." *Signs* 1 (1976): 33-49.

Lewis, Edwin C. *Developing Woman's Potential.* Ames, Iowa: Iowa State University Press, 1968.

Liebow, Elliott. *Tally's Corner.* Boston, Mass.: Little, Brown & Co., 1967.

Lipman-Blumen, Jean. "Changing Sex Roles in American Culture: Future Directions for Research." *Archives of Sexual Behavior* 4 (1975): 433-46.

Lipman-Blumen, Jean. "Toward a Homosocial Theory of Sex Roles: An Explanation of the Sex Segregation of Social Institutions." *Signs* 1 (1976): 15-31.

Lopata, Helena Z. *Occupation: Housewife.* New York: Oxford University Press, 1971.

Lynn, Naomi. "Women in American Politics." In Jo Freeman (ed.), *Women: A Feminist Perspective,* pp. 364-85. Palo Alto, Calif.: Mayfield Publishing Co., 1975.

McClendon, McKee. "The Occupational Status Attainment Process of Males and Females." *American Sociological Review* 41 (February 1976): 52-64.

Mead, Margaret, and Kaplan, Frances Bagley (eds.). *American Women: The Report of the President's Commission on the Status of Women.* New York: Charles Scribner's Sons, 1965.

Moss, Zoe. "It Hurts To Be Alive and Obsolete: The Aging Woman." In Robin Morgan (ed.), *Sisterhood Is Powerful,* pp. 170-75. New York: Vintage Books, 1970.

Oakley, Ann. *Woman's Work: A History of the Housewife.* New York: Pantheon Books, 1974.

Oakley, Ann. *The Sociology of Housework.* New York: Pantheon Books, 1975.

Paloma, Margaret M., and Garland, T. Neal. "The Married Professional Woman: A Study in the Tolerance of Domestication." *Journal of Marriage and the Family* 33 (August 1971): 531-40.

Papanek, Hanna. "Men, Women and Work: Reflections on the Two-Person Career." *American Journal of Sociology* 78 (January 1973): 852-72.

Pomper, Gerald. *Voter's Choice: Varieties of American Electoral Behavior.* New York: Harper & Row, 1975.

Pruitt, Dean. "Toward an Understanding of Choice Shifts in Group Discussion." *Journal of Personality and Social Psychology* 20 (December 1971): 495-510.

Roby, Pamela. "Structural and Internalized Barriers to Women in Higher Education." In Constantina Safilios-Rothschild (ed.), *Toward a Sociology of Women,* pp. 121-40. Lexington, Mass.: Xerox College Publishing Co., 1972.

Roby, Pamela. "The Condition of Women in Blue-Collar Jobs." In Jane Chapman (ed.), *Economic Independence for Women,* pp. 155-81. Beverly Hills, Calif.: Sage Publications, 1976.

Ross, Heather. "Poverty: Women and Children Last." In Jane Chapman (ed.), *Economic Independence for Women,* pp. 137-54. Beverly Hills, Calif.: Sage Publications, 1976.

Rossi, Alice S. "Job Discrimination and What Women Can Do About It." *Atlantic Monthly,* March 1970, pp. 99-103.

Rossi, Alice S. "Discrimination and Demography Restrict Opportunities for Academic Women." In Judith Stacey, Susan Béreaud, and Joan Daniels (eds.), *And Jill Came Tumbling After: Sexism in American Education,* pp. 366-74. New York: Dell Publishing Co., 1974.

Scott, Ann Crittenden. "The Value of Housework: For Love or Money?" *Ms.,* July 1972, pp. 45-59.

Shepard, Herbert. "Men in Organizations: Some Reflections." In Alice Sargent (ed.), *Beyond Sex Roles,* pp. 387-94. St. Paul, Minn.: West Publishing Co., 1977.

Shostak, Arthur. "Blue-collar Work." In Deborah David and Robert Brannon (eds.), *The Forty-Nine Percent Majority: The Male Sex Role,* pp. 98-106. Reading, Mass.: Addison Wesley Publishing Co., 1976.

Simon, Rita James. *Women and Crime.* Toronto: Lexington Books, 1975.

Stamm, Alfred M. "NASW Membership: Characteristics, Deployment and Salaries." *Personnel Information, NASW,* 12 (May 1969): 34-45.

Starr, Jerold, and Cutler, Neal. "Sex Role and Attitudes toward Institutional Violence among College Youth: The Impact of Sex-Role Identification, Parental Socialization, and Socio-Cultural Milieu." Paper presented at the 67th meeting of the American Sociological Association, August 1972.

Steinem, Gloria. "Women Voters Can't Be Trusted." *Ms.,* July 1972, pp. 47-51 and 131.

Stone, I.F. "The Offensive: Machismo in Washington." *The New York Times Review of Books,* May 18, 1972, pp. 13-14.

Straus, Murray. "Sexual Inequality, Cultural Norms, and Wife-Beating." In Jane Chapman and Margaret Gates (eds.), *Women into Wives: The Legal and Economic Impact of Marriage,* pp. 59-78. Beverly Hills, Calif.: Sage Publications, 1977.

Suelzle, Marijean. "Women in Labor." *Trans-Action* 8 (November-December 1970): 50-58.

Sullerot, Evelyne. *Women, Society and Change.* Translated by Margaret Scotford Archer. New York: McGraw-Hill Book Co., 1971.

Syfers, Judy. "I Want a Wife." *Ms.,* Spring 1972, p. 56.

Tillmon, Johnnie. "Welfare Is a Woman's Issue." *Ms.,* Spring 1972, pp. 111-16.

Time magazine staff, special edition on the American woman, March 20, 1972.

Tolchin, Susan, and Tolchin, Martin. *Clout: Womanpower and Politics.* New York: Capricorn Books, 1974.

Treiman, Donald, and Ferrell, Kermit. "Sex and the Process of Status Attainment: A Comparison of Working Women and Men." *American Sociological Review,* 40 (April 1975): 174-200.

Trey, J. E. "Women in the War Economy—World War II." *The Review of Radical Political Economics* 4 (July 1972): 1-17.

U.S. Bureau of the Census. *Statistical Abstract of the United States.* Washington, D.C.: U.S. Printing Office, 1976.

Vatter, Ethel. "Structural Change in the Occupational Composition of the Female Labor Force." In Jane Chapman (ed.), *Economic Independence for Women,* pp. 211-30. Beverly Hills, Calif.: Sage Publications, 1976.

Veblen, Thorstein. *The Theory of the Leisure Class.* New York: Mentor Books, 1953; first published 1899.

Walum, Laurel. *The Dynamics of Sex and Gender: A Sociological Perspective.* Chicago: Rand McNally & Co., 1977.

Wertheimer, Barbara. "Search of a Partnership Role: Women in Labor Unions Today." In Jane Chapman (ed.), *Economic Independence for Women,* pp. 183-209. Beverly Hills, Calif.: Sage Publications, 1976.

Whitehurst, Carol. *Women in America: The Oppressed Majority.* Santa Monica, Calif.: Goodyear Publishing Co., 1977.

Whyte, William H., Jr. *The Organization Man.* Garden City, N.Y.: Anchor Books, 1956.

Chapter 5

Personal Relationships and Gender Role Playing

The intimate relationships of most people with other humans are among the most important aspects of their lives, if they do not comprise the single most important one. Such relationships are undoubtedly colored strongly by gender roles, yet, ironically, this is precisely the subject on which social science has made available the least unbiased, relevant research information. Nonetheless, no discussion of gender roles can ignore their impact on interpersonal relationships. This chapter is an attempt to explore the issues, despite the relative paucity of relevant data. The basic question is: To the extent that males and females fulfill their respective gender role stereotypes, what are the implications for a variety of types of relationships?

Because few people of either sex "live up to" their stereotypes totally, the relationships discussed in the following pages are necessarily exaggerated. The issue is not how many people really behave in these ways. Rather, we can more profitably ask what aspects of people's relationships reflect, however dimly, the processes hypothesized as resulting from the pressures exerted by gender role stereotypes.

Theories of Human Relations

Dick and Jane interact with a myriad of people of both sexes, and they do so in a variety of ways. Human relationships have long been categorized as falling into one of two broad types: primary and secondary. Secondary relations are ritualized interactions between two or more individuals playing specific roles who come into contact for a limited purpose. The interactions that normally occur between salesclerk and customer, teacher and student, doctor and patient are all examples of secondary relations. One can rather easily predict the content of such exchanges, since they are generally prepatterned to a substantial degree, the behaviors are limited in scope, and emotional responses are minimal. Primary relations are exactly the opposite. They consist of interactions among people in a broad spectrum of ways and settings in which some degree of emotional commitment is usually present. Relationships between lovers, spouses, friends, and children and parents are all primary in nature. Naturally, the line between the two types is not clear-cut: many secondary relations shade into primary ones, while in some circumstances primary relations have certain secondary elements. The emphasis in this chapter is on primary relationships.

The same individual is never precisely the same in relationship to a number of other individuals, although there is a tendency toward consistency. We have all experienced the feeling that the Dick or Jane we know is "not the same person" as he or she is to someone else. The stoical, silent Dick we know is a loquacious, sensitive Dick to someone else; the scatterbrained, outgoing Jane to someone else is that bright but somewhat shy Jane we know. Are Jane and Dick hypocrites, hiding their "true selves" from us, someone else, or both? Probably not; they are merely performing in response to different circumstances, as well as differing perceptions and expectations of themselves. Stated in another way, we all have a very large repertoire of behaviors; other people elicit some elements of it, but not all. It is probably the case that no one person ever elicits the entire range of behaviors from another, regardless of how close the two may be or how long they have known one another. In primary relations, however, a substantial proportion of that repertoire is often revealed. Sooner or later, however, there will still come that time when we scratch our heads and wonder why Jane or Dick "acted out of character," i.e., showed us some part of their behavior repertoire we had not seen before.

Gender role playing constitutes one among several important factors that influence the behaviors an individual will exhibit in a given relationship. As a feminine person, Jane will tend to display somewhat different behaviors to males who might be romantic partners than to females or even to other categories of males. Some of this difference may be a conscious effort to fulfill certain assumed expectations; for example, she may "play dumb" to attract a certain male whom she believes feels threatened by bright females. This is called "impression management" (Goffman, 1959). More important, however, are those behaviors she does not consciously manipulate. She may actually *be* rather dependent vis-à-vis a given male, while fairly independent with her female friends. This results from the fact that she has somewhat different self-concepts when she is with that male and with her friends which developed because she was sanctioned differentially by them; she was "punished"—rebuffed or affection withdrawn—when she acted in an independent manner with her potential mate, but "rewarded" for the same efforts with her friends. Because the "definition of the situation" differed in the two instances, the behaviors rewarded differed, and the situations came to constitute self-fulfilling prophecies. The key is the nature of these situational definitions, and the point is that they are more or less strongly influenced by gender role stereotypes (see Aries, 1977).

There are a number of other social-psychological theories dealing with human interaction which may help us understand the possible effects of gender role stereotypes on various human relationships. People who remain in a close primary relationship either originally agree on most issues deemed important by those involved or evolve into such agreement over time. Stated another way, individuals who continue to participate in a close relationship feel the same way about most fundamental things (Newcomb, 1961). Thus, for instance, a female who rejects the traditional feminine role (or a political ideology) is not apt to be found in a stable, long-term relationship with a male who accepts that role as appropriate; sooner or later the "imbalance" will become too uncomfortable or "dissonant," and if neither changes, the relationship will usually terminate. Thus, there are basically two possibilities when a fundamental lack of agreement exists: the relationship may end, or one or both individuals' attitudes may change. Indeed, the feminine gender role encourages women not to become too committed to any attitudes that may conflict with those of a mate; that is, women are encouraged to defer to a male's opinion. Thus there is a built-in tendency for this kind of circumstance not to reach the point of real conflict in that particular type of relationship.

Which of these two possibilities in fact occurs in the face of conflict depends in large measure on the quantity and quality of other satisfactions being derived from a relationship. Exchange theory (Homans, 1961; Thibault & Kelly, 1959) postulates that in any human interaction the participants receive certain "rewards" and pay certain "costs." For an interaction to continue, the rewards must be equal to or greater than the costs for the parties involved. According to this approach, the motivation for people to remain in a relationship exists when there is a "net profit" or, minimally, no loss. The only exception is when individuals who are experiencing a loss nonetheless remain in a relationship because the alternatives appear even more costly (Thibault & Kelly, 1959). For instance, a wife who is quite unhappy in her marital relationship may fail to seek a separation or divorce if she thinks that the resultant loneliness, lack of father-presence, or financial situation will be worse (more costly) than her current misery.

The key to this approach resides in what people define as rewarding and what as costly. Such definitions are undoubtedly strongly influenced by gender role stereotyping. Females are systematically taught that one of the most important rewards they can receive is an overt display of warmth and affection; the withdrawal of this constitutes a cost. Past a very early age, males are not taught to value overt affection and, indeed, may even be taught it is "unmanly." It is not surprising that they are frequently embarrassed by, or at least oblivious to, the little signs of affection deemed so important by most females. One might say that giving these signs constitutes a cost for many males. Our folklore is full of jokes which center on precisely this phenomenon: husband forgets wife's birthday, their anniversary, or the morning goodbye kiss, or neglects to compliment her new dress or a new recipe she has tried. Marriage manuals routinely advise the male not to forget "afterplay" in sex, namely, a display of affection and warmth that is no longer explicitly directed at sexual fulfillment. Females are also taught to value dependency—psychological and financial—vis-à-vis males, for whom support may well come to constitute a cost.

Males, on the other hand, are systematically taught to value more concrete rewards, such as money or service, as well as power or dominance and prestige. Using the marital relationship as an example, Dick's rewards consist of such things as an orderly and well-kept home (children quiet, dinner ready, socks clean), an ear that will listen, a mouth that will compliment, and, perhaps more importantly, an overall impression that he is dominant (Laws, 1971, p. 507). Conversely, all these things may be said to constitute costs for many wives. Our folklore reflects this as well, with endless stories about the wife who manipulates her spouse while making it appear that he is dominant and competent.

This chapter analyzes the ways in which people seek to have their needs met by others and the effects that gender role stereotypes have on this process. Fulfillment of such needs certainly constitutes a reward, but it might well entail a cost for the interaction partner. The thesis to be developed is that gender role stereotypes tend to decrease the ability of individuals to achieve need satisfaction (rewards) and increase the costs of granting such satisfaction to others. In short, gender roles encourage the dissolution of a variety of types of interpersonal relationships.

Interpersonal Relations between the Sexes

In our society there is an ever-present tendency for relationships between a male and a female to either become "romantic" (i.e., sexual in the broadest sense of the word) or to dissipate; platonic or nonromantic relationships are seemingly very unstable. This phenomenon results from a limited and limiting view of love fostered by Hollywood, television, true-romance-type magazines, and indeed, our entire culture. Constantina Safilios-Rothschild (1977) argues that "sex has been labeled a 'masculine' pursuit and love a 'feminine' pursuit. . . . According to sex-role stereotypes, men are supposed to be afraid and often unable to love and commit themselves. They tend to mistake sex for love." She continues, pointing out that when men do "surrender" to love, "they tend to overromanticize and idealize women . . . and once sure of a woman's love, they are apt to lose interest" (pp. 23-23). Before male-female relationships of any type can be understood, it is crucial to examine our culturally accepted notion of this emotion we call "love."

Our language has but one word to cover a multitude of different emotional states: "love." We must then add adjectives to distinguish between the love parents and children have for one another from the love that is characteristic of close friends or romantic love, or, in some instances, forego the use of the word. We further distinguish between "infatuation," as a supposedly temporary, totally sexually based kind of romantic love; "liking," which is nonsexual love; and "TRUE LOVE," which is held out as the highest pinnacle of human emotion and sexuality and excuses all sins we may commit in its name.

Safilios-Rothschild (1977, pp. 6-11) distinguishes five different types of "love" pertaining only to the male-female relationships. The first is adventuresome love, or that which is oriented to fun, enjoyment, pleasure, and usually involves little commitment and responsibility. The second is friendship love which is usually asexual and often occurs after a more passionate kind of love has run its course. This kind of love is usually not possessive or exclusive according to her. The third type is passionate love, also known as romantic or "true" love. This is exclusive and in it one feels as if one were giving everything and expects everything in return. Affectionate love is the next type and it involves different mixtures of sexual attraction, friendship, intellectual exchange, understanding, tenderness, concern for the other's welfare, and so on. It involves constancy and predictability and is highly compatible with marriage. The final type is what Safilios-Rothschild terms mature love, which she says is rare, and it involves willful control rather than unbridled emotional expression. She concludes that our current socialization usually reinforces romantic or passionate love as the ideal male-female love relationship. Thus, "men and women are socialized to interact with each other as objects at the sexual level rather than as human beings who can relate with, like, and love each other in many different ways. . . . This alienating reduction of women-men relationships to sexual objects has . . . deprived love of its mature, fulfilling attributes" (Safilios-Rothschild, 1977, p. 25).

Perhaps because we basically have only one word for all these various emotions, we tend to treat love as a zero-sum game. A zero-sum game is any situation in which one person's gain automatically entails another's loss. If, for instance, one gains to the hypothetical value of + 1, the "opponent" loses to the value of —1, totaling zero when summed. In terms of love, this means the following. We begin with the very dubious assumption, rarely made explicit, that each person has a fixed, finite quantity of that emotion available to give. TRUE LOVE is assumed to take virtually all of it. Thus, if a person also "loves" someone else (not to mention many others), be it child, friend, or another romantic partner, he or she is automatically assumed to be giving less to the "legitimate" recipient. The result is a feeling called jealousy which is generally excused by society unless it is manifested in a fashion that is too dangerous (e.g., murder). Even then, as we saw in the preceding chapter, it is often excused. We frequently hear about the "problems" a new father experiences as his wife "withdraws" some of her love to focus it on the new child. It is not unusual for people to be jealous of a spouse's or lover's same-sexed friends. Mother-in-law "problems," about which so many jokes abound, are often reflecting the same phenomenon. Most serious are the problems that develop around one spouse's sexual and/or emotional "unfaithfulness" to the other. Why do we say that a married person who engages in sexual intercourse with another to whom she or he is not married is "cheating"? The very word carries the connotation that the "cheating" spouse is taking something that rightfully belongs to the cheated-upon person; one's gain constitutes the other's loss.

The emotion we call love is not a zero-sum game. We are just not that limited in our emotional energies. Humans are capable of loving many others at the same time as well as serially (and, in fact, often do so). Indeed, it is unlikely that any one individual can ever fill all of another person's emotional needs. To gain a full life and have a variety of their needs met, humans must develop deep emotional commitments to more than one individual and in more than one way.

Platonic Relationships

The widespread if subtle acceptance of a zero-sum concept of love helps to ensure that many loving relationships, especially platonic love for a member of the other sex, will be less rewarding and long-lived than they might otherwise be. Most Americans suspect that platonic relationships between a male and a female are something other than they appear. Husbands or male lovers, probably even more than their female counterparts, are apt to react to such relationships on the part of their mates with suspicion and jealousy. They are apt, in other words, to interpret such a friendship in terms of an increase in the cost of the relationship and a diminution of the rewards, thus creating an element of instability in both relationships. According to tradition and the masculine mystique, wives and female lovers are property not to be shared with others. Any hint of such sharing places the male in particular in an extremely embarrassing situation among his peers and undercuts his own feelings of masculinity. In most societies few insults are worse than accusing a man of being cuckolded by his wife or girl friend; it has been grounds for divorce in virtually every state even when no other grounds existed, although adultery has not always been automatic grounds for a wife seeking divorce. Moreover, jealousy and a zero-sum concept of love (i.e., strict monogamy) cannot possibly be inherent in our species, given all the societies in which polygamy and polyandry have functioned.

Thus any attempt at a close platonic relationship between a male and a female will elicit suspicions if either is romantically committed to someone else. If, however, there is no commitment to others, such a relationship will create ungrounded assumptions arising from stereotyped notions of how the sexes "ought" to relate to one another. Both male and female gender role stereotypes encourage individuals to define members of the other sex in broadly sexual terms. Females are taught to view males primarily as potential mates or husbands, namely, the objects of TRUE LOVE. Males learn to view females primarily as sex objects to be exploited if possible, married if necessary.

Indeed, it is not altogether unfair to view our cultural notions pertaining to sex, especially for males, in terms of war. Sex is often used as a method of proving dominance rather than a means of communication and mutual pleasure. In extreme cases we call this "rape," but the same general mentality exists in much of what passes for "normal" sexual activity, especially for males (Millet, 1970, p. 44). For many men the way to end an argument is to initiate sex. Our slang terms relating to sexual intercourse also generally reflect this attitude. "Screwing" refers both to copulation and exploitation, and one can be "laid" in bed or "laid out" in a fight; "balled" in love or "balled out" in punishment; "fucked" sexually or in terms of being "taken" or exploited; "banged" in bed or with a gun. The male sexual organ is also characterized by slang expressions emphasizing dominance: a "cock" is a fighting bird; a "prick" is something that produces pain.

In short, the one way in which neither sex is taught to view the other is as potential friends and peers. Thus in any platonic relationship there is a built-in dynamic encouraging one or both participants to redefine the situation by "falling in love." Generally, either both do, in which case TRUE LOVE results, or one alone does, in which case the relationship becomes uncomfortable and is usually terminated.

Even though platonic relationships between males and females tend to be short-lived and unstable, they cast a very interesting light on gender role phenomena. Often, the relationship begins with the male approaching a female he knows in order to confide something and/or seek advice. Or he asks her for a date and they then discover that, although they are not sexually attracted, they do like one another. In either case the stereotypical prerogative of male initiation of cross-sex interaction is usually maintained, even when the purpose is clearly not sexual or romantic. Many males confide things to female friends they would never broach with other males. Basically the masculine stereotype discourages males from speaking openly with one another about their fears, anxieties, or weaknesses. It fosters intellectualizing, bravado, and competitiveness among males, all of which are directly antithetical to more intimate personal exchanges. As a result, males often seek the ear of a nonthreatening female for such purposes. But notice how strongly the two gender-role stereotypes are reflected in this. His expectation is that she will function basically as a compassionate, even ego-boosting listener and make relatively few such demands in return; she often supports such expectations. If, perchance, she attempts to elicit the same attention from him that she gives to him, she may find a bored expression, an attempt to change the subject, or a quick excuse for leaving. His rewards in the relationship are obvious, his costs few. Her motivations are more difficult to comprehend. Probably she remains in it because her ego is boosted simply by virtue of the fact that a member of the superior caste has "chosen" her—for whatever purpose. Moreover, she is being given the opportunity to perform the kinds of expressive functions she has been taught to value so highly (see Safilios-Rothschild, 1977, pp. 94-98).

Romantic Relationships

However influential gender roles are in shaping platonic relationships, they are that much more powerful in their effects on romantic male-female interactions. It is probably the case that truly open and honest communication, mutual respect, and the concomitant emotions of warmth and deep affection can only result from interaction among equals (O'Neill & O'Neill, 1972). Yet the sexes are anything but equal in this society and most others. To put it bluntly, in most such relationships the male has considerably more power, resulting from his financial advantages, from those myriad personality differences instilled in the two sexes by socialization, and, if need be, from his superior physical strength. Sexual attraction, protectiveness, dependency, and a host of other emotions can all develop among people who are unequal (even masters and slaves in times past sometimes held such feelings for one another), but not the equalitarian, companionate relationships lauded in the media and found so rarely in reality (Gillespie, 1971; Safilios-Rothschild, 1972). As long as our culture maintains two different and unequal gender role stereotypes that enable people to explore a mere half of their human potential, interpersonal relations, and most especially those between males and females, will fall far short of our ideal norms concerning love relationships (Firestone, 1970, chap. 6).

Compounding the inequality of the sexes is the fact that our gender role stereotypes have left virtually the entire realm of emotional expression and human caring to femininity. It is difficult to imagine a genuine loving relationship involving the stoical, unemotional, instrumentally oriented, dominating, aggressive, and competitive creature of the masculine stereotype. Moreover, both males and females view a man's primary function as that of economic provider; there is no socially defined and sanctioned expectation that he will confide, comfort, or share with a romantic partner, and without these there is scarcely "love" (see Balswick & Collier, 1976). It is, of course, equally difficult to imagine a male developing deep respect for the scatter-brained, passive, dependent, vain creature who would be "feminine."

Regardless of how contradictory gender roles are to establishing a love relationship, when Dick and Jane come together they generally share many, if not most, of the stereotypical notions of masculinity and femininity. These ideas shape their expectations of one another and themselves. On the one hand, if they live up to these expectations, their behaviors will often prove costly to one another, because of the types of considerations discussed above. On the other hand, if either one fails to live up to these expectations, that failure may be defined as a cost or a diminution of rewards by the other. Dick may have a very real need to express his emotions, maybe even to cry; he may have dependency needs and a whole host of other traits that belie his masculinity. And Jane really may not be all that passive; moreover, she might be a straight A student and very competitive and aggressive. As their relationship deepens and a broader range of their behavior repertoires is revealed (often long after marriage), they begin to see signs of these unexpected traits in one another.

From that point the relationship may go in a number of directions. It may simply end as one or both find that the costs of having their expectations unmet is too high. When this occurs people later look back and wonder what it was they ever saw in the other person. Such a response usually results only if the pair has not yet made a binding commitment to one another, but the relatively high divorce rate today attests to the fact that it may occur even after such a commitment has been made. If, however, the mutual "profits" derived from other aspects of the relationship are great enough, the couple may grope toward redefining those expectations and ultimately rejecting society's stereotypes. Although this solution may bring with it real human growth and a more satisfying relationship, it is painful. Nevertheless, today an increasing number of couples appear to be making such an effort. Probably the most common solution in the past, especially if the two were married and had children, has been the sort of compromise that eventually shatters whatever emotional ties may have existed: they have simply attempted to ignore the discrepancies and to work around them.

The Marital Relationship

In the past, the creation of a new family through the marriage of two people was considered too serious an enterprise to be left to the whims of the marriage partners. The family had as its primary functions the rearing of children and the provision of the basic necessities of life. Parents chose a marriage partner for their own child on the basis of how well they thought the partner, given his or her family, could fulfill the relevant functions (i.e., bearing and rearing children for females, and provision of necessities for males). Romantic love was not a consideration; it was nice if the spouses came in time to love one another, but this was not of central importance. In the traditional family there was a relatively clear-cut division of labor, and by law and custom, decision-making authority was vested in the male.

In traditional societies today marriage sometimes essentially still fits this description. However, in many societies, including our own, it has changed drastically in the past 100 years. Today most Americans feel that the only legitimate basis for forming a marriage is romantic love. Potential partners seldom admit to economic or other "practical" motives in their mate selection (which is not to say that such considerations are never present). The term "gold digger" is applied to people suspected of pecuniary motives in their selection of a mate, and this term (or its equivalent) is clearly pejorative. Not only has the culturally legitimate basis of mate selection changed, but so have our definitions of family function, division of labor, and decision-making authority.

Largely because of the primacy of romantic love in considerations of mate selection, we have come to define the purpose of a marriage primarily in terms of the individual satisfaction of the spouses. Marriage is supposed to provide each of the partners with companionship, affection, and a sexual outlet, in short, a way to lead life that is more satisfying than singleness. In this kind of marriage, the emphasis becomes personal expression and "growth." However, largely because of our gender roles, in reality marriages rarely resemble this ideal. In fact, they are often little more than economic units with child-rearing responsibilities. The disjuncture between the realities of marriage and our ideals probably helps to account for the high divorce rates not merely in our own society, but in virtually all industrialized, modernized societies. In essence, we form marriages on the basis of a type of feeling that is intrinsically unstable, namely, romantic love. This feeling has very little to do with whether or not two people are capable of living together comfortably and creating a life-style that is mutually satisfactory over time. When, in later years, the reality of living together is compared with an idealized version of what marriage ought to be, we too often conclude that there is a rather radical discrepancy.

One major contributor to this discrepancy is the fact that the division of labor within the family is still very stereotyped in terms of gender roles. As we have seen, men are still expected to be the breadwinners, despite the increasing numbers of wives employed outside of their homes, and women are still expected to be homemakers and primarily responsible for child rearing. Determining the division of labor on the basis of sex rather than individual interest is inherently contradictory to a view of marriage which emphasizes personal satisfaction. Indeed, in the past several years many people have begun to question the assignment of tasks or functions on the basis of sex. However, recent research (Dworkin & Chafetz, n.d.) shows that in the minority of cases where spouses do not divide household labor in a traditional fashion, females are found doing traditionally masculine tasks (e.g., lawn and yard care, earning money) without reciprocity. In other words, males have not begun to engage in any numbers in such tasks as care of sick children, laundry, or daily cooking as opposed to occasional barbecues. In this respect change appears to constitute added responsibilities for women, and very little more. This development can scarcely be interpreted as movement toward a more personally satisfying marriage for women.

Although, as we have seen, there are still legal vestiges of the tradition that defines the male as chief authority in the family, in fact we, as a society, no longer automatically vest all decision-making authority in the husband. As a concept, authority entails the notions that the person in authority has the right to make decisions, and those for whom decisions are made feel morally obligated to abide by those decisions. This feeling of obligation is called "legitimacy"; when it is no longer present, authority ceases to exist. If a person is still able to make binding decisions unilaterally anyway, we call it "power." In order to exercise power, a person needs superior resources, such as physical strength or financial clout. These resources can be used by one party to coerce the other. Males have traditionally had, and in large measure they continue to have, superior power resources, physically and financially. They can thus continue to make binding decisions even though their wives may no longer think it appropriate (legitimate). Even when wives are employed they are usually considered "junior partners" rather than equals, since they earn less and are defined (and often define themselves) as less career committed than their husbands. Thus, major decisions, such as the decision to move geographically or to make or forego major purchases, are typically made primarily according to the husband's wishes. Research has consistently indicated that employed wives, especially those with a strong career commitment, have more power vis-à-vis their mates than housewives do (Scanzoni, 1972, p. 69). It is also reasonable to assume that such women are better able to find more fulfillment of their own needs within the marital relationship, and indeed, research rather consistently shows employed wives to be happier than full-time homemakers (see Tarvis & Offir, 1976, p. 223).

When people lack power (or authority) in a relationship, they often must resort to manipulation in order to get their needs fulfilled. Wives have long been defined as manipulative ("the power behind the throne"), getting their way by tricking their husbands rather than by direct or assertive behavior. Manipulation requires that those employing the technique have sufficient knowledge of the reactions of others that they can elicit the desired response by their own behavior. For instance, a wife who wants a new dress for a party may manipulate her husband into providing the money for it by "trying on" the most ill-fitting, out-of-date piece of clothing she owns and then proclaiming that she plans to wear it when the boss comes to dinner on Saturday. If she knows her husband is sensitive about her appearance and wishes to impress his boss, she may be successful in getting her way without even directly expressing her wish. This form of accomplishing one's ends is time-consuming, often unsuccessful, and, for many, a humiliating experience. In the face of superior power or authority it may be the only technique available, however. It is not surprising that other groups said to use this technique include children and, in the Old South, blacks. One result of powerlessness is thus that the manipulators know their interaction partners more intimately than their partners know them. Women know more about men than vice versa; southern blacks knew more about whites than vice versa. In the absence of such knowledge, successful manipulation is almost impossible.

Myth would have us believe that marriage is more beneficial to women than to men. After all, it has traditionally been females who have sought marriage, and men who have sought to remain bachelors. As Jessie Bernard (1971, 1972) points out, however, there are really two marriages, his and hers, and they are not equal. His is, by all indications of mental and physical health, a lot happier than hers. Given our discussion of the division of labor and the locus decision making, this is scarcely surprising.

Let us examine a bit more closely what can happen in a marriage when the "romance wears off" and the husband and wife are unwilling or unable to redefine their expectations concerning appropriate gender role behavior. At this point they turn to manipulation, play-acting, withdrawal, and a variety of means of displacement in an attempt to have their needs and expectations met. Suppose that Jane is really a very aggressive and competitive person. She cannot directly manifest these traits and still appear "feminine" to herself and her mate. What she can do, often quite unconsciously, is express these personality attributes by nagging, flattering, and manipulating Dick; she uses "feminine wiles" to get her way (Hacker, 1951, p. 65). She nags him to do better on the job, pushing him ever harder to "succeed" while belittling his efforts. She does this not so much because of the new car she claims to want as for the vicarious thrill of experiencing competition and success through him. Hanna Papanek (1973) has coined the term "two-person career" in examining the vicarious ways in which wives share their husbands' occupational fortunes. Were Jane out competing in the world herself, she would have no need to displace her needs by badgering her husband. Or maybe Jane likes to dominate. She cannot go out and obtain a position of power; moreover, Dick refuses to be directly dominated. Her response is to develop timely "headaches" when he wants to engage in sex; she openly flirts with his best friend at a party; she belittles him in public or gives away the punch line to the joke he is telling. In short, those unpleasant qualities of nagging, whining, manipulating, perhaps even frigidity attributed so often to wives result largely from the fact that in trying to conform to their gender role stereotype many Janes find that they are left without direct expression of much of their personality (Greer, 1970, especially pp. 281-89).

What is Dick doing in response to Jane's behavior and to his own unsatisfied needs? In the first place, unlike Jane, Dick never expected his entire life to revolve around the marital relationship. Thus he is psychologically in a position to use both her behavior and his needs as a justification for various forms of withdrawal. He withdraws affection from her; spends his time at home glued to the TV, a book, the newspaper, a hobby; stays late at work or takes a second job. All of these can be forms of withdrawal from an unpleasant relationship. Ultimately he spends less and less time at home and more time with "the guys" or a succession of "girl friends" who "understand him" and his needs. Another reaction Dick may have is to engage in never-ending "put-downs," denigrating his mate's abilities and intellect and thus her "right" to belittle or even disagree with him. In turn, this behavior feeds back and exacerbates his wife's nagging and whining. It is also not uncommon for him to react to his mate with various degrees of physical violence or threats of violence (see Friedman, 1977; Straus, 1977). In all of this Dick has one strong advantage over Jane. He, unlike she (if she is a housewife), has the world outside the home in which to seek satisfaction of his needs. Given the current isolated nuclear family structure, if he can't satisfy her needs she has very few options.

Thus the war between the sexes goes on in millions of homes, each skirmish helping to ensure that the next will be worse (Jones, 1970). A vicious circle develops in which her unpleasant behavior elicits withdrawal, denigration, or violence from him, which in turn results in worse behavior by her and more reaction by him. Communication, respect, and affection are all casualties of trying to live within the straitjacket of the gender role stereotypes. Moreover, many of these spouses, especially the wives, spend their lives thinking "if only (I was different, he or she was different, etc.), life would be bliss."

While this picture of marriage may represent something of an extreme, elements of it are undoubtedly present in a very large proportion of marriages. Given this, the relatively high divorce rate can be viewed with optimism: it may represent an attempt on the part of millions to opt out of relationships that bring out the worst human traits and seem to grant little by way of rewards for so many (Scanzoni, 1972, chap. 4). From this point of view divorce is hardly the "failure" it is frequently pictured. Rather, it may represent significant human growth for one or both of the former spouses.

There are also many cases where one or both partners comfortably conform to the relevant gender role stereotypes and have so strongly internalized them that the kinds of displacements suggested above do not occur. If both have done so, conflict is probably minimal, but so too are genuine sharing and two-way communication; the masculine role, particularly, has hardly prepared a male to enter a close, open relationship, nor would the power differential encourage it. The situation in which both gender role stereotypes are conformed to is probably increasingly rare in today's world of flux, although it might possibly have been the norm in more traditional times and places. Such a relationship would tend to be quite stable. If only the female has truly internalized her role, her partner will face different kinds of problems than those already discussed. Instead of a bitchy, nagging, manipulative spouse, he will find himself saddled with a human being who is virtually totally dependent upon him for the fulfillment of all her needs, for making all the decisions, and so on. Moreover, such a wife will be of little help to him in coping with whatever insecurities he may have. What starts out to be an ego trip quickly becomes a heavy burden for many modern men. Few honest males today would deny that such overwhelming responsibility is extremely difficult and unpleasant, as well as constricting to their own lives. If only the male has fully internalized his role, his mate is likely to respond in the manner delineated earlier and become manipulative and nagging in an effort to extract more open affection and attention, as well as more power in the decision-making process.

In general, the less similar the daily activities and interests of the male and female (or of any two people) (i.e., the more stringent the sexual division of labor), the more difficult communication and understanding between the two are likely to be. Perhaps ironically, males have been found to be more willing to engage in household and child-rearing activities than females are willing to allow them to do so, especially as the years go by in a marriage (Safilios-Rothschild, 1972, p. 67). By the time children arrive, most couples have developed a fairly precise and stereotyped division of labor that often serves to encourage further deterioration in the relationship. Wives and mothers jealously guard the only realm of activity that is socially defined as their legitimate preserve, resisting any but the most minimal efforts by their husbands to engage in them ("because they are inept"). After a while the husband who has been ejected from the kitchen and nursery no longer offers his services at all. This provides the harried wife with an excuse to play the "martyr" and proclaim his lack of appreciation for her efforts, and the husband with the opportunity to complain about the disorganized state of their home. Again, we have come full circle to find her complaining and him withdrawing.

It is increasingly unlikely today that either partner truly conforms to these stereotypes and hence to the other's expectations. Nor is our accepted courtship system likely to reveal many of these disparities until after a binding commitment between the pair has taken place. When you add to this the fact that many males have the opportunity to grow and change in their daily contact with the world, while many females find themselves mentally shrinking in the isolation of their homes and the heavy menial requirements of housework, the probability of any real understanding between the two shrinks even further. The result is millions of families in which frustrated women who feel unappreciated, unloved, and impotent face hostile men who feel exploited as "meal tickets" and react by withdrawing psychically and physically from the relationship.

Parents and Children

Soon after an American couple marries, pressure by parents and friends to produce children begins, to become a clamor within a few years. As Ellen Peck put it, people don't ask *if* you are planning to have children, they ask *when* (1971, p. 171). The child-free couple has been considered almost as socially deviant as the husbandless woman. Couples who choose not to ever have children have been labeled selfish, immature, immoral, or just plain peculiar. Most, of course, desire children; even if the husband does not, his wife has learned to view this as her primary mission in life. Among those who don't, most eventually succumb to the pressure and have them anyway.

In the past few years the pressure on couples to have children has probably declined somewhat, and certainly the pressure to have them soon after marriage has declined. Our national birth rates declined in the 1970s to their lowest levels in history. In recent years they have averaged less than two children per family, and, if they continue at this rate, eventually our population will begin to shrink. Furthermore, the age at which women have their first children has risen in recent years, as couples increasingly postpone this event into their late twenties and even early thirties. Couples also are postponing marriage, and the age of first marriage likewise has been rising. Also, there is an increasing, though still small, minority of women who are choosing to have and keep babies born out of wedlock.

Thus, in the future, we can expect people to marry later, if at all, have children later, if at all, and complete their families with two children or less. These trends are especially important to women, since they allow them time to complete their educations and to make career commitments before they are burdened with family responsibilities. Such commitments in turn will lead some women not to marry at all and many to choose to have no children or only one child so as not to interfere unduly with their careers.

Despite these trends, however, society still expects people to marry and to have children, and in a variety of ways it pressures them to do so. Once a couple conforms in this respect, the same society that encouraged their parenthood and prides itself on being so child-centered proceeds to do very little by way of manifesting any further interest in the child. Unlike most European societies, we have no children's allowance (except the humiliating AFDC); few inexpensive, well-run child-care centers; little provision for ensuring adequate health care for children; and a penchant for turning down school bond issues. In short, once a couple has had a child it becomes solely their responsibility and, in reality, *hers*. This is not an irrelevant fact, given estimates that for a family to raise two children, send them to college, and forego the wife's potential income costs between $80,000 and $150,000! Before the society will intervene in any way the parents must abuse the child to the point of near murder, a not infrequent occurrence which has only recently come to public attention as a major social problem.

Most couples probably need to make fewer adjustments to marriage than they do to parenthood (Lopata, 1971, chap. 4). Husband-wife roles may flow fairly smoothly from the girlfriend-boyfriend ones. This is especially true if, as is typically the case today, the female continues employment or schooling and if the couple lives in an apartment where housekeeping chores are relatively minimal. The assumption of father and mother roles, however, is usually a completely new experience, and it often entails radical adjustments in both of their individual lives as well as in the nature of their interaction.

For couples who desire the pregnancy (and with legal abortions available this proportion is probably increasing), the news is often greeted with euphoria. The husband may become extremely attentive to his spouse and to her "mystical" condition. Indeed, females often desire pregnancy precisely to elicit such attention. Very soon after the birth, if not somewhat before, this situation starts changing. The husband begins to resent the intrusion of the newcomer on his previously exclusive "turf," and the wife often ceases employment (at precisely the time expenses have increased) and begins to perceive the realm of the house and child as more or less exclusively hers—in short, it is at this juncture that she has traditionally turned into the typical housewife (Gavron, 1966, p. 135). All of the problems enumerated in the preceding section either surface at this time or are exacerbated if they have been already manifested. Far from "bringing a couple close together," as myth would have it, the arrival of a child strains any but the most solid relationships between parents (Peck, 1971, pp. 15-16 and 20 ff.). Bernard (1972, chap. 4) cites substantial research that demonstrates that child-free couples, especially the women, are much happier than parents. Scanzoni and Scanzoni (1976, pp. 375-77) found the same conclusion in research among both black and white couples. They also point out that a child-free couple will feel more free to separate than one with children, in the event marriage proves unsatisfactory.

Gender roles affect the way men and women fulfill their roles as parents no less than in other types of human relationships. In the discussion below, the assumption is made that the parents are enacting their traditional roles. Increasingly, however, it is becoming clear that many mothers, at least, are no longer completely conforming to their role, as they choose to return to employment quickly after childbirth. Moreover, many mothers today are not married, either because they chose not to marry the fathers of their children or because they have been divorced.

Mother-Child Relations

Young Jane begins learning the mother role when she receives her first doll at about age 2 or 3. If she has a younger sibling, she is probably encouraged to aid in its care. As just about the single most important aspect of the total feminine role complex, motherhood is romanticized and taught to a greater or lesser extent from early youth (Peck, 1971, p. 18 ff.). MOTHERHOOD IS FULFILLMENT! shout the media, the "helping professions," Madison Avenue, and the corporations which see babies as consumers and a high birth rate as a business bonanza. As a social role motherhood is relatively precisely defined, and its obligations are broadly agreed upon by members of the many diverse subcultures that comprise American society. Mother is expected to be responsible for the daily physical and health care of the child from birth until at least adolescence. She is responsible for monitoring the child's emotional and intellectual development. She is expected to function as the chief mediator between the family on the one hand, and school, church, and the families of the child's friends on the other. Particularly during the preschool years, she is chiefly responsible for amusing the child or seeing to it that someone else does. Above all, mother is held to be the major, emotional mainstay of the child: the constant provider of unconditional affection, understanding, and moral support. These things are expected of mothers regardless of their education, social class, interests, abilities, mental health, and so forth. As Laurel Walum (1977, p. 179) points out, fathers aren't asked "Well, if you don't want to stay home and raise children, why did you have them?" Walum also notes that if we say a baby was fathered by someone, the meaning attached is biological. If we say a baby was mothered by someone, it is assumed we mean the child received "tender loving care" from that person.

The theoretical basis of these social expectations of mothers is the simple fact that, usually, it was the woman's body that carried and eventually gave birth to the child. Myth has it that the process of being pregnant and giving birth magically results in instant "mother love," namely, an overwhelming desire to nurture and care for all the needs of her offspring for the next 15 or 20 years of life (Lopata, 1971, p. 35). If, indeed, "nature" provided such an urge we could scarcely account for the large numbers of mothers who neglect, abuse, and abandon their children, not to mention the even larger number who perform their maternal tasks poorly. Nor could we account for the deep "maternal" love people of both sexes often develop for children they did not physically conceive. The fact of the matter is that a *social* injunction is placed on virtually all females to be mothers, to do the required types of things and develop the "appropriate" emotions, as outlined above (Peck, 1971, chap. 5). The context in which the role of motherhood is normally played in contemporary America is that of the small, isolated nuclear family with only one to three children. When grandparents are present in middle-class, white families, they tend to be excluded from serious participation in family life, although they probably play a more important role in some social and ethnic subcultures, such as those of blacks and Chicanos. Moreover, most "experts" and public opinion have maintained that the only way in which the mother role can be played adequately, especially when children are young, is for the woman who is the mother to be constantly accessible, that is, not employed outside the home. This again is enjoined without regard to the particular mother's interests or abilities, unless she is poor.

The ramifications of these circumstances for children and for mother-child relations (not to mention the mothers themselves) are relatively disastrous. Until quite recently in history most people lived in extended families consisting usually of at least three generations, a number of adults of both sexes, and a number of children of various ages and both sexes. A child was reared in a microcosm of the world in which it would probably live as an adult. It had a variety of role models and a variety of inputs to its developing behaviors and attitudes. With a number of adults and older children to share the responsibility, a young child was not an overwhelming burden to any one individual; its many needs could be easily met because there were many people to meet them. If the biological mother lacked in any way the interest or ability to fulfill the many and varied responsibilities entailed in child rearing, there were always others to make up for the deficiency. Larger families precluded concentrating close attention and scrutiny on every move of the child; they discouraged an intense, all-consuming interest in any one individual. In this way they encouraged cooperativeness and discouraged extreme ego-centeredness. Moreover, they necessitated active contributions on the part of all but the very youngest, thus giving all family members functional roles and a concomitant sense of importance. In fact, the very concept of "childhood" as a distinct stage during which individuals are treated in a markedly different manner from adults is only a few centuries old at most (Firestone, 1970, chap. 4).

Bernard (1975, p. 219) points out that motherhood, as we know it today in middle-class America, is historically unique and the product of an affluence which allows women to be spared other productive labor. The modern middle-class mother has little choice but to lavish attention on her few children, and she is strongly encouraged by society to focus on the most minor details of their daily existence. Barraged by a constant stream of "expert" opinions on child development, she scrutinizes every aspect of the child's life, apprehensive lest she damage its psyche or fail to recognize and correct some "abnormality." Ironically, in the process she probably works harder than her predecessors, with their larger families and lack of modern conveniences. The children, in turn, have few other adults present during their waking hours to turn to or emulate. They exist, by and large, in a world of children their own age and even their own sex which bears little resemblance to that outside the home, and they can fulfill few if any functional roles to give them a sense of worth. Young mothers, bound to children during virtually all their waking hours and almost solely responsible for fulfilling all their needs (as well as performing all the other household duties), quite frequently find themselves harried, exhausted, and frustrated. They periodically explode with anger for minor infractions of rules by their offspring and subsequently feel guilty at their own reactions. Survey the midafternoon or late-morning scene at any supermarket and you will see this drama endlessly played. Years later, these same mothers are reluctant to allow their children the independence that spells the end of their only major functional role in life.

But the problem only begins here for many women. The aggressive, dominant, ambitious wife who must live vicariously through her husband because she is prohibited by her gender role from direct and constructive expression of these traits will do the same to her children—and especially her male offspring. If she can dominate no one else, she can at least wield power over her young (Sexton, 1969, chap. 3). Little Dick *must* be the best athlete, get top grades, be most popular, in short, *succeed;* little Jane *must* be the prettiest girl in her class with the best wardrobe, best in dancing and piano lessons, have the most dates, and so forth. Mother vests all of her pent-up energies and needs on her two or three children, dragging them from one organized activity to another, lavishing attention on their "progress" like a horticulturist in a hothouse. She ends up putting incredible pressure on them to be not themselves but some version of her own dreams. Her self-definition becomes that of her offspring (the final insult occurs when her husband begins referring to her as "mother" or "mom"). Dick can't grow up to be a plumber rather than a lawyer, nor can Jane marry the former rather than the latter; it would reflect badly on mother. She comes to expect that the costs in terms of work and "sacrifice" for her children will be repaid in terms of rewards accrued from a vicarious thrill in their successes.

Middle-class adolescents (and even younger children) often express their reactions to all this close scrutiny and pressure in a variety of destructive ways. Suicide rates among the young have been steadily climbing, as have rates of juvenile delinquency. Drug and alcohol abuse periodically reach epidemic proportions among the young. In the 1960s youth created its own counterculture, designed to flout the most cherished ambitions of the adult world. These reactions probably reflect, at least in part, a pressure-cooker environment in which young people are pressured to perform well a series of nonfunctional activities. Without the daily inputs of a variety of adults, without the independence that can only arise from a studied *lack* of attention to all aspects of their daily existence, without meaningful roles to fulfill during the many years before they finish school, youths have a difficult time trying to develop a clear sense of themselves as self-reliant, independent, responsible human beings with some sense of purpose in life (Friedan, 1963, chap. 12; Grønseth, 1971-72, p. 13).

Motherhood cannot be an all-encompassing activity, for the sake of both the mothers and the offspring. Quantity of attention (past some absolute minimum) is simply not an important consideration in how children "turn out." A few hours a day of intensive, loving, "high-quality" attention to a child by a mother who is happily fulfilling herself the rest of the time are worth infinitely more than the never-ending hours of incessant bickering that pass for child rearing activities in many homes. Try as they might, researchers have failed to document any substantial differences in adjustment, happiness, and so forth between children of employed mothers and those of housewives. In fact, it seems to be the case that children of nonemployed mothers who wish they *were* employed suffer the most, and youngsters whose mothers are employed are generally more self-reliant than others (Bird, 1968, p. 182; Friedan, 1963, p. 186). Recent research (Stewart, 1976) shows that daughters especially profit from the decreased protectiveness that is typical of employed mothers. If mother love means anything, it must involve encouraging children to fulfill their own potentials—not to live the lives their mothers would have liked to live had they not been bound by social convention. It means raising children who are capable of functioning without mothers (by providing a model of an independent person) and then encouraging them to do just that. It is difficult to imagine how our current family structure, combined with our traditional definitions of motherhood and of the feminine gender role, could function to permit that kind of mother love to thrive.

Father-Child Relations

The role of fatherhood is very dissimilar to that of motherhood in three crucial ways. First, it is a very minor part of the total masculine role constellation; it ranks relatively low on the list of priorities a male is likely to have, and the father is not strongly sanctioned socially for playing this role either well or poorly. Second, our society does not have a precise, agreed-upon definition of the components of this role, beyond the ever-present obligation to "provide" in economic terms. Finally, almost nothing in the prefatherhood learning of most males is oriented in any way to training them for this role (see Brenton, 1966, p. 130 ff.; Bernard, 1975, pp. 220-23; Fasteau, 1976; Fein, 1977). Males are actively discouraged as children from play activities involving baby surrogates, and, except in rare instances of large families with few or no older sisters, they are not usually required to help much in the daily care of younger siblings. In short, a new father has only the vaguest idea of what he is expected to do and how he ought to do it, and often his commitment to the role in the first place is marginal.

Females are prompted in part to have babies because society has continually informed them that their primary function in life is motherhood. Males are under little such direct social pressure to become parents, except as it is exerted through their wives. It is not surprising, then, that males are generally somewhat less enthusiastic about the prospect of parenthood (Peck, 1971, p. 19) and may in fact face it with grave trepidation. They may fear the added financial obligation and the decreased freedom to come and go at will, as well as a decline in attention from their wives. Counterbalancing this is the vague notion, especially within some ethnic subcultures and the lower classes, that to father a child "proves" one's potency, hence one's "masculinity." Indeed, much opposition to vasectomy or male sterilization results from an erroneous confusion (not altogether at the intellectual level) of male fertility and sexual potency. Related to this is the masculine emphasis on "productivity"; fathering children comes to be viewed as a kind of sexual productivity, and later the offspring themselves may be viewed as products more or less "owned" by the father.

In the past fatherhood was a rather more clearly defined role than today. Father was the chief disciplinarian; mother's threat of "wait 'till your father comes home and hears of this" was enough to quell the most obstreperous child (see Fein, 1977, p. 192). Today mother is more willing and father less so to engage in such tasks; discipline is no longer a critical component of the father role as distinct from parenthood in general. Before the Industrial Revolution, father was also the chief mentor of his sons, passing on his craft or trade through an apprenticeship program begun early in the child's life. In the remote and complex work world of postindustrial society this task has been virtually abandoned, devolving instead on formal institutions, most notably the schools. In simpler times father was the fount of all knowledge, the primary educator of his children. Today his well-educated spouse is usually more available and as well equipped as he to answer children's questions, if indeed anyone in the family is capable of so doing.

In recent decades countless popular articles and books have encouraged father to be a "pal" to his children—especially his sons, who spend their days in a virtually maleless environment (Fasteau, 1976, p. 61). Simultaneously, the "experts" have warned him not to be "*too much of a pal*"—to remain authoritative and, when needed, capable of discipline. He is enjoined to somehow avoid both being an ogre and being "permissive," yet he is given little time or opportunity to learn how to walk this tightrope (Brenton, 1966, pp. 120-21). His major responsibility remains his work, and now he has even greater financial needs than before he had children (see Bernard, 1975, pp. 220-23). For the up-and-coming middle-class businessman or professional, this means that he will rarely even see his young children awake. The working-class father, pressured by financial need to work overtime or at a second job, will also rarely see his children. Yet when such fathers find that their eight-year-old sons are incapable of throwing a ball decently or are too "tied to mother's apron strings," they react with guilt and a sudden burst of attention. Even then they are hampered by their gender role. The "masculine mystique" has discouraged males from learning to relate to people, including children, in a compassionate, warm, open, affectionate manner (Fasteau, 1976, p. 62). The instrumental orientation they have been taught all their lives leads them to praise their children's successes but ill equips them to sympathize with their bumbling errors. They are thus able to offer "conditional affection" only.

Moreover, if father is not very successful at work, he (like his mate) is apt to pressure his children, especially the males, to succeed in order to enjoy a vicarious compensation for the failures and frustrations he has experienced. Caught in the "success ethic" himself, he is likely to stress achievement more strongly than just about anything else (Brenton, 1966, p. 138 ff.; Fasteau, 1976, p. 63), thus perpetuating this component of the masculine mystique. When father proudly proclaims "This is *my* son," he is engaging in an "ego trip" that says, "If I have succeeded in nothing else, look at what I have produced." In the process he forgets that he took little part in the actual upbringing of the child, not to mention the fact that the child was the one who actually accomplished whatever is being proclaimed.

By and large most fathers, especially in the white middle class, probably relate very little to their children during infancy and early childhood, perceiving them as more or less of a nuisance (Peck, 1971, chap. 6). Later, often much to the anger of the mother, they may return slightly from their withdrawal. They take the children (usually the sons) to interesting places and engage them briefly in the kind of exciting play for which the harried and exhausted mother has little time or energy. They buy them special things (not their everyday needs like clothes and school supplies). They occasionally "flirt" with and heap praise upon their dressed-up daughters (one of the few things many fathers actually do with daughters). They teach their sons sports and hobbies. They badger them to succeed in school and in sports and tend to reward them only contingent upon such success. In short, fathers do not actively partake of the petty, daily problems and needs of their offspring; they remain tangential to the intimate lives of their children, involved only in the "special" moments of excitement or disaster. In most cases, fathers refuse to even engage in physical contact with their sons past infancy, preferring the handshake to the kiss (see Balswick & Collier, 1976, pp. 58-59). All too often a divorce between the parents reduces the quantity and quality of the father's interaction with his children little, if any (assuming they all remain in the same geographical vicinity), and occasionally even increases it because of the guilt involved.

Motherhood is often said to have a humanizing effect on women because of their intimate daily contact with a developing child, with all its strengths and frailties. To the extent that fathers do not actively engage themselves in their children's daily growth process or the minor changes in their abilities and activities, the experience of paternity will not result in their own human growth. Once again the gender role stereotype is responsible for a vicious and unrewarding circle: ill equipped by the masculine stereotype to deal with children on a deep emotional ("expressive") level, caught in an often all-consuming devotion to work and economic success, the father fails to involve himself in his child's life to the extent necessary to ultimately develop the more humane and compassionate aspects of his personality which might, in turn, make him better able to relate to his offspring.

Men in general profit from not being burdened with the daily care of children. However, those who do wish to be involved in the daily upbringing of their children are largely denied the opportunity to do so (Walum, 1977, p. 182). On the basis of impressionistic evidence, it seems that more young fathers today are seeking such involvement. Fein (1977, p. 193) reports research which shows that when a father begins immediately, at the child's birth, to involve himself in its care, he develops a deep emotional bond which is enhanced if he was also closely involved in the pregnancy and delivery. The natural birth movement and the small but growing interest in home births involve fathers closely with the entire process. It may be that in the near future the father's role will come to be defined socially as involving far more than financial provider. If this occurs, children should benefit, mothers should benefit, and, despite the added burdens for fathers, so should they. However, the nature and costs of both gender role stereotypes, combined with the isolated nuclear family structure characteristic of this society, have generally resulted in parent-child relations that fall far short of our cherished social ideals and, in the process, create numerous problems for the next generation of adults.

Same-Sexed Friendships

It might seem that if gender role stereotypes are irrelevant to any type of interpersonal relationship, it would be in friendships between members of the same sex. The fact that this is not the case underlines the all-pervasive quality of such stereotypes in virtually every aspect of human existence.

Male Friendships

From early childhood males are encouraged to form friendship and peer groups with other members of their sex and to cooperate with other males for the achievement of mutually desired goals, often in competition with other all-male groups. In Chapter 3 it was shown how the play activities of young males foster the formation of such relationships, and they scarcely end at adolescence. "Bonded males," or all-male groups, as Lionel Tiger (1970) argues, persist throughout life, be they for work, war, sport, poker, or "drinking buddies." When Jean Lipman-Blumen (1976) analyzed the same phenomenon more recently, she called it "homosociality." She argues that men "commonly . . . seek satisfaction for most of their needs from other men." They seek women primarily in order to meet the one need other men cannot satisfy: paternity, which "in most societies [is] the ultimate claim to masculinity" (pp. 16-17). A rudimentary kind of superior "caste consciousness" that begins in childhood encourages males to shun the companionship of females for ordinary friendship purposes. It is not unusual for females to be informed more or less explicitly by male colleagues or fellow students that they have enough (male) friends; what they want is a sexual partner, or nothing. When they find their family life becoming unpleasant, males look to other males even more for companionship, often developing a virtual woman-hating fraternity (Fast, 1971, chap. 2).

The same masculine stereotype that encourages male friendships, however, often seriously limits the scope and content of such relationships (Booth, 1972, p. 186), as suggested in the discussion above on male-female platonic relationships. Male friendships are character-ized by a kind of rough-and-ready camaraderie. Males will usually be found *doing* something together (fishing, bowling, tinkering with machinery, working). When they are "merely" talking to one another it will usually be on a "light" subject (sports, some "dish" who works in the office), or they may engage in generalized "bitching" about their mates; other topics are approached in an abstract, intellectualized manner. What they are very rarely found doing is talking to one another on an intimate basis about their deepest needs and insecurities. As Robert Fein (1977, p. 195) puts it, "males in the United States are socialized more for sociability than for intimacy." A male attempting to organize a men's consciousness-raising group similar to those existing among feminists, found that:

> A salient observation . . . involved an increasing awareness of how annoying the employment of men's values can be. Among such traits observed were dominating, interrupting, condescension, disrespect, aggression, obsession with sex, ego, intellectualization, put downs, and a lack of empathy, emotion, openness, warmth and contact with persons as human beings rather than as competitors for power and position (Farrell, 1971-72, pp. 21-22).

Two major aspects of the masculine sex role discourage intimacy among American males. First, they are taught it is "unmanly" to show most emotions or to express dependency needs. Second, the aggressiveness and power orientation of the masculine role encourages males to view each other as competitors for status, and one hardly reveals weaknesses to a competitor. "One-upmanship" is primarily a masculine game. A pervasive fear of being labeled "homosexual" that is particularly endemic to American males exacerbates these tendencies further; a male who approaches another male on too intimate a basis fears being interpreted as making an improper "pass" (Fast, 1971, pp. 19 and 104-7). Men are particularly uncomfortable touching other men, except in highly ritualized ways such as a handshake, a slap on the shoulder, or, among athletes, a slap on the rump (see Fein, 1977, p. 195).

The old adage that males will talk to one another in quite explicit terms about females they don't care much for but say little if anything about those they love is also indicative of the level of communication in all-male groups. Sexual prowess is acceptable conversation, emotional commitment is not; the former grants prestige, the latter, if anything, takes it away. The many hours that males spend in one another's presence are rewarding in that they serve primarily to satisfy their needs for amusement, the accomplishment of instrumental goals, and prestige. Status and prestige, however, are relative; by definition someone is always on the bottom. Those males whose prestige among their peers is low are thus impelled to look to the lower caste to resurrect their bruised egos, a role most females know only too well. At any rate, the nature of males' expectations of one another often makes it appear far too costly to attempt to push such relationships to a deeper level (Fasteau, 1972). Thus many are left with unmet emotional needs which, as we have seen, are not easily satisfied in their long-term relationships with females, either.

Female Friendships

Females face almost exactly the opposite problems from males in their friendships. They have a more difficult time forming relationships with members of their own sex and do so with less frequency than males, but when they succeed such friendships tend to be qualitatively deeper and more intimate (Booth, 1972). In a study of the aged, Marjorie Lowenthal and Clayton Haven (1968) found that females were more likely to have a confidant than males, and that the younger the respondents the more pronounced the differences between males and females in this regard. Moreover, among women, husbands were least frequently mentioned as confidants, while among males, wives were most frequently so designated (p. 28). The nature of such female friendships is strongly rooted in the gender role stereotype.

Girls are not encouraged to participate in games that foster cooperation and camaraderie. More importantly, from adolescence females are taught that their major task is to outshine other members of their sex sufficiently to attract and then hold the best possible mate. In centering the female's self-definition around that of the male she will eventually attract and wed, the feminine role encourages a kind of constant competition between all members of the sex; the most important aspect of their entire lives rests directly on a never-ending war of all against all. We have all heard the stereotype that women "hate" other women. Unlike the kind of competition fostered among males, this in no way entails group cooperation for the purpose of competing. Indeed, best friends among young females often specifically and explicitly exempt the realm of "boys" from their friendship. Males will usually avoid dating a friend's girl friend, to preclude rejection by peers. Females are bound by no such code. From early childhood females learn to size themselves up relative to other females, especially in appearance and "charm," and this habit becomes lifelong for most (Pogrebin, 1972). When matrons enter a party, while their spouses eyeball the other sex they scrutinize the "competition," namely, members of their own sex, always insecure lest they lose their mate to a younger or better looking woman. The clothing and cosmetic industries have been extraordinarily successful in extracting huge sums of money from females for constant fashion changes precisely because of this mentality.

The isolation caused by this orientation is further encouraged by the isolation of the daily activities of the housewife. Each little nuclear family lives in its own "cell"—be it a 3-room apartment or a 20-room mansion—and each is more or less self-contained as to the tools and appliances needed for its functioning. Housewives need not cooperate with any other females to accomplish their daily tasks, except perhaps in rare emergencies. The result is that the only females many housewives know are the wives of their husbands' friends and the mothers of their children's playmates, with whom they may or may not have much in common personally. Tied to their homes and to a heavy, time-consuming schedule of household and child-rearing duties, many women have little opportunity to meet other females who share their own interests and points of view, as distinct from those of other family members. It is here that the female's submergence of her own identity in those of her husband and offspring becomes most evident and most costly.

Against all these odds, most females do get to know other females and form close friendships. Housewives often find that they have a lot in common with their husbands' friends' wives and their children's playmates' mothers, if for no other reason than that they are all in the same leaky boat. Especially as children grow older, females get out of the house and join voluntary organizations where they meet others with similar interests. Increasingly, they are going to school or to work and finding friends there. Because the feminine gender role encourages women to express their emotions, needs, and problems without feeling threatened, when and if they get beyond worrying about competition over appearance and males the way is clear for a deep, intimate association. Females talk to females about the males they love—not about those with whom they have had fleeting and casual relations. They discuss their own dreams and insecurities, their marital and even sexual problems (often to the profound embarrassment of their mates, if they discover it). The kaffeeklatsch, afternoon of shopping, or weekly bridge game is often an excuse to gather and talk rather than an activity for its own sake. The telephone has greatly aided such interaction among isolated housewives and, in the process, has spawned its share of male jokes about the female's presumably excessive use of that instrument.

Ironically, some of those very qualities that handicap females most in the world of work and in interactions with males enable them to experience far richer interactions with others of their own sex. Precisely because of their insecurities and general feelings of inferiority and incompetence, it is possible for them to avoid power plays, dominance, ego trips, and abstracted intellectualizing in their interactions, while openness, empathy, and compassion can readily flourish. However, all of this is possible only *if and when* they surmount the initial hurdle of competing over appearance and male attention. Nowhere is this more evident than in the relative ease with which the growing numbers of feminist "rap groups" have been able to elicit their members' deepest feelings, compared to the great difficulty experienced by the few male groups that have attempted to do the same.

Before leaving the subject of same-sex friendships, the findings of a laboratory experiment conducted by Elizabeth Aries (1977), in which all-male and all-female groups comprised of white, middle-class college students spent one and one-half hours getting to know group members, are worth reviewing. Among these findings were the following:

1. ". . . all-male groups established a more stable dominance order over time than all-female groups" (p. 294).
2. "Significantly more interaction was addressed to the group as a whole in the all-male groups than in the all-female groups" (p. 294).
3. "Men in the all-male groups talked very little of themselves, their feelings, or of their relationships with persons of significance to them. In the all-female groups . . . members shared a great deal of information about themselves, their feelings, their homes, and their relationships with family, friends, and lovers" (p. 295).
4. "One of the greatest concerns expressed by members of the all-male groups was where they stood in relation to each other. . . . The themes of superiority and aggression were often merged in the male groups." These traits were not manifested by the all-female groups (p. 296).
5. The content of their discussions differed too, with "more frequent male references . . . for sports and amusements, physical hostility, action, and the category describing what someone may have seen, read, or heard" (p. 296).
6. "Stylistically the male and female groups differed: . . . males engaged in dramatizing and story telling, jumping from one anecdote to another, and achieving a camaraderie and closeness through the sharing of stories and laughter. Females discussed one

topic for a half hour or more, revealing more feelings, and gaining a closeness through more intimate self-revelation" (p. 296).

In short, Aries found "the themes of intimacy and interpersonal relations for women, and themes of competition and status for men" (p. 296).

Sexual "Deviance" and Gender Roles

The term "sexual deviance" covers a multitude of behaviors which share in common only the fact that a particular society at a moment in history defines them as "abnormal," "wrong," and often illegal. According to the laws of contemporary America, about the only nondeviant form of sexual behavior is genital intercourse between a male and female married to one another. Our social mores do not really consider such things as masturbation, adultery, premarital and extra-marital intercourse, and heterosexual oral-genital contact as "sexually deviant," although some of these are not condoned behaviors, either. Prostitution and pornography are considered "more deviant" and homosexuality, transvestism, sodomy, rape, self-exposure, sadomasochism, and other fetishisms are "very deviant" (Gagnon & Simon, 1967). It is impossible and possibly irrelevant to explore all these varied expressions of human sexuality in the context of a book on the sociology of gender roles. However, some of these types of behaviors are probably strongly affected by gender role stereotypes and warrant discussion here.

There is no such thing as a particular expression of human sexuality that is universally "normal" or "natural"; deviant and nondeviant forms alike are learned behaviors (Marmor, 1971, p. 166). When we speak of "sexual deviance" we do not mean the same thing as when we use the term "pathology." The latter implies that the pathological individual is "sick" or "unnatural," and sick people generally want to be and ought to be "cured" if possible. The former term simply connotes that the deviant is doing something that most people in the society define as bad or wrong; from the vantage point of the deviant that is no reason in and of itself to change. Indeed, today the term "variant life-styles," especially with reference to homosexuality, may be used rather than deviance.

Broadly speaking, in this country today the mores (although not yet the laws) accept as "normal" adult sexuality almost any behavior between consenting members of the two sexes that does not inflict pain and is not directly sold for money. This is the message taught directly and indirectly to members of our society, and most behave in this manner most of the time. What is problematic is why some do not, and part of the answer lies in the pressures exerted by the two gender role stereotypes, beginning in early childhood.

Males and females share some varieties of sexual deviance, but most types are more or less sex-specific. Homosexuality is engaged in by members of both sexes, although it is given a special name, lesbianism, among females. Heterosexual prostitution is primarily a female phenomenon; the male counterpart, the gigolo, is relatively rare and in most places is not even considered to be engaged in an illegal activity. On the other hand, homosexual prostitution is generally a male phenomenon. Rape is, of course, a male activity and so is transvestism, for all practical purposes. Pornography is more frequently consumed by males, but the subject matter is more often female. Finally, sadomasochism probably most frequently follows the pattern of a male sadist and a female masochist, although the converse is by no means unknown.

Most research and writing pertaining to homosexuality has concerned itself with the psychodynamics of the origins of this form of "deviance" as understood on the highly suspect basis of clinical samples. Even in this corpus of work, however, there seems to be little agreement. Moreover, until the past few years, virtually all professional attention was focused on the male. In the decade of the 1970s more material has begun to appear about lesbians. First, there was a spate of personal accounts written by radical feminist lesbians (Abbott & Love, 1972; Aldrich, 1972; Damon, 1970; Koedt, 1972; Martin & Lyon, 1972a, 1972b; Shelley, 1970, 1971). More recently research studies have begun to appear (e.g., Chafetz et al., 1976; Rosen, 1974; Hedblom, 1972, 1973). It is clear that our society and the professionals it supports react far more strongly to male than to female homosexuality. Indeed, there has been scarcely any recognition that lesbians exist in any numbers worthy of note. The major reason for this one-sided view of homosexuality probably resides in the fact that society places a higher value on masculinity than on femininity. Males form a superior caste, and "defections" from masculinity appear less comprehensible and more reprehensible than parallel behavior by females (Lehne, 1976). Moreover, male homosexuality is often more public than female, and therefore most of the arrests for this activity are male. In addition (as discussed in Chapter 3), the masculine gender role is learned in such a way that males tend to experience far more insecurity about it than do females about their gender role. Since most professionals who study sexual deviance have been male (like the police who arrest homosexuals), their own insecurities might be responsible for the lopsided attention that has been given to homosexuality among members of their own sex.

Popular imagination depicts the male homosexual as "effete" or "feminine" in appearance and behavior; homosexuality and a limp wrist are almost synonymous to Americans. Many even confuse homosexuality with transvestism or female impersonation. In fact the latter are often not homosexual at all, while the former more often than not are quite "masculine" in demeanor. Similarly, popular imagination pictures lesbians as "bull dykes" who are very masculine in behavior and appearance. "Queens" and "bull dykes" do exist, but they comprise a small, if conspicuous, proportion of practicing homosexuals. Homosexuals are homosexual because they react more positively (that is, are attracted more) to members of their own sex than to the other one. What possible reason would they have for being attracted to an impersonator of the other sex rather than a member of that sex? From the perspective of a gender *role* orientation, homosexuals are drawn to members of their own sex because they find their behavior more appealing, and/or they reject those of the other sex because the behaviors and attitudes characteristic of that sex are in some way offensive or repellent to them. The research evidence, however, demonstrates that neither male nor female homosexuals dislike members of the other sex any more than their heterosexual counterparts do (see Chafetz et al., 1976, chap. 7; Lehne, 1976, p. 68).

If we may believe lesbians' accounts of their own experiences (Martin & Lyon, 1972a), not infrequently at the outset of a relationship one partner will assume the "butch" or stereotyped masculine role, the other the "femme" or stereotyped feminine role. They do so because they too have learned the stereotypes about lesbians. However, in lasting relationships (often characteristic of lesbians although somewhat less so of male homosexuals), such role-playing tends over time to decrease and eventually disappear. More systematic research supports this conclusion (Chafetz et al., 1976, chap. 9). Most writers on the subject seem to agree that lesbians, like "straight" females, enter "love" relationships before they find themselves actively engaged in sexual behavior (Hedblom, 1972; Martin & Lyon, 1972b, p. 75; Simon & Gagnon, 1967, p. 251; Chafetz et al., 1976, chap. 8). Indeed, many lesbians are sexually passive, disinterested, even frigid before they find themselves in a close relationship with another female. In short, they have internalized the feminine role injunctions concerning sexuality. From their study of a "small sample" of lesbians, William Simon and John Gagnon conclude:

> Most lesbians, apparently, are not exempt from the constraints and norms that regulate the development of female sexuality in general. This appears to be particularly true of the timing or phasing of entry into active sexual roles, as well as of the quality of relationships required to facilitate the entry (1967, p. 253).

Moreover, these same authors found that entry into lesbianism was rarely contingent upon "seduction" by an older woman (see also Chafetz et al., 1976, chap. 8). In short, females become lesbians primarily because they find they develop more meaningful emotional attachments to other females than to males, and such relationships eventually come to be expressed in sexual terms. Given the problems endemic to male-female relationships discussed earlier in this chapter, it might be considered surprising that there are not many more lesbians, especially since open communication, emotional expression, an absence of exploitation, and real equality between partners is easier between two females than between a male and a female or two males.

In a comparative study of 65 homosexual and 81 heterosexual women, Chafetz et al. (1976) found that the lesbian women were more idealistic about sexual relationships than their straight counterparts. In addition, lesbians were highly sensitive to the tendencies of males to fail to treat females as equals, to force women into stereotyped roles, and to relate to females as sex objects. Lesbians claimed that sexual relations ought to be predicated on love relationships, but typical masculine behavior makes it difficult to love males. Heterosexual women were nearly equally negative in their assessments of males, but they were willing to accept males as sexual partners in exchange for a variety of goods and services, as well as social acceptability. The major drawbacks of a lesbian life-style, therefore, are the societal definitions which label it as sick, bad, or illegal and the resultant abuse and discrimination lesbians face outside of their own community. These disadvantages probably function as powerful preventatives for most females in translating friendship into a sexual relationship (Shelley, 1970; Damon, 1970; Chafetz et al., 1976, chaps. 6 and 8).

Female homosexuality thus often reflects an attempt to fulfill the feminine role injunction to base sexuality on the prior formation of an emotional attachment, but its male counterpart tends to reflect the very different injunctions that arise from the masculine stereotype. Compared to lesbians, male homosexuals seem to be less frequently involved in a long-term, loving dyad. Their sexual encounters, like those of "straight" males, are likely to be many, fleeting, and exploitative. The one-night stand resulting from a pickup at a gay bar, or what one author referred to as a "market mentality," is far more typical of male than female homosexuals (Hooker, 1967, pp. 176-77); so too is the seduction of an adolescent by an older man. In general their behavior reflects the masculine emphasis on sex divorced from emotional commitment; sex used for status, dominance, and so forth (Simon & Gagnon, 1970). The male homosexual may be narcissistic, sometimes engaging in long hours of body-building exercises; he is often the picture of robust masculinity. In fact, many of the societies in which male homosexuality has been relatively widespread and overt have been those most dedicated to the sexual caste system and a masculine mystique, including ancient Greece (especially warlike Sparta), Imperial Germany, and Imperial Britain in the Victorian era. It is possible too that male homosexuality reflects a need on the part of some males to be the object of sexual desire. Females have been trained to suppress their desire for males, or at least not to demonstrate it overtly. The more narcissistic the male, the more he might experience such a need, and therefore the greater the likelihood that he would turn to other males for its fulfillment.

Male homosexuals who play a more "feminine" role (at the extreme, "queens"), along with transvestites, who are not homosexual, are often subject to cruelty and exploitation at the hands of straight males and even "masculine" homosexuals. These are the real sellouts to their superior caste position. Their behavior may reflect a feeling that only in assuming the outward appearance and mannerisms of females are they free to engage in the kinds of emotional expression barred to "masculine" males. At any rate, they are more visible to the general public, which thus mistakes them for the norm.

The transsexual, who is sometimes mistaken as a homosexual, represents the epitome of the negative effects of gender roles on sexuality. Transsexuals (almost always males) are those who choose to undergo hormone treatment and surgery in order to become, physically, members of the other sex. They claim that they really *are* members of the sex into which they are changing but were trapped at birth in the "wrong body." If we had no gender role stereotypes, and people were able to express their own personalities freely, irrespective of sex, there would be no need to change one's body in order to express one's "true self."

Male prostitution is generally homosexual in nature and takes particular advantage of the more "feminine" homosexuals. To be more precise, the patron is homosexual, although the seller or prostitute may not be, indeed usually is not (Reiss, 1967). Typically, the prostitute is a lower-class male, often an adolescent and, increasingly, a runaway, who engages in this activity as a quick, easy way to earn money. He strictly limits his behavior to an active role, refusing to receive sexual pleasure in return. By so doing he is able to maintain a self-identity as heterosexual (Reiss, 1967). Not infrequently such encounters (as portrayed in the movie *The Midnight Cowboy)* end in the beating and robbery of the homosexual patron, who, given his inability to call upon the police, is completely defenseless. In behaving this way, the prostitute reaffirms to himself his own "masculinity." This situation arises for male homosexuals but not for the female counterparts, primarily because of the males' "marketplace mentality" concerning sex.

Homosexual rape also casts an interesting light on the masculine gender role. This behavior has grown to nearly epidemic proportions in many of our nation's prisons. A study of this phenomenon in one prison system by Alan Davis (1970) shows that the victims are generally young, relatively small males who have committed minor offenses. Their aggressors are older, larger, and guilty of more major transgressions. Most crucially, the rapist does not define himself as homosexual. Indeed, he does not even see himself as engaging in a homosexual act. The author states that this "seems to be based upon his startlingly primitive view of sexual relationships, one that defines as male whichever partner is aggressive and as homosexual whichever partner is passive" (pp. 122-23).

Male heterosexual prostitution is a very different kind of phenomenon. The male prostitute, or gigolo, is, in the most fundamental sense, betraying the masculine stereotype. He is doing so in two ways: by functioning as an economic dependent of a female and by acting as the sexual object and recipient of a female's initiative. It is likely that few males stand lower in prestige in the masculine world than the gigolo, except in some subcultures where the behavior is defined as a "con" and perceived as an acceptable form of exploitation of females.

Unlike lesbians, female prostitutes have been the subject of much discourse for literally eons. They seem to simultaneously intrigue and disgust members of society, yet no form of "sexual deviance" arises so completely from either gender role as this (Nadle, 1970; Strong, 1970). When mother and Ann Landers tell teen-age Jane that if she "gives" her boyfriend "everything" he will have no "reason" to marry her, they are teaching her, albeit subtly and usually unconsciously, to trade her sexual "favors" for economic support. In a thousand ways females are taught to view themselves as sexual objects and informed that males relate to them in these terms. Moreover, they are seriously handicapped in an effort to earn a decent living in most legitimate occupations. It is hardly surprising, then, that even some well-educated females take the relatively small step of translating these messages into a decision to make a living by being sexual objects, namely, going into prostitution. Whether she is a $100-per-hour call girl or a $10-per-job whore, the prostitute is selling femininity and a willingness to be and do that which their clients are often too afraid to request from their mates. The male purchases not merely a willing and sometimes glamorous body to use as his fantasies dictate but often a "sympathetic" companion to assuage his loneliness and to listen to his problems, his hang-ups, his hatreds. The fact that he is usually married underscores the nature of much of what passes for love and communication between spouses. The only disgrace he faces from his peers is the fact that he can't exploit a female in this manner for free (see Laws & Schwartz, 1977, pp. 180-96 for a good, brief discussion of prostitution).

Many prostitutes have male "pimps" who protect them from abuse by clients, procure clients for them, manage their finances, and handle their legal problems. The pimp is financially dependent on the prostitute, with whom he may or may not also have a sexual relationship (not surprisingly, a number of prostitutes are lesbian in personal preference). However, the pimp usually has nearly total domination of the life of the female (and often a number of them) and is thus able to maintain his self-definition as masculine. It is not uncommon for prostitutes to be drug addicts; some pimps are able to maintain tremendous power over such women by also serving as their supply source. Increasingly, prostitutes are also young runaways who seek the protection of streetwise pimps to afford them feelings of security (see Laws & Schwartz, 1977, pp. 196-200).

If female prostitution reflects the feminine role emphasis on woman as a sexual, exploitable object, so probably does sexual masochism. Females are socially devalued and taught to devalue themselves. In its extreme, the feminine stereotype teaches women that their bodies and their sexuality are dirty; that they exist primarily for the gratification of males; that they have little intrinsic worth. What more crystalline expression for this could there be than receiving sexual gratification through pain? To a greater or lesser degree, most females have masochistic personalities, a characteristic well noted, if poorly explained, by Freud and his followers. Many seem to enjoy playing the martyr role—the sacrificing mother (Mother Portnoy) or wife who claims her "reward" is to be ignored and unloved. Like other suppressed peoples, females tend to turn their frustrations, anger, and hatred not toward those who directly create the problems and who are often members of the superior caste, but inward, upon themselves. Such a trait, common in mild form to perhaps most females, is manifested in its extreme as sexual masochism.

Sadism, or the propensity to derive sexual pleasure by inflicting pain on others, can be viewed as an extreme outgrowth of the masculine role. Earlier in this chapter it was mentioned that males tend to view sex, to a greater or lesser degree, as a tool for expressing power and dominance. In its extreme this mentality is manifested in rape. The rape of a stranger may be interpreted as a male's proclamation that he can exercise his will over any member of the female sex he selects, and, therefore, it asserts his superiority over the entire sex. Our movies, books, and folklore are filled with stories in which the hero "subdues" an independent, unresponsive heroine by the force of "THE KISS," or a more or less explicit rape. Male fantasy pictures the heroine as melting in response, totally captivated by the hero and henceforth completely attached and subservient to him. The same mentality is reflected in the often-heard opinion that all an aggressive woman needs is "a good lay." In very recent years, spurred largely by the Feminist Movement, public and scholarly attention alike have been drawn to the phenomenon of rape, its meaning, the treatment of the victim after the rape, and the outcome for the rapist. Susan Brownmiller's instant classic *Against Our Will* (1975) is an excellent source of detailed information on all aspects of this topic.

Until the recent establishment of rape crisis centers, inspired by the Feminist Movement, raped women frequently reported that male police officers, as well as the courts, treated them with marked contempt and disrespect, virtually blaming the victim for the crime. Such treatment has been sufficiently prevalent that many rapes, if not the majority of them, are never even reported to the police (see the discussion concerning the treatment of rape victims by the law in Chapter 4). This attitude toward rape victims was manifested in hideous form in Bangladesh (Goldman, 1972). During the civil war Pakistani soldiers raped nearly a quarter of a million women whose husbands refused after the war to accept the "damaged goods" back. For most of these females, this meant that they were faced with virtual starvation, and many responded by committing suicide. In fact, rape has, over the millenia, accompanied war. As Brownmiller (1975) points out, "War provides men with the perfect psychologic backdrop to give vent to their contempt for women. The very maleness of the military . . . confirms for men what they long suspect, that women are peripheral, irrelevant to the work that counts . . ." (pp. 24-25). Griffin (1975, p. 35) notes that "rape is a kind of terrorism which severely limits the freedom of women and makes women dependent on men" for protection against other men.

Combining this general mental orientation toward sex with the masculine emphasis on aggression and even violence, it is not difficult to see how some males would come to depend on producing pain in order to receive sexual gratification. Where members of the subordinate caste impotently turn their fury inward, those in the superordinate caste are in a position to externalize their frustrations and hostilities. Regardless of the source of such feelings, males can, if they choose, vent their fury on the other, physically weaker sex, an option not readily available to females.

Another form of sexual deviance, one which our society has only come to recognize as prevalent in the past two years or so, is incest. By far the most frequent forms of incest are those between fathers or stepfathers and daughters, uncles and nieces, or grandfathers and granddaughters; mother-son incest is rare. The average age of the girls is 13, of the men about 40 (Laws & Schwartz, 1977, p. 211). Judith Laws and Pepper Schwartz see this as yet one more way in which defenseless females are victimized sexually by males. Given the youth of the females, combined with the family relationship, such victimization may continue unreported for years. Indeed, when the incest is discovered, often both parents blame the girl by defining her as seductive and, rather than pressing chages against the male, they institutionalize the girl (Laws & Schwartz, p. 212).

The final form of "sexual deviance" to be discussed, pornography, is not really deviant at all. The primary consumers of pornographic materials have been males, homosexual and heterosexual alike. Perhaps this, too, results from an orientation to sexuality that is exploitative and basically divorced from considerations of the quality of interpersonal relationships, traits characteristic of the masculine but not the feminine stereotype. However, it could simply be a function of the double standard by which males receive fewer negative sanctions than females (and even some positive ones) for engaging in anything relating to sex. Moreover, until the liberalization of laws and mores pertaining to pornography and the concomitant increase in their availability, many males viewed the acquisition of pornographic materials as an illegal "adventure" designed to prove one's "bravery," hence "masculinity."

The subject matter of pornography consists of essentially four types of activities: heterosexual behavior (group or dyadic), lesbian activity, male homosexuality, and masturbation (mostly female). Heterosexual males will consume with equal relish material on heterosexual activity or that concerning females only (alone or in lesbian relationships); they are repulsed (and possibly threatened) by male homosexual material. Material that is devoid of females seems to appeal almost exclusively to male homosexuals. Male heterosexuals are predictably attracted to the female depicted in pornography, regardless of what she is doing or with whom she is doing it. What makes less sense is the fact that heterosexual female consumers also are "turned on" by the female figures. It appears that our cultural definition of females but not males as sex objects is so pervasive that women who would never engage in lesbian activities are sexually stimulated by consuming material depicting such behavior. In short, our culture has conditioned all of us, females as well as males (except homosexuals), to perceive the female form in terms of a stimulating sexual object.

Conclusions

This depressing litany of the effects of gender role stereotyping on a wide variety of primary relationships and on human sexual expression is somewhat exaggerated. This has been done in part as a response to the pervasive romanticization of such relationships. However, there can be little doubt that to varying degrees we all relate to other humans in a much constricted manner because of those cultural definitions of masculinity and femininity which have been emphasized and reinforced throughout our lives. We are none of us free to develop truly multifaceted personalities and behavior repertoires in relationship to a number of significant others. Nor are we free to develop our full potential as humans vis-à-vis other humans. Another conclusion may also be drawn from this discussion. It would appear that where femininity exacts a high price in the realm of functioning in instrumental roles outside the context of the home, masculinity extracts its greatest toll in the development of rewarding interpersonal relationships within and outside of the family. Were this book written a decade or more ago, it might well have ended on this bleak note. However, a number of recent developments encourage hope that the heavy burdens of the gender role status quo are decreasing. In the next and final chapter, these changes will be discussed.

References

Abbott, Sidney, and Love, Barbara. *Sappho Was a Right-on Woman: A Liberated View of Lesbianism.* New York: Stein & Day, 1972.

Aldrich, Ann. *Take a Lesbian to Lunch.* New York: MacFadden Bartell, 1972.

Aries, Elizabeth. "Male-Female Interpersonal Styles in All Male, All Female and Mixed Groups." In Alice Sargent (ed.), *Beyond Sex Roles,* pp. 292-99. St. Paul, Minn.: West Publishing Co., 1977.

Balswick, Jack, and Collier, James. "Why Husbands Can't Say 'I Love You.'" In Deborah David and Robert Brannon (eds.), *The Forty-Nine Percent Majority: The Male Sex Role,* pp. 58-59. Reading, Mass.: Addison-Wesley Publishing Co., 1976.

Bernard, Jessie. "The Paradox of the Happy Marriage." In Vivian Gornick and Barbara Moran, *Woman in Sexist Society,* pp. 145-62. New York: Signet Books, 1971.

Bernard, Jessie. *The Future of Marriage.* New York: Bantam Books, 1972.

Bernard Jessie. *Women, Wives, Mothers: Values and Options.* Chicago: Aldine Publishing Co., 1975.

Bird, Caroline. *Born Female: The High Cost of Keeping Women Down.* New York: David McKay Co., 1968.

Booth, Alan. "Sex and Social Participation." *American Sociological Review* 37 (April 1972): 183-93.

Brenton, Myron. *The American Male.* Greenwich, Conn.: Fawcett Publications, Inc., 1966.

Brownmiller, Susan. *Against Our Will: Men, Women and Rape.* New York: Simon & Schuster, 1975.

Chafetz, Janet S.; Beck, Paula; Sampson, Patricia; West, Joyce, and Jones, Bonnye. *Who's Queer? A Study of Homo and Heterosexual Women.* Sarasota, Fla.: Omni Press, 1976.

Damon, Gene. "The Least of These: The Minority Whose Screams Haven't Yet Been Heard." In Robin Morgan (ed.), *Sisterhood Is Powerful,* pp. 279-306. New York: Vintage Books, 1970.

Davis, Alan. "Sexual Assaults in the Philadelphia Prison System." In John Gagnon and William Simon (eds.), *The Sexual Scene,* pp. 107-24. Chicago: Aldine Publishing Co., 1970.

Dworkin, Rosalind J., and Chafetz, Janet S. "The Mop and the Mower: A Study of the Division of Labor Among White, Middle Class Spouses." Unpublished manuscript, University of Houston.

Farrell, Warren T. "Male Consciousness-Raising from a Sociological and Political Perspective." *Sociological Focus* 5 (Winter 1971-72): 19-28.

Fast, Julius. *The Incompatibility of Men and Women.* New York: Avon Books, 1971.

Fasteau, Marc. "Men: Why Aren't We Talking?" *Ms.,* July 1972, p. 16.

Fasteau, Marc F., "Men as Parents." In Deborah David and Robert Brannon (eds.), *The Forty-Nine Percent Majority: The Male Sex Role,* pp. 60-65. Reading, Mass.: Addison-Wesley Publishing Co., 1976.

Fein, Robert. "Examining the Nature of Masculinity." In Alice Sargent (ed.), *Beyond Sex Roles,* pp. 180-200. St. Paul, Minn.: West Publishing Co., 1977.

Firestone, Shulamith. *The Dialectic of Sex.* New York: Bantam Books, 1970.

Friedan, Betty. *The Feminine Mystique.* New York: Dell Publishing, 1963.

Friedman, Kathleen O'Ferrall. "The Image of Battered Women." *American Journal of Public Health* 67 (1977): 722-23.

Gagnon, John, and Simon, William. "Introduction: Deviant Behavior and Sexual Deviance." In Gagnon and Simon (eds.), *Sexual Deviance,* pp. 1-12. New York: Harper & Row, 1967.

Gavron, Hannah. *The Captive Wife: Conflicts of Housebound Mothers.* London: Routledge and Kegan Paul, 1966.

Gillespie, Dair L. "Who Has the Power? The Marital Struggle." *Journal of Marriage and the Family* 33 (August 1971): 445-58.

Goffman, Erving. *The Presentation of Self in Everyday Life.* Garden City, N.Y.: Doubleday Anchor Books, 1959.

Goldman, Joyce. "Women of Bangladesh." *Ms.,* August 1972, pp. 84-88.

Greer, Germaine. *The Female Eunuch.* New York: McGraw-Hill Book Co., 1970.

Griffin, Susan. "Rape: The All American Crime." In Jo Freeman (ed.), *Women: A Feminist Perspective,* pp. 24-39. Palo Alto, Calif.: Mayfield Publishing Co., 1975.

Grønseth, Erik. "The Husband Provider Role and Its Dysfunctional Consequences." *Sociological Focus* 5 (Winter 1971-72): 10-18.

Hacker, Helen M. "Women as a Minority Group." *Social Forces* 30 (1951): 60-69.

Hedblom, Jack. "Social, Sexual, and Occupational Lives of Homosexual Women." *Sexual Behavior* 2 (October 1972): 33-37.

Hedblom, Jack. "Dimensions of Lesbian Sexual Experience." *Archives of Sexual Behavior* 2 (1973): 329-41.

Homans, George. *Social Behavior: Its Elementary Forms.* New York: Harcourt, Brace & World, 1961.

Hooker, Evelyn. "The Homosexual Community." In John Gagnon and William Simon (eds.), *Sexual Deviance,* pp. 167-84. New York: Harper & Row, 1967.

Jones, Beverly. "The Dynamics of Marriage and Motherhood." In Robin Morgan (ed.), *Sisterhood Is Powerful,* pp. 46-61. New York: Vintage Books, 1970.

Koedt, Anne. "Can Women Love Women?" *Ms.,* Spring 1972, pp. 117-21.

Laws, Judith Long. "A Feminist Review of Marital Adjustment Literature: The Rape of the Locke." *Journal of Marriage and the Family* 33 (August 1971): 483-516.

Laws, Judith, and Schwartz, Pepper. *Sexual Scripts: The Social Construction of Female Sexuality.* Hinsdale, Ill.: Dryden Press, 1977.

Lehne, Gregory. "Homophobia among Men." In Deborah David and Robert Brannon (eds.), *The Forty-Nine Percent Majority: The Male Sex Role,* pp. 66-88. Reading, Mass.: Addison-Wesley Publishing Co., 1976.

Lipman-Blumen, Jean. "Toward a Homosocial Theory of Sex Roles: An Explanation of Sex Segregation of Social Institutions." *Signs* 1 (Spring 1976): 15-31.

Lopata, Helena. *Occupation: Housewife.* New York: Oxford University Press, 1971.

Lowenthal, Marjorie Fiske, and Haven, Clayton. "Interaction and Adaptation: Intimacy as a Critical Variable." *American Sociological Review* 33 (February 1968): 20-30.

Marmor, Judd. "'Normal' and 'Deviant' Sexual Behavior." *Journal of the American Medical Association* 217 (July 12, 1971): 165-70.

Martin, Del, and Lyon, Phyllis. "Lesbian Love and Sexuality." *Ms.,* July 1972 (a) 74-77 and 123.

Martin, Del, and Lyon, Phyllis. *Lesbian/Woman.* New York: Bantam Books, 1972 (b)

Millett, Kate. *Sexual Politics.* Garden City, N.Y.: Doubleday Publishing Co., 1970.

Nadle, Marlene. "Prostitutes." In Sookie Stambler (ed.), *Women's Liberation: Blueprint for the Future,* pp. 51-56. New York: Ace Books, 1970.

Newcomb, T. M. *The Acquaintance Process.* New York: Holt Rinehart & Winston, 1961.

O'Neill, Nena, and O'Neill, George. *Open Marriage: A New Life Style for Couples.* New York: M. Evans & Co., 1972.

Papanek, Hanna. "Men, Women, and Work: Reflections on the Two-Person Career." *American Journal of Sociology,* 78 (January 1973): 852-72.

Peck, Ellen. *The Baby Trap.* New York: Pinnacle Books, 1971.

Pogrebin, Letty Cottin. "Competing with Women." *Ms.,* July 1972, pp. 78-81 and 131.

Reiss, Albert J., Jr. "The Social Integration of Queers and Peers." In John Gagnon and William Simon (eds.), *Sexual Deviance,* pp. 197-228. New York: Harper & Row, 1967.

Rosen, David. *Lesbianism: A Study of Female Homosexuality.* Springfield, Ill.: Charles C Thomas Publisher, 1974.

Safilios-Rothschild, Constantina. "Companionate Marriages and Sexual Inequality: Are They Compatible?" In Safilios-Rothschild (ed.), *Toward a Sociology of Women,* pp. 63-70. Lexington, Mass.: Xerox College Publishing Co., 1972.

Safilios-Rothschild, Constantina. *Love, Sex and Sex Roles.* Englewood Cliffs, N.J.: Prentice-Hall, 1977.

Scanzoni, John. *Sexual Bargaining: Power Politics in the American Marriage.* Englewood Cliffs, N.J.: Prentice-Hall, 1972.

Scanzoni, Letha, and Scanzoni, John. *Men, Women and Change: A Sociology of Marriage and the Family.* New York: McGraw Hill Book Co., 1976.

Sexton, Patricia Cayo. *The Feminized Male.* New York: Vintage Books, 1969.

Shelley, Martha. "Lesbianism and the Women's Liberation Movement." In Sookie Stambler (ed.), *Women's Liberation: Blueprint for the Future,* pp. 123-29. New York: Ace Books, 1970.

Shelley, Martha. "Women of Lesbos." In *Up Against the Wall, Mother: On Women's Liberation.* Beverly Hills, Calif.: Glencoe Press, 1971.

Simon, William, and Gagnon, John. "The Lesbians: A Preliminary Overview." In Gagnon and Simon (eds.), *Sexual Deviance,* pp. 247-82. New York: Harper & Row, 1967.

Simon, William, and Gagnon, John. "Psychosexual Development." In Gagnon and Simon (eds.), *The Sexual Scene,* pp. 23-41. Chicago: Aldine Publishing Co., 1970.

Stewart, Vivian. "Social Influences on Sex Differences in Behavior." In Michael Teitelbaum (ed.), *Sex Differences: Social and Biological Perspectives,* pp. 138-74. Garden City, N.Y.: Anchor Books, 1976.

Straus, Murray. "Sexual Inequality, Cultural Norms and Wife-Beating." In Jane Chapman and Margaret Gates (eds.), *Women into Wives: The Legal and Economic Impact of Marriage,* pp. 59-78. Beverly Hills, Calif.: Sage Publications, 1977.

Strong, Ellen. "The Hooker." In Robin Morgan (ed.), *Sisterhood Is Powerful,* pp. 289-97. New York: Vintage Books, 1970.

Tarvis, Carol, and Offir, Carole. *The Longest War: Sex Differences in Perspective.* New York: Harcourt Brace Jovanovich, 1976.

Thibault, J. W., and Kelly, H. H. *The Social Psychology of Groups.* New York: John Wiley & Sons, 1959.

Tiger, Lionel. *Men in Groups.* New York: Vintage Books, 1970.

Walum, Laurel R. *The Dynamics of Sex and Gender: A Sociological Perspective.* Chicago: Rand McNally & Co., 1977.

Chapter 6

Conclusion: Masculine/Feminine or Human?

It was the best of times, it was the worst of times; it was the age of wisdom, it was the age of foolishness; it was the epoch of belief, it was the epoch of incredulity; it was the season of Light; it was the season of Darkness; it was the spring of hope; it was the winter of despair; we had everything before us; we had nothing before us; we were all going direct to Heaven; we were all going direct the other way.

Charles Dickens, *A Tale of Two Cities* (1859)

In the same manner that Charles Dickens introduced his classic novel about the French Revolution, we can begin our discussion of the social ferment of the past decade and a half in our own society, especially as it pertains to changing gender roles. Dickens's message is that periods of radical social change are never easy for a society. They cause despair and frustration in proportion to the hopes they raise, and they spawn wickedness and stupidity to match the moral upsurge and intelligence that also emerge in such times. Times of social ferment force members of a society to examine the presuppositions upon which they have based their lives and the collective activities of the whole, causing people to question their deepest values, their most habitual responses, and the very reasons for their existence.

221

In the decade of the 1960s, a time of social ferment, the legitimacy of virtually all social institutions came under question. Only in the closing years of that decade, however, did gender roles and the sexual caste system begin to be subjected to widespread examination. Because of this relatively late start compared to the examination and critique of many other social phenomena, such as racism, poverty, and war, issues pertaining to the gender role status quo remain hotly debated even now, when many other issues have slowly faded from mass public consciousness. (This is not to say that the problems concerning these issues were "solved," however.) Beginning only in about 1967 or 1968 a social movement took form which questioned the legitimacy of the gender roles and the sexual caste system—in short, the status quo as it pertains to both masculinity and femininity. By the mid-1970s a vocal countermovement had also formed. Far from quieting down, social, legal, and political ferment on this topic continues unabated in the late 1970s.

Social change is a difficult concept with which to come to grips. How much change in institutional structures, norms, values, and individual behavior needs to occur before we can say that there has really been a radical alteration in the status quo? Incremental, evolutionary change is always occurring in every society, no matter how static that society may appear on the surface. The total effect of such changes, however, may only amount to "adjustments" by which the most fundamental aspects of the status quo are buttressed. Such, for instance, was the basic impact of the New Deal vis-à-vis capitalism; changes necessitated by economic disaster served in the long run to give new life and vigor to the institution of private enterprise. Moreover, there is a very real question as to whether it is possible for social institutions to alter themselves radically in response to social strains or new social currents, or whether such change can only result from conflict between these institutions and forces outside the system. Will those who profit from the status quo willingly alter the situation in any way that might seriously undermine their own position, or must such changes be wrested from them by the "have-nots"?

Most of this book has been devoted to documenting the existence of gender role stereotypes and a sexual caste system, examining the many ways by which they are reinforced and passed on through the generations, suggesting who profits from them, and delineating the individual as well as social costs of the gender role status quo. The future of our species depends in large measure on our collective ability in the next several decades to control our consumption of nonrenewable resources, prevent further ecological deterioration, and avoid war, especially a nuclear holocaust. To accomplish these in the context of modern technology, our age-old notions of masculinity and femininity must be fundamentally altered. Moreover, given the fact that our major social institutions reflect and support the gender role stereotypes and profit from their continuation, to the extent that such stereotypes significantly change, our institutions will be altered in profound ways. In short, such changes, if they occur, will constitute a veritable "revolution." The questions for this final chapter thus concern those trends already existing in American society that may encourage or discourage such gender role changes. What are they? Who is involved in them? What kinds of changes are likely to produce what kinds of results?

Before attempting the difficult task of surveying the contemporary scene for indications of such trends, a crucial point that is all too frequently ignored in sociological writing and even activistic planning must be made. This is the need for utopian thinking. Change does not mean the same as progress; our society has too long obscured the difference, to its own detriment. When social institutions, norms, or values are altered, things do not become ipso facto better. First of all, what is defined as better or progress is a matter of values, of who is doing the defining. From the vantage point of one person's or group's values and/or interests, a given change may represent progress; to someone else it spells disaster. When we actively engage in efforts to bring about some sort of change in the status quo we should have in mind some idea of what we would define as progress, or a better state of affairs. In other words, it is not enough to reject the present. To guide the future we need a positive image of how it might look if our goals and values should be embodied. That is utopian thinking.

In the context of this book, understanding the damage created by our current gender role stereotypes constitutes an impetus to change the situation. Next we need to develop some alternatives: a utopia. This cannot consist merely of concrete suggestions like "equal pay for equal work" and more day-care centers, important as such things may be. We need a vision of what it would mean to be a society comprised not of feminine and masculine creatures, but of humans. The truth of the matter is that we have very little understanding of what it means to be human, divorced from notions of masculinity and femininity. Traditionally, "human" has largely meant masculine; all too often today we make the same error, and, for many, women's liberation becomes merely a question of how females can acquire those prerogatives traditionally allocated to males. I for one do not wish to avoid the disadvantages of the feminine role simply to be burdened with those of the masculine role. Therefore, in reviewing recent trends it is important to search for an emerging definition of humanness and to try to envision a world in which we might want to live in the magical year 2000.

A Brief History Lesson

Before we can assess where we might be going, we must examine where we have been and are. In the preceding chapters historical changes that have occurred in recent decades and even centuries have been suggested in passing. These will be brought together here to develop a somewhat more systematic picture.

The secular changes brought about by the Industrial Revolution of the 19th century and the postindustrial "revolution" of the 20th have profoundly altered the way in which members of Western societies function in virtually every aspect of their social existence. Some significant changes even date back to the sharp increase in trade and urbanization in Northwestern Europe in the 17th century. Those most relevant for our purpose include: (1) changing demographic rates, (2) change in family structure and functioning, (3) alterations in the nature of productive work, (4) sharply increased production in the quantity of goods and services available to most members of society, and (5) the development of new forms of institutional organization. These are all highly interrelated phenomena; incremental changes in one tend to produce alterations in the others which, in turn, feed back in an almost perpetually accelerating progression.

Before about 1650 Europeans and the few "Americans" typically lived in extended family networks in primarily rural settings. The birth and death rates were very high; it was not uncommon for a woman to bear 10 or 15 children, of whom only a couple would survive to reach reproductive age themselves. Thus, the rate of growth of the total human population was incredibly slow. The population of the entire world in 1650 totaled only about a half a billion, of which only about 100 million inhabited Europe and North America. In the next three centuries the world population increased sixfold, while that of Europe and North America increased to more than eight times what it had been (Wrong, 1968, p. 13). This demographic "revolution" began primarily because better sanitation facilities and methods of food distribution resulted in a slow decline of the death rate, while the birth rate remained stable. Death rates dropped off even more sharply in the West with the advent of modern medicine in the first part of the century and in the so-called underdeveloped countries after World War II. In Europe and the United States birth rates also finally began to decline, and during the Great Depression of the 1930s total population actually decreased in some Western nations (for a discussion of the effects of these trends on women specifically, see Ridley, 1972).

Many demographers attribute the declining birth rate in the West to the combined effects of urbanization and industrialization. On the farm, children were an economic asset and cost very little to rear. After the passage of child-labor laws, the situation for urban dwellers was reversed: children earned nothing and cost a lot. In addition, parents began to understand that they could provide the resources for their children to become upwardly mobile, but only if they kept their families small. Members of urban industrialized societies ceased, by and large, to produce large numbers of children because they were provided with increasingly effective birth control methods, were assured that most children would survive to adulthood, and were offered the prospect of economically prosperous offspring. Families became as we know them today: small, mobile units free to follow economic opportunities from city to city, leaving kin behind in the process.

While families were shrinking and becoming geographically mobile, they were also losing most of their functions. In the eons before modern times, families functioned as a productive *unit* in which all but the very youngest were involved in activities needed to supply the goods and services upon which their lives depended. Training and "education" were part of life; children learned from older people—parents, kin, and older siblings—in the course of their everyday lives. The Industrial Revolution took production out of the family, moved it spatially, and later restricted the entry of children into the factory. Thus one's life work (other than housekeeping for females) could no longer be learned within the bosom of the family. Moreover, the age at which it was learned was increasingly postponed. Together, childhood and adolescence were created as a long period of dependence without serious responsibility.

The nature of productive labor also changed with industrialization. Most people were henceforth restricted to a single, repetitive task, usually requiring little skill and, increasingly over time, little physical strength. Nothing in most jobs intrinsically required one sex rather than the other. A minority controlled the daily functioning of the work force in the ever more complex, immense, and powerful bureaucratic structures of technocratic society. Organizations came to "own" their employees, especially those at the top, moving them at will and often impinging on many aspects of their private lives. Economic institutions and bureaucracies developed their own paradigm of rationality based on a cost accounting ethos in which corporate profits and the machinelike efficiency necessary to produce them became the most important considerations, even long after individual entrepreneurs had ceased to own companies (Harrington, 1969, chap. 1; Roszak, 1969, chap. 1). For society as a whole this became translated into an overwhelming emphasis on a rising gross national product and a balanced budget.

"Rational" administration, coupled with science, has brought us to a stage of technological development that is truly astounding. It has created the weaponry to destroy ourselves, a glut of goods designed to be replaced every three years (to "keep the economy going"), foul air and water, and the marvelous potential to someday shape our lives to gain maximum personal fulfillment. Technology has opened up the future possibility and, to a considerable extent, the present reality of large quantities of leisure and a decent standard of living for all. Everyone need not be productive today, and producers need not spend 70 or more hours a week at their labor, as they did in the past. But the system that has done this has allowed a sizable minority to continue to exist in poverty. It has led many of us to lose our capacity to enjoy leisure. It has provided most of us with goods that obviate the necessity of hard work and increase the potential pleasure we can derive from our hobbies and pastimes, but it has ruined the land, air, and water we would want to use in doing so. It has frustrated, bored, and alienated many of those who staff its assembly lines and offices. In short, our species has created a radically new world for itself but has not yet learned how to use it to develop its human potentials; it is strangling us rather than being controlled by us.

While the very foundations of human existence have been altering in such radical ways, our gender role stereotypes, as we have had ample opportunity to note, have long remained pretty much the same as those extant eons ago. Females are still enjoined to devote their lives to families, shrunken and stripped of functions though they may be, and despite the fact that women may expect to live for at least 40 years after their children are in school full time. They are not taught to develop the attributes that would enable them to function well in the economy, although those attributes are irrelevant to sex. Males are still enjoined to be rugged, aggressively competitive, and productive in a nation gagging on its affluence, a world threatened by nuclear holocaust, and a society ruled by all-powerful institutions that are no longer under identifiable human control. We are enjoined to do things with the bulk of our lives that no longer make any sense. Indeed, in some ways, at least the feminine role is ironically more "traditional" than tradition itself! To understand this we need to look more closely at the recent past, particularly the post-World War II history of our society.

Demographers are hard pressed to explain the postwar "baby boom" of the late 1940s and 1950s in this, the most industrialized nation of the world, but it really isn't difficult to understand if we go back a bit in time. Beginning with the Seneca Falls Convention of 1848, or even earlier with Mary Wollstonecraft's *A Vindication of the Rights of Women* published in 1792, women's rights has been a public issue. The history of the first Woman's Rights Movement is as frustrating to read about as it is glorious to contemplate (Flexner, 1975; O'Neill, 1969; Sinclair, 1965). The important fact for our purposes is that gradually this social movement spawned many young women who, especially after World War I, were anxious to create a place for themselves outside the home. During the closing years of the 19th century and first two decades of the 20th, educational institutions and many occupations and professions were opened to women for the first time, and the vote was finally gained. The cultural heroine of young women in the era between the two World Wars became the ambitious career woman, as demonstrated by the popular movies of this era. Even if most females continued to marry, have children, and stay home, models of females doing other things were evident and increasingly acceptable.

Women entered the job market in tremendous numbers and attained positions new to their sex during World War II when *man*power was short. It looked like a new era had finally arrived for females. The very small families characteristic of the depression years, coupled with new employment opportunities, seemed to herald a time when females could truly enter the mainstream of society. Then V-J Day arrived and the soldiers came home. Ultimately millions of women were fired from their jobs to be replaced by these veterans, even though many of them had earlier expressed a desire to continue working after the war (Trey, 1972). In the two years following the termination of hostilities, the number of females in the labor force declined by about two million. The marriage rate soared and so did the birth rate, as if to make up for lost time. But it did more than that. The middle-class family that had two children in the 1930s gave way a decade or so later to an ever-expanding number of families averaging almost four children.

With the help of a more advanced, less labor-intensive technology developed during the war, the economy had little need for female employees over and above males. Moreover, it did not take industry long to discover that prosperous families with females at home producing lots of children spelled marvelous profits. If the housewife was bored and frustrated in her suburban "cell," she would buy goods in those shiny new suburban shopping centers to relieve her frustrations (bad moods could always be changed with the acquisition of a new hat, it was suggested). Insecure females, isolated in their homes, could be counted on to try that new hair product or deodorant that promised a "new, more lovable you." Create a product, create a new female insecurity, and increase your profits. Children? You can't deny them the many material benefits technology has to offer. And so we got the feminine mystique, which encourages females to stay home and have children—created by industry and Madison Avenue, nurtured by all the media, supported by "science," and believed by almost everyone: housewifery, motherhood, but, most of all, *consuming* is FULFILLMENT. Never before had these tasks been expected to alone fill the lives of most females; never before had they been so romanticized and glamorized. But then, never had they been so profitable, either.

The so-called "sexual revolution" that was also occurring in these years, far from liberating females, bound them more tightly to the mystique. Sure, women, like men, were freed to enjoy sex, and thank heaven for that. But mostly this simply meant that the housewife had to spend the money and effort to appear the glamorous mistress to her husband after spending up to 90 hours a week on household drudgery. "Respectable" women were freed to enjoy sex, but the price they paid was to add "sex object" to the list of their obligations to males.

What was happening to males during this period? The masculine mystique was little changed during any of the period under consideration. Perhaps males' dedication to work increased slightly, if for no other reason than to supply the funds for their burgeoning families' burgeoning consumption habits. Male executives were encouraged by the new human relations school of corporate management to develop some expressive skills in order to function better in bureaucratic settings, and these undoubtedly carried over to their private lives. Males were under increased pressure to perform well sexually in order to satisfy the newly liberated sexuality of their partners. Males, however, with crew-cut hair styles and attired in grey suits, white shirts, and nondescript ties, and tied to their corporate offices or an assembly line, continued to be suppressed by age-old notions of masculinity based essentially on an agrarian existence.

By the late fifties and early sixties some things started happening that were to burgeon, in a very few years, into a veritable social upheaval. One of the first of these things was that the postwar brides, now with children mostly grown and realizing that they still had 35 years or so to live, began returning to the job market to help the family acquire all the "goodies" shown on TV. In a decade the employed wife went from a statistical rarity to practically a majority. Likewise, women began returning to school in dramatically increasing numbers. But it was the children of this generation, the enormous generation of the baby boom now grown, who became most intimately involved in the social ferment of the 1960s.

Decade of Upheaval

Significant numbers of the baby-boom children took two directions upon reaching adolescence which, among other things, represented the start of an attempt to redefine traditional gender roles. Some males became members of the counterculture, which emphasized sensuality and emotional caring and expression. Many members of both sexes became active in a variety of social movements which served to develop and give expression to a social conscience. Both of these changes developed in part as direct reactions to the stifling existence these young people knew as children in affluent, middle-class homes, and in larger part as the logical expression of the point to which our society has come. For social scientists, the most appalling thing is that in the late fifties and early sixties the discipline apparently had no inkling of what was brewing; it expressed little more than smug satisfaction with the state of affairs that existed.

Given the isolated nuclear family and contemporary gender roles, parent-child relationships suffer from a variety of pressures tending to produce strain, as noted in the preceding chapter. First Elvis Presley and later acid rock and the Rolling Stones, marijuana, long hair on males—all of the symbols of the youth subculture—were designed to infuriate middle-class parents trapped in their own roles. If father and mother sought their vicarious thrills from junior's academic and economic successes and constantly applied pressure toward the accomplishment of these goals, what better rebellion than "turning on and dropping out"? If father were a chemical engineer, how better could you reject him than by turning anti-intellectual, rejecting science, and reading your stars? If mother wanted young Jane to snag a prosperous WASP lawyer, her daughter could say no by sleeping around and ending up living with a dropout, or better yet, a black man.

But mere rejection of parents cannot entirely explain the "youth phenomenon" that occurred in most industrial societies in the sixties and early seventies. The nature of the technocratic society in which this generation grew up was radically unlike that which existed in their parents' youth, and their parents' own behavior at least dimly reflected the changes that had occurred. Nurtured on a work ethic crucial to earlier stages of industrial development, the fathers continued to half-heartedly espouse productivity and economic success as the highest virtues. Yet increasingly the work week was shortened and the quantities of consumer goods available were vastly increased, along with the pressures to consume, and the parents' lives and behaviors reflected these phenomena. They pampered their children, gave in to their whims, supplied them with huge allowances, and gave them little if any real responsibility. Moreover, postwar babies grew up watching television and receiving the message that to *consume* is the highest good; leisure is the most meaningful part of life; constant adventure is fun and available to all. The realities of postindustrial (capitalistic) society are such that the role of humans in productivity is increasingly less important and consumption more so (for the sake of the GNP), and youth learned that "message." Moreover, life, as depicted on the TV screen, is constant excitement and new experience, a far cry from the daily routine of middle-class existence. The baby-boom children themselves never knew financial adversity, the most formative experience of their parents, who reached maturity during the depression. In addition to substantial allowances, these young people enjoyed considerable leisure, arising in large measure from virtual enforced absence from the labor market until well into their twenties. It is little wonder, then, that this generation was characterized by a mentality that said work is acceptable only if it is personally satisfying and challenging and that held consumption, leisure, and action to be the highest values.

This mentality, which for want of a better term will be called a "consumption mentality," is very different from the older production-oriented one. The latter is usually associated with a kind of Puritanism (very evident today in such production-oriented societies as the U.S.S.R. and Communist China) which calls for a denial of both sensuality and emotional expression. Work is done because it must be done, and those who will not work at whatever job is available are morally culpable. A consumer orientation encourages hedonism; enjoyment of life becomes the highest value, and such pleasure is bound to be linked to sensuality and freer emotional expression, as it has long been for our primary consumers, females. It is equally bound to be divorced from the straitjacket of a rigid work schedule, not to mention the alienation of the assembly line. Work per se is not rejected, only the dullness of fixed schedules, routine or "irrelevant" tasks, and so forth. To be worth doing, work must be "meaningful" to the worker, and substantial numbers of young people in the 1960s were willing to live in poverty rather than work under circumstances not to their liking. To their own generation they were not morally culpable in refusing routine work.

This general shift in orientation became evident when first the beatniks and later the hippies appeared on our TV screens and in the press. Young, white males were shown rejecting serious study as promulgated in our educational institutions, as well as the straitjacket of formal jobs, not to mention careers. They were depicted as sensual, emotional, and free-spirited, given to enjoying sun, nature, and bright colors, drifting around the country and the world "grooving" on some wild musical form, and escaping from rationality through a mystifying variety of drugs. Their parents' tentative steps toward the consumer mentality, with martinis, barbiturates, high levels of material consumption, and long weekend parties in the country, found a logical extension in their children, with pot, LSD, and full-time leisure. The straight male world was carried along to a limited degree, as bright colors replaced grey flannel and white shirts, and hair was allowed to reach to the collar and sprout on the face, and many turned to marijuana, at least on Saturday night. These changes may be seen as first, tentative, and, in retrospect, mostly short-lived attacks on the masculine mystique as it had been practiced in the 1950s.

If jewelry-bedecked, emotionally expressive male hippies represented a new kind of male, their female counterparts did no such thing with reference to the feminine gender role. Garbed in long peasant dresses, making their own bread, the "flower girls" were steeped in "femininity." Indeed, the entire phenomenon was one of reinforcing "feminine" values and extending them to males. They may have been more sexually liberated than their mothers or straight sisters, but in practice for most that merely meant that the legalities were dispensed with, not monogamous (if serial and somewhat short-lived) relationships, and not their relative caste position.

While many male youths were becoming emotionally and physically free of a number of the arbitrary restrictions under which their fathers labored, young people of both sexes were also becoming more socially conscious. The adults of the fifties had centered their entire existence on the family and its status and security—on "togetherness." Smugly convinced that the United States was then the "best of all possible worlds," white adults during the Eisenhower years virtually ignored social issues, until Martin Luther King began forcing the nation to open its eyes. The Civil Rights Movement of the early sixties gave to many white middle-class youth of both sexes a sense of excitement and purpose for the first time in their routinized, organized, and overplanned lives. Unlike their parents, many postwar youths had known nothing but physical security and comfort since infancy. Thus they were psychologically equipped to (temporarily) reject material comfort in the name of "social injustice." Indeed, it may be precisely because of boredom induced by a lack of challenge that they were so willing to take up a social cause. Their parents' most meaningful experiences had been depression and war. They had to fight to acquire material goods, and to them "heaven" was withdrawing into the comforts of a financially secure family life. To the most energetic offspring there seemed to be no challenge in taking up where their parents had left off and continuing to chase economic success, material comfort, and security. Opulence bred its own antithesis.

The Civil Rights Movement was the impetus for this social conscience, but it took Vietnam to produce a relatively widespread involvement, at least among middle-class college youth. It was at this juncture that the developing social conscience of the generation linked up with its developing sensuality and emotional expressiveness. Males openly proclaimed in large numbers that war, far from being a test of one's masculinity, was (in this case, at least) immoral; that the heretofore "feminine" values of peace, love, and sensual enjoyment were more important. Most were probably not pacifists opposed to all wars; they were opposed to what they perceived to be an aggressive war based on some antiquated notion of honor. Their view of war began to coincide with what has long been the characteristic female response, as discussed in Chapter 4. Here again their parents' generation tentatively followed suit, until the majority of the population began to disown the war.

The new generation was now "tuned in" to social issues, and it did not take long for their analysis of the corporate role in war, racism, and poverty to spread to the environmental rape that was rapidly destroying our national resources. Ecology became an issue as some youths began to question the right of corporations to pursue profits at the expense of our national environmental heritage. The entire notion of continued productivity for its own sake, the ever-expanding GNP, became suspect as another fundamental aspect of the masculine stereotype came under fire.

Closely related to ecological questions were those pertaining to population growth. It became clear that 200 million Americans consuming resources at ten times the rate of peoples in underdeveloped lands was, if not too many people, at least enough. Serious questions were raised about the morality of having more children than the two who would replace the parents, regardless of how well the parents could "afford" children. The value of motherhood was questioned as people began wondering if it is wise to advocate that all females must engage in it—and often. A chip was chiseled out of the feminine stereotype.

Young females had been involved in these various social movements from the beginning. However, as pointed out in Chapter 4, they were relegated to the more boring tasks, perceived as sexual objects, and refused entry into the decision-making ranks. The human rights for which the multitude of different groups were ostensibly fighting were increasingly being viewed as equal rights and freedom for males only. And so in the midsixties a handful of activist women skilled in organizational techniques withdrew to their own enclaves to discuss their status and role as females. They began to realize that while they were fighting male death in Southeast Asia, no one was fighting the greater number of female deaths resulting from bungled illegal abortions; while they were clamoring for better jobs for blacks, females were receiving less pay than white *or* black males. Simultaneously, beginning about 1960, a group of older career women was reaching essentially similar conclusions about the relative position of women in the economy and in society. By the early 1970s these two streams had coalesced into a full-fledged social movement with hundreds of groups around the nation and rapidly increasing numbers of adherents. In early 1972, when the initial edition of *MS.,* the first major national women's liberation magazine, appeared, all 300,000 copies were sold off the newsstands in eight days. By 1973 the National Organization for Women had over 50 chapters, and there were chapters in more than half the states (Yates, 1975, p. 6). The social movement that had died after passage of women's suffrage, leaving most of the crucial issues unsettled, was given new life by the suffragists' granddaughters and was quickly joined by females of all ages, marital statuses and, to a lesser degree, social classes and racial and ethnic groups.

The New Feminism: Movement and Countermovement

It is impossible to make truly accurate generalizations about any social movement. With that in mind, I will nonetheless attempt to generalize about the new feminism and, later in this section, about the countermovement as well. Women's liberation is today a full-blown social movement, many if not most of whose adherents are oriented to nothing less than changing the basic values, as well as the norms, of this society. While involved in attempts to bring about a wide variety of specific legal and institutional changes, this movement goes further, to question some of the core values of our society and its definition of appropriate behavior for both sexes. Rather extensive normative changes can occur without basic value alterations in a society; in fact, they can serve to bolster the most fundamental aspects of the status quo. However, the opposite is not possible; value changes will, sooner or later, necessarily entail normative ones. Another way of looking at the overall goals of the movement was expressed by Constantina Safilios-Rothschild (1971-72) in these terms:

> Liberation . . . means freedom from stereotypic sex-linked values and beliefs restricting the range of socially acceptable options for men and women because some options are considered to be inappropriate for one or the other sex. Liberated men and women living in a liberated society have equal access to the range of options and may make any choice according to their particular inclinations, talents, wishes, and idiosyncratic preferences. . . . A major goal . . . of emancipation was to give women as many privileges as men, while the major goal of liberation is the elimination of social, cultural and psychological barriers in the way of *both men and women's* realization and, therefore, benefit both men and women (p. 71).

In his theory of collective behavior, Neil Smelser (1962, p. 124) delineates a number of stages which, if followed sequentially, will give rise to a value-oriented belief system as the basis of a value-oriented social movement. The first of these pertains to the existence of a social strain, which, as we have seen, clearly emerges from both gender roles. In Stage 2 this strain gives rise to anxiety. It is clear, again, that both sexes manifest anxiety over their respective gender roles in contemporary society. Stage 3 consists of a "generalized belief that agents are responsible for [the] anxiety-producing state of affairs." It is here that the sexes part ways. Today it is primarily females involved in some way with women's liberation who attribute their gender role problems to specific agents, namely, male-dominated institutions and/or males in general ("male chauvinism"). The next two stages consist of a "generalized sense of social disharmony [and] failure of institutional life," and a "generalized belief in [the] degeneration of values." Such beliefs characterize the thinking of most females involved in the movement, who view both the norms and the values of the society as wrongly reflecting masculine interests and supporting patriarchy to their own detriment and that of society at large. Stages 6 and 7 stress the belief in the possibility of regenerating values and norms, in short, some degree of optimism in the possibility of meaningful social change. The last two stages involve the conviction that value changes will in fact "destroy, remove, damage or restrict the responsible agents," and a new and better society will be forthcoming.

Smelser goes on to explain that value-oriented social movements, as opposed to social movements merely directed to altering norms, "arise when alternative means for reconstituting the social situation are perceived as unavailable." He gives as examples of this the following:

> *(a)* The aggrieved group . . . does not possess facilities whereby they may reconstitute the social situation; such a group ranks low on wealth, power, prestige, or access to means of communication. *(b)* The aggrieved group is prevented from expressing hostility that will punish some person or group considered responsible for the disturbing state of affairs. *(c)* The aggrieved group cannot modify the normative structure, or cannot influence those who have the power to do so. (1962, p. 325)

As we have seen, females rank as a lower caste, generally deprived of wealth, power, and prestige. They are trained psychologically so that direct expression of hostility toward males is often impossible. Excluded from the power structure of all major institutions, their opportunities to change the normative structure of the society are very limited. In short, they are prime candidates for a value-oriented movement.

Social movements represent a collectivity of different groups plus many people who support some or many of the general goals of the movement but are not affiliated with any specific groups. There is typically too a diversity of ideological orientations to be found in a large social movement. Gayle Yates (1975, p. 21) has identified three types of ideologies that exist within the Women's Movement, which she calls the feminist, the women's liberationist, and the androgynous. She compares these three ideologies in terms of eight characteristics.

The ordering principles of the different ideologies are "women equal to men" for the feminists, "women over against men or separate from men" for the women's liberationists, and "women and men equal to each other" for those with an androgynous ideology. The second characteristic Yates considers is "source of standard." For the feminists this is "established by men, adopted by women"; for the liberationists it is "arrived at by women"; and for the androgynists it is "arrived at by men and women together." In terms of their analysis of the problem, the feminists claim that women are "subordinate or secondary to men"; the women's liberationists claim that women are "sex objects, property, laborers"; those who adhere to the androgynous ideology speak of the "loss of legitimacy of traditional male/female roles." Each ideology identifies an enemy; for the three ideologies, in the same order, that enemy is: "socioeconomic attitudes and institutions"; "men, other women, capitalism, the family"; and "cultural value orientations, institutional structures." The techniques for change advocated also differ: "court cases, electoral process, information dissemination, voluntary groups" are advocated by feminists. The women's liberationists advocate "consciousness-raising, separation from men for female psychic support, awareness and exercise of woman power." Those attached to the androgynous model call for "educational process, voluntary groups, information dissemination." Each also is characterized by a different primary focus of change: political, social, or cultural. Each pursues a different strategy: pressure, conflict, or conversion. Finally, each is characterized by different goals. The feminists want "integration (collapse of diversity into unity)"; the women's liberationists seek "segregation (diversity at the expense of unity)"; and those ascribing to an androgynous ideology call for "pluralism (diversity within unity)."

In summary, Yates explains that:

> . . . the feminist paradigm evolved from the . . . quest of the historical feminists to achieve the values, rights, privileges, and opportunities that men had established as good. . . . The women's liberation paradigm is a pro-woman, anti-masculinist model. . . . The androgynous paradigm . . . takes the position that values should be arrived at, decisions made, and society ordered on the basis of women and men together. (1975, pp. 18-19)

In the early years of the new Feminist Movement two rather distinctly different types of groups were formed (see Carden, 1974, for a good discussion of the early history of the recent Feminist Movement). Some, like the National Organization for Women (NOW), Women's Equity Action League (WEAL), the national and local women's political caucuses, welfare rights groups, and the women's caucuses of a variety of professional associations were oriented primarily to normative changes or "bread and butter" issues. They were the rough counterparts of the National Association for the Advancement of Colored People and the Southern Christian Leadership Conference. These task-oriented groups have generally been patterned on the usual structure of voluntary organizations in our society, with elected officers, dues, newsletters, and often constitutions. They have addressed themselves to legal changes, such as the Equal Rights Amendment and, earlier, abortion repeal legislation. Some have engaged in litigation, such as suits against corporations for failure to comply with the Civil Rights Act. Most have proposed new programs such as the creation of low-cost day-care centers or the revision of school texts and curricula. Generally, these organizations have consisted of a relatively large number of usually white, middle-class females. The bulk of the members are employed outside the home, many as "career women." Most of the organizations have allowed male membership.

A much larger number of usually nameless women's liberation groups or "cells" were quite different in nature, however. They often numbered little more than a handful of females at any one time (usually 10 to 15), and they barred male membership or even presence. They lacked formal structure or formalized national ties, although they were in communication with one another. Characteristically, they had a constantly shifting "membership." With some frequency they came into being and broke up, only to form again with somewhat different people. Such groups were primarily composed of young females, often college students or dropouts who were generally politically radical and who came together first and foremost to "rap" and "raise consciousness." Their concern was less with normative changes (which they did, however, usually support actively) than with "head" changes, namely, alterations in the value premises upon which our gender role stereotypes and patriarchal institutions are based, as well as our day-to-day behavior. They ranged from the overly publicized, militant, man-hating groups to the far more prevalent type consisting of many females who are trying to live with males and still break out of the old stereotypes they have internalized. Some groups had quotas establishing the proportion of "members" who could be living with males at any given time; some were lesbian groups; some were communes.

Many of these rap-type groups have attempted to put into practice the kinds of radical changes they proposed for society at large. Such groups have functioned primarily for what Barbara Polk (1972, p. 322 ff.) has termed "personal liberation/consciousness raising" purposes (also see Kravetz & Sargent, 1977). The members have attempted, by rapping, to come to a more complete understanding of what the gender role status quo (male chauvinism) has done to their own personal thinking and behavior, in which they ultimately hope to make fundamental changes. In short, these groups have served a resocializing function. However, Polk notes that "The purpose of these groups is not therapy; it is to develop both an analysis of the society and an appropriate politics based on the experience of being female—the personal becomes the political" (pp. 323-24).

Because many female participants in the rap-type groups were found to be more or less passive, afraid to express their opinions, and so forth, a variety of techniques were developed to help alter these traits. The traditional organizational structure, defined as a masculine, middle-class phenomenon in which a small number of articulate members compete for dominance over a larger number of passive followers, was rejected. Formal structures were conspicuously avoided; there were no presidents or chairpersons, and tasks were frequently allocated by lottery, rotating among all members. Each had to take her turn at the dull typing and stamp licking, as well as at public speaking. In addition, some form of system to ensure broad participation was often instituted (Polk, 1972, p. 327). In the disk system, each member received a limited number of disks upon arrival at the meeting. Each time she spoke she spent a disk; when she ran out she could no longer speak. This system encouraged all members to develop confidence and poise in speaking to a group, while discouraging dominance by a few. Thus some feminists attempted on a small scale to develop new modes of organization and interaction that they felt would help put their beliefs into practice.

After a few years the two different types of groups were no longer so clearly distinguishable. Many of the formal organizations discovered that they too needed to raise the level of consciousness among their members, especially as new members kept joining. Therefore they began forming rap groups to help their members overcome the passivity and submissiveness they had been taught as girls. Despite the fact that the organizations themselves permitted male members, they often found that they had to exclude men from these groups if the women were to be able to work through their gender role problems effectively. Meanwhile, the more loosely structured groups were finding that their very looseness was an impediment in accomplishing anything beyond consciousness raising. Many of these groups evolved into semistructured, single-purpose organizations, such as women's health collectives, rape-crisis centers, organizations to help battered wives, child-care collectives, and groups oriented to pointing out sexism in school texts and attempting to correct the situation. These groups often maintained many of the organizational innovations of the consciousness-raising groups but found that they also needed some structure if they were to accomplish their goals. Also new, highly organized single-issue groups have arisen in the 1970s, such as those fighting for passage of the Equal Rights Amendment. Thus a wide array of group types, differing in terms of both their stated functions and their organizational structures, continue to exist as part of a loosely interrelated social movement.

As the decade of the 1970s has progressed, a Men's Liberation Movement has also begun to emerge which shares the feminists' goals of eliminating both the gender role stereotypes and the sexual caste system. Small groups of men with such objectives are now to be found in most major cities, although this movement today is probably about the size of its female counterpart a decade ago.

The Women's Liberation Movement continues to be perceived as largely a white, middle-class phenomenon. Minority women are often sympathetic to at least some of the goals of this movement, yet many choose to devote their energies and talents to the struggles being waged by their own minority communities (see Walum, 1977, pp. 212-16). Besides efforts to broaden the base of involvement beyond the white middle class, the Women's Movement faces other problems. There is the ever-present danger that, like the earlier Woman's Rights Movement, it will succeed in extracting certain concessions (more and better jobs for equal pay, more and better child-care centers, and abortion law repeal) at the expense of truly fundamental alterations in the gender role status quo. In short, there is the danger that feminists will be "bought off" with what amount to token changes, as they were when women's suffrage was passed. Avoiding this entails, at a minimum, emphasizing the value-oriented aspects of the movement as the ultimate goal and viewing the normative or utilitarian goals as mere beginning steps.

The Antifeminist Countermovement

In the middle years of the 1970s the most obvious problem faced by the Women's Movement became a growing countermovement, manifested chiefly by groups actively fighting the passage of the Equal Rights Amendment and others oriented to once again outlawing abortions. The rapid rise of such groups has prompted many to proclaim the imminent decline of the Women's Liberation Movement. I think this prediction is premature. Whenever a segment of society organizes to attempt sociopolitical change, there is a strong tendency for a countergroup to organize. Naturally, this takes time. The Feminist Movement grew, at least in part, out of the general liberal-radical ferment of the 1960s. In that decade, the most obvious and outspoken political groups were those of the left (i.e., those seeking change). It often appeared that, because they were organized and outspoken, they represented the vast majority of people. It is easy now to see that they merely had a historical headstart over conservatives (i.e., those opposed to change). As the nation moved into the 1970s, groups opposed to all types of social change began to organize. In short, there are no fewer feminists today, in fact there are probably many more than there were five years ago. Nor are there more people opposed to ERA and abortion; they are only organized, hence visible now.

My argument that the nation is, if anything, more inclined now to accept many of the ideas promulgated by the Women's Liberation Movement than it was earlier is based in part on opinion survey data. For instance, in a study of nearly 200,000 college freshmen in 373 institutions, Bayer (1975) found that the percentage who believe that "the activities of married women are best confined to the home and family" declined from 47.8 in 1970 to 30.4 in 1973. For males, the decline was from 57 percent to 40.9; for females from 36.7 to 18.8. These students also were more likely to agree that "women should receive the same salary and opportunities for advancement as men in comparable positions." The percentages went from 81.3 in 1970 to 91.9 in 1973. Data from other attitude surveys also demonstrate increasing support for various feminist goals (see Brown, 1976). Poll data reveal that the proportion of Americans who would vote for a female for president increased from 54 percent in 1969 to 66 percent in 1971, and in just one year, between 1971 and 1972, the proportion of women who supported "efforts to strengthen or change women's status in society" increased from 40 to 48 percent (Kirkpatrick, 1974, pp. 248-49).

In part, the reason I argue that the countermovement is not representative of future or, indeed, even present widespread thinking is also based on the nature of the people, primarily women, who are involved in it. David Brady and Kent Tedin (1976) studied a group of women opposed to ERA and found that they were largely nonemployed housewives who were rural or small-town in background and overwhelmingly church members, specifically members of fundamentalist Protestant churches to whom religion was a "very important" part of their lives. They were also found to be extreme conservatives in their general political attitudes, who "believe in a domestic communist conspiracy, feel big government in the United States is a menace, and are very preoccupied with the state of morality." Maren Carden (1974, pp. 164-65) also reports that antifeminists are typically conservative Republicans who feel that we must return to old values in our society. Since the vast majority of Americans today do not grow up in small towns or rural areas, are not conservative Republicans, are not fundamentalist Protestants, and are increasingly not unemployed housewives, it is clear that antifeminists are drawn from a small and declining segment of our nation's population.

Altering the Value Premises

The Anti-ERA Movement is currently causing difficulties for the efforts of the Women's Liberation Movement to have states ratify that amendment. In the long run, however, I believe that the success of the Women's Liberation Movement, in terms of eliminating the sexual caste system and the gender role stereotypes, hinges more strongly on its ability to create a variety of nonlegal changes in society. The real question, for which there is no pat answer, pertains to how the movement could bring about changes in the value premises underlying the gender role stereotypes. Females are increasingly in a position to extract some normative changes by the use of traditional conflict strategies and tactics. As more come to understand their caste position, they are utilizing the ballot box to extract legal changes and the courtroom to follow up on them. The legal changes of the past half-dozen years, discussed in Chapter 4, reflect this development. As women continue to increase their proportion of the labor market, especially if they continue to be concentrated in a relatively small number of occupations, they can use the labor strike as a tool. As they have more disposable income of their own, they can use the economic boycott. The trade boycott of states which have failed to ratify the ERA called for by NOW cost such cities as Chicago, Atlanta, and Miami tens of millions of dollars in lost conventions in its first year alone. Women can refuse to buy products whose advertisements degrade and insult their sex or to patronize stores that discriminate against females in hiring, promotions, salaries, or the granting of credit.

Most men have yet to become seriously involved in any *collective* way with the issues inherent in the sociology of gender roles. Many individual males are quite ready to advocate some or many of the goals of feminism (although not necessarily of "male liberation"), sensing that their future prospects will be far happier if a few changes are made. Increasingly, husbands can see that bored, frustrated wives trapped at home lead to poor marital relations and severe emotional burdens. They can see that their collective disposable income would be much increased if wives worked and received equal pay for their labors. Many support child-care centers so their wives can go to work. Some even perceive the fact that a wife with a decent-paying career can relieve them of the necessity of engaging in highly paid occupations which they don't like rather than pursuing their own "thing," regardless of income. Some men support the goals of feminism because they want to be more involved in child care or because they have lost custody of their children in divorce proceedings on no other basis than their sex.

Thus, on the basis of personal interest and perhaps a twinge of conscience, increasingly males are paying at least lip service to many of the concrete demands made by feminists. However, these same men, when acting as corporate employees or union members instead of thinking as husbands, often maintain the kind of mental set and priorities that result in de facto discrimination against women. They are frequently unwilling to accept truly *equal* responsibility for and involvement in housekeeping and child rearing; without this, the result is a double burden for women, who must carry the full-time household role on top of their full-time jobs. The habits of a lifetime continue to encourage these would-be supporters of feminism to attempt to dominate the females with whom they personally come in contact.

Feminists may find males useful allies in some concrete endeavors, but until the latter begin to collectively reexamine their own masculine behavior patterns and value premises and perceive the *long-term* advantages to be gained by changing them, such an alliance will be fragile at best. The *short-term* advantages to males in maintaining the most fundamental aspects of the gender role status quo are simply too great to expect most men to knowingly and willingly undermine them. Most will gladly trade the necessity of opening the car door for females for the knowledge that they need not compete with them for their jobs.

The question of how fundamental *value* changes can be wrought has not been answered. This process, which will probably involve at least a generation or more, may result from the confluence of a wide variety of changes, many of which are ostensibly based on other issues. Earlier in the chapter we saw that the various social movements of the past decade contributed to chipping away some of the traditional stereotypes of masculinity and femininity and the values implicit in them. In addition, the demographic and economic realities of contemporary society encourage women to seek new roles outside the home, most especially in the labor force.

To the extent that the concrete, utilitarian demands of feminism are met, there is a fair probability that values will also be altered to some extent. For instance, if females are the equal of males in the economy, the idea that masculinity is mainly expressed through the function of provider will probably decrease. If, given increased opportunities for rewarding careers, females take work outside the home seriously as a major life commitment, then there is a good chance that many will simply refuse to carry the lion's share of responsibility also for the full-time job of housekeeping and child raising, and thus they will question the overwhelming emphasis on being a good homemaker. If females function outside the home, in school, office, politics, and so forth, as the equal of males, they are less apt to defer to male opinion just because it is male and are more apt to question the feminine "virtue" of passivity vis-à-vis males. In short, because of normative changes people may come to behave in ways that belie the stereotypes, and there is a good chance that their attitudes will follow suit.

The social-psychological theory of cognitive dissonance (Festinger, 1957) maintains that in an attempt to avoid that uncomfortable psychological state known as dissonance, once we have made some sort of commitment to a course of action we will readjust our thinking to support it. However, the other implication of this theory is that those who have had long-standing commitments to established patterns will avoid considering changes that would create dissonance. Thus, for instance, the middle-aged housewife is hardly in a position to redefine the role of females when in so doing she risks seeing her life as in some manner a waste or failure.

The crucial changes, however, will come about (if, indeed, they do) because we rear a new generation with different values. If mother has a commitment (not necessarily a "job") to the world beyond the home, children of both sexes will no longer be taught that "woman's place is in the home" and that the greatest virtue a female can have is to stay there. If mother earns as much as father or more, children will learn that earning and providing are irrelevant to sex. If we have male kindergarten teachers, homemakers, and secretaries, and female astronauts, plumbers, and corporate executives, children will learn that all manners of life are open to all who are suited by inclination and aptitude. If father cooks dinner regularly and transports the children to the dentist (because mother's outside commitments are less flexible than father's), the message will be clear: housework and child rearing are everyone's responsibility. If parents disavow aggressive wars fought for "honor" and corporations that pollute for the sake of expanding profits, children will learn that, regardless of sex, production without social conscience or purpose and fighting for reasons other than defense are wrong. If boys as well as girls get dolls to play with, if both are given Erector sets and science kits and neither receive toy weapons, if everyone is encouraged to develop their bodies for pleasure and to keep healthy, children will learn radically new notions about "appropriate" behavior.

Children learn from the *actions* of their parents and other adults with whom they come into contact. What we do, often with great effort and psychological cost, to overcome gender role stereotypes will become our children's habitual responses. Changes in our behavior today will create new values in our children which, in turn, can be expected to lead to further changes in norms and institutions.

It is not easy for parents to encourage attitudes and behaviors in their offspring that essentially make the latter "social deviants" among their peers and in their schools. In fact, the pressures on children outside the home may all but cancel many lessons being conveyed by parents. In many neighborhoods today the boy with his doll or the girl who demands of the boys the opportunity to play the doctor, not always the nurse, will either spend many lonely years as an outsider or change to conform to traditional patterns. There is undoubtedly some critical proportion that must be reached before such children can find enough others reared the same way to reinforce the messages being taught by parents who would radically change gender role stereotypes. Without that proportion of peers, such children are asked to pay a substantial personal price. There is no assurance that such a critical level will be reached in many places. Moreover, there are segments of our population to whom any social change appears threatening, and changing gender roles may appear more dangerous to them than most other phenomena. However, the number of young females in the childbearing years, and even many of their mates, who espouse an ideology based on change in both gender roles has been rapidly increasing in recent years.

It should be clear that the costs of *conformity* to both gender role stereotypes are terribly high for individuals and for society at large. Nonconformity is never easy, and the costs entailed in it are only too obvious to all who have ever broken relatively important social mores. The problems arising from conformity are far less obvious; indeed, they are usually not perceived as such by most members of society. Moreoever, particularly in the case of the feminine role, recent changes and suggestions for change are very threatening to substantial numbers of people of both sexes. The threat to males is obvious; change entails a loss of many concrete prerogatives and an automatic ego haven, namely, their designation as intrinsically "superior" to half the human species. The threat to females is less obvious. First, women who conform need not seriously question the manner in which they have spent their own lives or those of their loved ones. Although a woman may be unhappy due to the pressures of her role, she also basks in an illusive kind of security. She need never explore the limits of her abilities, and in so doing risk failure; she need never live under personal or social pressure to fully exert herself in any endeavor; she need never, in the final analysis, take the full and terrifying responsibility for her own personal destiny. That she receives none of the immense personal satisfactions of standing as a self-defined, independent adult may be, for many, unnoticed, or at least of little importance. In short, to ask people who have been trained to be dependent and of whom little has been expected to make the real effort to be independent and competent is to ask a lot; to ask this when it also entails the obvious costs of nonconformity seems almost ridiculous. Yet the fact of the matter is that increasing numbers of females are demanding precisely this of themselves.

The types of changes that have been discussed here will take one or more generations to accomplish on a widespread basis, and there is no assurance that they will indeed come to pass. As a nation we are impatient. We tend to become involved in social and political movements with the expectation that the millenium is just around the corner. We have an insufficient understanding of the time involved in historical processes. Thus we tend to lack the patience to make a lifetime commitment to a social or political cause that will probably not be fully realized during our own lives. Movements come and go with great rapidity in our society, as most members, failing to see significant, immediate change, drift away. The Feminist Movement experienced substantial dispiritedness during the midseventies, as the first bloom of sisterhood and success wore off. Perhaps the major problem facing the Women's Movement is maintaining sufficient dedication among its adherents so that they will be willing to devote a lifetime to a cause whose fruition may only be experienced by their grandchildren.

New Migrants to the Rat Race?

The preceding discussion may have conveyed the general impression that many of the changes witnessed in recent years concerning gender roles and the sexual caste system are here to stay. However, we have seen how women's roles and fortunes have swung back and forth in this century. Equality for women is not a foregone conclusion; indeed, there are reasons to believe it is problematic.

Edna Bonacich (1972) developed a theory of the "split labor market" which applies to social minorities generally, including women. She argues that business interests seek to minimize labor costs but are blocked by high-priced labor. High-priced labor is comprised of members of the socially dominant group (white males), which is sufficiently powerful to block the entrance of minorities into high-paying occupations. R. D. Barron and G. M. Norris (1976) use essentially the same approach in discussing the sexual division within the labor force, but they speak of a "dual labour market." Such a labor market has the following attributes:

1. There is a more or less pronounced division into higher paying and lower paying sectors.
2. Mobility across the boundary of these sectors is restricted.
3. Higher paying jobs are tied into promotional or career ladders, while lower paid jobs offer few opportunities for vertical movement.
4. Higher paying jobs are relatively stable, while lower paid jobs are unstable. (p. 49)

As an ascriptive characteristic, sex has been used traditionally to assign men and women to different halves of the dual labor market.

Janet Chafetz, Rosalind Dworkin, and A. Gary Dworkin (n.d.; also see Dworkin & Dworkin, 1976, pp. 41-43; Chafetz, 1978, Exemplar) have attempted to develop a model to explain the conditions under which changes are effected in the power that higher priced, majority group labor exercises over lower priced minority group labor. They seek to explain under what conditions women (as well as other minority groups) tend to become more or less equal to men in the labor force. The assumption is that historically change can and has taken place in both directions—toward greater equality and toward greater inequality. Further, it may be assumed that as equality in the labor force changes, so too does equality in other aspects of our social and political life.

Basically, this model postulates that there is always a large supply of women available for the labor force. Whether or not they participate, and the extent to which those participating are treated equally, depend largely on the demand for labor. Such things as population size and structure, the state of the economy, the availability of natural resources, and the level of technology determine the demand for labor. As long as the social majority (white males) have sufficient numbers to fill this demand, especially the demand for higher paid jobs, others will not be brought into the labor force, or they will be kept segregated in the lowest level positions. When majority group labor becomes scarce, minority labor is sought.

As minorities begin to enter the labor force or to move up somewhat into the higher paid jobs, according to this model, they perceive more clearly that they have been and continue to be discriminated against. It is at this point that they may develop a social movement in an attempt to exert political pressure on the dominant majority to cease discrimination. From this perspective, social movements arise in response to socioeconomic change, which can then be pushed further by the activities of the movement. Thus, for instance, the rise of the new Feminist Movement *reflects* changes initiated in the early 1960s in the labor force participation of women, as well as helping to *create* further changes. However, if the state of the economy changes such that the demand for labor decreases, it is the newcomers, the minority group members, who are pushed down and out of the employment market. In short, women constitute a reserve labor pool to be manipulated as the economy requires. To the extent that this model is accurate, the future in terms of sexual equality rests less with movement activities than with economic forces, which are often not amenable to control by anyone in the nation. Thus, the new migrants to the rat race may, in future years, once again become the new migrants to the homestead.

Social Institutions and Changing Gender Roles: A Glimpse at Utopia

Despite, or perhaps because of, the problematic nature of the future in terms of changing gender roles, it is important to speculate about what our society might be like if indeed androgyny were to replace the gender role stereotypes and sexual caste system. If nothing else, if utopia can be made to look good enough, it could spur people to devote more energies to helping create change.

What might some of our most fundamental social institutions look like in the year 2000 *if* significant changes occur in the gender role status quo? To the extent that males and females are truly released from their stereotyped roles, the family, economic, and political institutions at the least, will very likely be altered in the process. In turn, such institutional changes would feed back and further reinforce the changes in our gender role definitions.

The Family

The most basic social institution is usually considered to be the family. Already a wider diversity of living arrangements is being tried than existed a decade and a half ago (see Safilios-Rothschild, 1977, chap. 7). There are a larger number of one-parent families, due to the rising divorce rate and an increasing willingness on the part of unwed mothers to keep their children, thus questioning the sexual double standard that labels them immoral and their offspring illegitimate (see Kornfein et al., 1977, and Scanzoni & Scanzoni, 1976, pp. 140-60). Communal living arrangements, ranging from the "back to nature" rural communes of the counterculture to small urban communes consisting of a few, usually young, often professional, families, continued into the 1970s after their proliferation in the late 1960s. Even within the nuclear family, many are attempting to alter the old presuppositions radically and to create what Nena and George O'Neill (1972) have termed "open marriages." Increasing numbers of young people are choosing not to have children, and many are also no longer bothering to legalize their sexual relationships. The minority now experimenting with a variety of new forms of living together can be expected to grow into a large number by the year 2000, when living arrangements may reflect the personal needs of those involved more than the social and legal prescriptions surrounding the contemporary nuclear family and stereotypical gender roles.

Young people in the past decade have become increasingly aware of the necessity to restrict the number of children they have to two or fewer. Moreover, as females increasingly take life outside the home more seriously, they are further encouraged to have few or no children. It has long been recognized that employed women have fewer children than homemakers, and it seems to be the case that women with interesting jobs choose to restrict family size, rather than that women with small families choose to seek employment. As young, educated females increasingly postpone their entry into marriage to a later age and put off birth of the first child as well, we can expect that many will find themselves in sufficiently interesting and challenging jobs that they will not wish to impede their careers with large families or, in some cases, any families at all. In the past decade our birth rates have plummeted, and they now stand at the lowest point in our history.

In Chapter 5 the argument was made that the kind of "hothouse" attention that almost necessarily becomes focused on children in small families can result in disaster for both parents and children. Many solutions to the dilemma of how to raise children in small families are possible. The society could encourage a small number of couples to have large families, make that their "livelihood," and encourage everyone else to have none. That is an unlikely solution, however, and one that would deprive most people of the very real rewards entailed in child rearing. More promising are various communal arrangements consisting of a number of adults, married and single, with and without children, living as an extended family based on choice rather than "blood." This is already occurring, but the practice is not widespread. Not only do our forms of residential architecture discourage communal living, but most Americans have not been brought up with the kind of values that would make them want to sacrifice their privacy. Communes tend to be rather unstable and short-lived; people live in them for a year or two, then move on, often to be replaced by others. Typically, the commune itself eventually ceases to exist. Some people probably will live communally in the future, but it is unlikely that this will become a dominant pattern.

The advantages of communal living are potentially enormous, however. Those without children can benefit by partaking of the experiences of child rearing, and those with children can benefit by sharing its burdens. The children benefit from daily contact with other children and a variety of adults. The burdens and expenses of housekeeping can be lightened for everyone. As a society, we would benefit by decreasing the rapid expenditure of our resources; only one of each appliance would be needed, instead of one per family if each family were living separately. Presumably, all tasks pertaining to home and children would be assigned or rotated without regard to sex, thus releasing all to function more readily in the world outside the home. Finally, the kind of ingrown relationship that springs up between mates and often serves to stifle both parties can be avoided more readily in a group. Everyone can be freer to pursue his or her own interests without worrying about a mate's "sacrifices." Dick is less apt to demand that Jane be home for dinner every night if Alice and Ted and Bob and Mary also eat with him; Jane is less apt to get angry that Dick is too tired to listen to her or go to a movie or a party if someone else is readily available.

In the year 2000, as today, most people will probably live alone as singles, as single parents with custody of children, or in a nuclear family comprised of two adults, with or without children. For those with children, the changes which will occur will involve the greater use of

child-care centers and the greater sharing of child-rearing responsibilities by fathers. To the extent that child-care centers are adequately
funded and staffed with members of both sexes who are emotionally
stable, competent people who enjoy their work, they have tremendous
advantages over the home. The child has better recreational and
educational facilities, more playmates, and probably as much real
attention from adults. Since it is not a burden to a harried mother, the
child will not find itself cast in the role of the most available recipient of
her frustrations. Infant and child centers need not turn out assembly-
line children who think and act alike, although they might if such centers
continue to be funded at the abysmal level characteristic of most social
services. There is nothing *inherent* in such centers, however, that must
result in this. The children of Israeli kibbutzim are not drab,
maladjusted, totally conformist, or emotionally disturbed, as visualized
by many Americans contemplating collectivized child rearing for
anyone other than the poor. Indeed, children raised in such settings are
probably more socially adept and adjusted and less egocentric than
those brought up in an isolated nuclear family (Bettelheim, 1962). In
such centers, child rearing would no longer be learned by the young as a
"feminine" function (not to mention the primary one), and there is the
obvious freedom to engage in other activities that these centers provide
for the parents. Perhaps the greatest benefit, however, arises from the
fact that parents and children, being less of a burden to one another,
would probably relate better during the time they did spend together.

Thus we can anticipate that in the utopia that could develop if
androgyny were to replace gender role stereotypes and the sexual caste
system, most children (past a very early age) would be raised in a
collectivized setting of one variety or another. It is likely that more
people will spend more of their adult lives unmarried, before their first
marriage, or, for many, after divorce or widowhood. As people forego
the assumption that relationships will last "till death do us part"; as
many opt not to have children; as females become economically
independent of males; and as the sexual double standard finally
crumbles, there will be less and less reason to become involved in the
legal and often financial hassles that surround marriage and ultimately
divorce for so many. Men and women will increasingly come together as
independent human beings who truly love and respect one another's
individuality, form close relationships, live together, share together, and

sometimes marry. This relationship will last until one or the other changes or moves geographically and they find it to be no longer tenable. Serial monogamy, already the fact for many, will be yet more prevalent.

Such relationships, which are already relatively widespread among the young, tend to be more "open" than marriage. Each feels more free to pursue independently her or his own interests, to spend time with others of both sexes, to share equally in the housekeeping tasks. Legalizing the union, however, as the O'Neills point out (1972, pp. 139-40), often produces profound changes as both become psychologically bound by traditional notions of matrimony (the "closed" marriage). Such notions include a more strict division of labor by sex and the presentation of a "couple front," in which each is more or less bound to be with the other and share all activities and relationships. An open *marriage* is prescribed by these authors as the solution to the stagnation and ultimate deterioration of such relationships. Increasingly, people are questioning the need to legalize it at all.

If the outward *form* of the traditional family is valued as intrinsically sacred, then the kinds of changes discussed above will, by and large, be repugnant. However, if the *substance* of family living is considered more important, such changes should be greeted with cautious optimism. In postindustrial societies, the fundamental function left to the family is the provision of warm, open, close, primary relationships. Secondarily, the family is supposed to provide a modicum of security. Taken together, these functions should enable the family to serve as a springboard from which individuals can develop their own personal potentials and interests. The isolated nuclear family structure increasingly fails to fulfill these functions. It seems to me that any hope for their fulfillment must reside in the emergence of a variety of new forms, offering more choice to people to suit their changing personal needs at various points in their life cycles. (For other speculations concerning the future of the family, see Yates, 1975; Scanzoni & Scanzoni, 1976; Bernard, 1972.)

The Economy

The logical question that arises at this point is: If we free everyone from full-time housework, how is the economy going to absorb all of the adults in our society? The answer is that it will not. Moreover, our definitions of work, occupation, and leisure will have to be changed quite substantially. It is common today to predict that technological changes will, within the next several decades, restrict the number of jobs in the economy. Indeed, the facts that we have been forcibly retiring most people at age 65 and keeping young people out of the labor force and in educational institutions (where they learn little if anything directly pertaining to their future work) until well into their twenties indicate that this trend is well underway. So too do the continuing relatively high rates of unemployment, as well as the shortened work week and the increasing amount of holiday and vacation time being provided to workers.

In the year 2000 many people may spend their time "unemployed" in the sense that they will not be in the labor force because it will have no jobs for them. However, if gender role stereotypes have disappeared, there would be no reason why it should be females who absent themselves from the labor market more frequently than males. Both will be equally free not to work. There are also a variety of arrangements by which more people could be employed in a given number of jobs. For instance, a male could work mornings, his mate or friend afternoons; or she could work January through May, he the other six months; or two or a group of people could work six months together while another couple or group were off, and not be part of the labor force for the remainder of the year when the second crew was. Such arrangements would clearly require the cooperation of industry to hire and train two or more people to do essentially one job. This would not be the most profitable course, but, as shall be argued shortly, if gender role stereotypes have really changed, other considerations may enter corporate policy decision making (see Chafetz, 1976; Kreps & Leaper, 1977).

Whether or not the members of our society approve, we have to support people at a decent standard of living who are either not part, or are only intermittently part, of the labor force. Society will also have to "create" jobs, which, given pressing social needs, should not be too difficult. Well-staffed child-care centers will require relatively large numbers of people to run them; school classes could be cut to an educable 10 to 15 students; jobs could be created involving reading to the blind, transporting the disabled, and providing similar services. In short, the affluence created by cybernetics could be used in the service sector of the economy to help people, thus employing large numbers of both females and males. To cope with the economy of the future, however, involves a willingness on the part of members of our society and its leaders to relinquish some of our most cherished notions about rewarding productivity and punishing those who are not employed. Similarly, it will involve a willingness to increase government spending radically to finance new types of jobs which will yield no one individual or group a profit in strictly economic terms. Such changes almost presuppose the demise of some aspects of the masculine mystique, among other value changes.

There exists, however, a more profound question: Just what do work and productivity mean? Today we tend to define these in terms of having a paid job: you do some work, have an occupation, and in return receive income and some degree of social recognition and prestige. The person who is doing volunteer work at a hospital today is not "working"; he or she does not have this activity as an occupation. The same is true of the individual who sews at home for family members or makes a cabinet foɪ the house.

It can be assumed that, given our level of intellect as a species, humans are somehow impelled to try to express themselves creatively by making an impact, however small it may be, on their world. Our mental health probably requires some sort of challenge which demands a physical and/or mental expression of our abilities. If society fails to provide such challenges, it risks creating a vast number of alcoholics, drug addicts, mentally ill, and so on, due largely to boredom. Technological society poses relatively few challenges for many people, and it is not difficult to discern the effects of this shortage. As more people spend less time on jobs, there is an increasing likelihood that this problem will increase. This is because, the multibillion-dollar entertainment and leisure industries notwithstanding, Americans have not learned how to use large amounts of leisure in noncompulsive, personally satisfying ways. Our culture encourages us to do only those few things we do well. Many people drop pastimes which give them joy but which they nonetheless do poorly, or at least not as well as professionals from whom they could purchase similar goods or services.

In adjusting to the future, the concepts of occupation, work, and leisure would essentially disappear. Most humans would have to learn to spend most of their time doing what they enjoy (of course, first they would have to discover what that might be), regardless of whether or not it is rewarded monetarily; in utopia, income would no longer be an indicator of the value of an activity. If we are all occupied less, we will need to redefine the bases upon which we distribute scarce and valued resources such as prestige and income. Humans of both sexes could engage in activities that are meaningful and challenging to them, but they might or might not be engaged in occupations.

There is another way in which the economic complexion of our society could change if role stereotypes disappear. Assuming that as females enter the decision-making ranks of corporations they do not become totally engulfed in the essentially masculine emphasis on productivity for its own sake (and that males retreat from this orientation), there is the possibility that the kinds of policies characteristic of our contemporary economic institutions may change. Goods may be built to last rather than to wear out and require replacement; safety and ecological issues may become more central to policy decisions, not just advertisements. In short, industry may become more humane and socially oriented, as it already proclaims it is, and considerations other than spiraling profits based on spiraling production may come to play a major role. If that comes to pass, efficiency would not be the only concept determining work schedules and the deployment of our human resources. The probabilities of this occurring are not great, since businesses typically recruit their leaders from those who accept the dominant philosophy of the corporation. Thus, women who succeed, like their male counterparts, are most likely to reflect the profit/productivity mentality. However, since we are speaking of utopia, it is worth speculating on a more desirable outcome, despite its improbability.

Political Institutions

As gender roles change, females should take their place as leaders in the various political units of society. Again the assumption is made, despite the low probability of this occurrence, that in doing so they will not become completely "masculine" and that males will have lost some of their stereotyped attributes while taking on some aspects of the "feminine" personality. If this is the case, wars for honor and aggressive purposes should decrease, and decision making in the context of saving face would no longer be salient to our national heritage (see Kirkpatrick, 1974; pp. 244-52).

These changes would make a greater proportion of our national resources available for government to steer into human development rather than arms development. Schools, social services, hospitals, day-care centers for the very young and very old, housing, and public transportation are likely candidates for the lion's share of expenditures. In all likelihood the firearms many American males cling to as an expression of their virility would be stringently controlled, if not altogether outlawed. And, perhaps most generally, politicians would begin to seek power not as a goal in itself but as a means to accomplish social goals.

To Be Human

The last sections of this chapter have focused on the probable consequences of females taking on previously male functions and vice versa, as females enter the mainstream of life outside the home and males learn to partake more fully of both the dull tasks of housekeeping and the potentially rewarding and enriching duties of child rearing. Changing gender roles mean males become more sensual and emotional as females become more rational and psychologically and intellectually confident and competent. Evolving into a society of humans undoubtedly entails the breakdown of the traditional division of labor and personality by sex, as the choices open to all are expanded. The term "androgyny" is used to express this phenomenon, a possibility which, depending on the person, is greeted with glee or dismay. I feel that progress in achieving a better society will only be made when and if *all* ascribed characteristics, including sex, are irrelevant to the opportunities afforded people, the way in which people spend their lives, the manner in which they are taught to view themselves and others, and the kinds of emotional and intellectual responses that are deemed appropriate (see also Deaux, 1976, pp. 137-42; Kaplan & Bean, 1976, conclusion; Sargent, 1977, pp. 275-78).

A mere swapping of gender role traits, however, is not enough. Are we any better off in the long run, individually or collectively, if females begin to fight for glory; if they learn to dedicate their lives to productivity for its own sake and to compete for power, dominance, and status at the cost of all else? For that matter, is monetary payment for housekeeping chores more to be desired than questioning the values that place so much emphasis on money in the first place? Would it be any improvement if males, in the process of rediscovering their expressive faculties, surrendered their willingness and ability to be analytical on occasion? Does it help if they learn to be so vain about their appearance that they spend billions on it; if they ignore completely the joys that can come from creative production, embrace passivity, and forsake all competition, even that which spurs humans to their finest endeavors?

In short, we, as a society, must develop a set of humanistic and socially conscious values that embraces the best of both traditional masculinity and traditional femininity. And we must expect people, regardless of sex, to embrace them. Merely allowing males to get into the costly "bag" females have long been in, and vice versa, is no solution. We must also unlearn some traits almost completely, while tempering others. It is the task of the future to come to grips with this problem; to develop and teach a viable definition of humanness and equality that will enable us to live in personally and collectively rewarding ways in postindustrial society. It is the task of all of us to decide whether our society is to be comprised of people who are masculine/feminine or human.

References

Barron, R. D., and Norris, G. M. "Sexual Divisions and the Dual Labour Market." In Diana Barker and Sheila Allen (eds.), *Dependence and Exploitation in Work and Marriage,* pp. 47-69. London: Longman, 1976.

Bayer, Alan. "Sexist Students in American Colleges: A Descriptive Note." *Journal of Marriage and the Family* 37 (May 1975): 391-97.

Bernard, Jessie. *The Future of Marriage.* New York: Bantam Books, 1972.

Bettelheim, Bruno. "Does Communal Education Work? The Case of the Kibbutz." *Commentary* 33 (February 1962): 117-25.

Bonacich, Edna. "A Theory of Ethnic Antagonisms: The Split Labor Market." *American Sociological Review* 37 (October 1972): 547-59.

Brady, David, and Tedin, Kent. "Ladies in Pink: The Anti-ERA Movement." *Social Science Quarterly* 56 (March 1976): 564-75.

Brown, Bertram. *How Women See Their Roles: A Change in Attitudes.* Report from the Director, National Institute of Mental Health, U.S. Department of Health, Education, and Welfare, 1976.

Carden, Maren Lockwood. *The New Feminist Movement.* New York: Russell Sage Foundation, 1974.

Chafetz, Janet Saltzman. "The ERA and Redefinitions of Work: Toward Utopia." In California Commission on the Status of Women, *Impact ERA: Limitations and Possibilities,* pp. 108-15. Millbrae, Calif.: Les Femmes Publishers, 1976.

Chafetz, Janet Saltzman. *A Primer on the Construction and Testing of Theories in Sociology.* Itasca, Ill.: F. E. Peacock Publishers, 1978.

Chafetz, Janet Saltzman; Dworkin, Rosalind J., and Dworkin, Anthony Gary. "New Migrants to the Rat Race: A Model of Rates of Labor Force Participation and Patterns of Occupational Deployment by Gender, Race and Ethnicity." Unpublished manuscript, University of Houston, n.d.

Deaux, Kay. *The Behavior of Women and Men.* Monterey, Calif.: Brooks/Cole Publishing Co., 1976.

Dworkin, Anthony Gary, and Dworkin, Rosalind J. *The Minority Report: An Introduction to Racial, Ethnic, and Gender Relations.* New York: Praeger Publishers, 1976.

Festinger, Leon. *A Theory of Cognitive Dissonance.* New York: Row Peterson, 1957.

Flexner, Eleanor. *Century of Struggle: The Woman's Rights Movement in the United States.* Rev. ed. Cambridge, Mass.: Belknap Press, 1975.

Harrington, Michael. *Toward a Democratic Left.* Baltimore, Md.: Penguin Books, 1969.

Kaplan, Alexandra, and Bean, Joan. *Beyond Sex Role Stereotypes: Readings toward a Psychology of Androgyny.* Boston: Little, Brown & Co., 1976.

Kirkpatrick, Jeane. *Political Woman.* New York: Basic Books, 1974.

Kornfein, Madeleine; Weisner, Thomas, and Martin, Joan. "Women into Mothers: Experimental Life Styles." In Jane Chapman and Margaret Gates (eds.), *Women into Wives: The Legal and Economic Impact of Marriage,* pp. 260-91. Beverly Hills, Calif.: Sage Publications, 1977.

Kravetz, Diane, and Sargent, Alice. "Consciousness-Raising Groups: A Resocialization Process for Personal and Social Change." In Alice Sargent (ed.), *Beyond Sex Roles,* pp. 148-56. St. Paul, Minn.: West Publishing Co., 1977.

Kreps, Juanita, with Leaper, John. "The Future for Working Women." *Ms.,* 1977, pp. 56-57.

O'Neill, Nena, and O'Neill, George. *Open Marriage: A New Life Style for Couples.* New York: M. Evans & Co., 1972.

O'Neill, William. *The Woman's Movement: Feminism in the United States and England.* Chicago: Quadrangle Books, 1969.

Polk, Barbara Bovee. "Woman's Liberation: Movement for Equality." In Constantina Safilios-Rothschild (ed.), *Toward a Sociology of Women,* pp. 321-30. Lexington, Mass.: Xerox College Publishing Co., 1972.

Ridley, Jeanne Clare. "The Effects of Population Change on the Roles and Status of Women: Perspective and Speculation." In Constantina Safilios-Rothschild (ed.), *Toward a Sociology of Women,* pp. 372-86. Lexington, Mass.: Xerox College Publishing Co., 1972.

Roszak, Theodore. *The Making of a Counter Culture: Reflections on the Technocratic Society and Its Youthful Opposition.* Garden City, N.Y.: Anchor Books, 1969.

Safilios-Rothschild, Constantina. "The Options of Greek Men and Women." *Sociological Focus* 5 (Winter 1971-72): 71-83.

Safilios-Rothschild, Constantina. *Love, Sex and Sex Roles.* Englewood Cliffs, N.J.: Prentice-Hall, 1977.

Sargent, Alice. *Beyond Sex Roles.* St. Paul, Minn.: West Publishing Co., 1977.

Scanzoni, Letha, and Scanzoni, John. *Men, Women and Change: A Sociology of Marriage and the Family.* New York: McGraw Hill, 1976.

Sinclair, Andrew. *The Emancipation of American Women.* New York: Harper & Row, 1965.

Smelser, Neil J. *Theory of Collective Behavior.* New York: Free Press, 1962.

Trey, J. E. "Women in the War Economy—World War II." *Review of Radical Economics* 4 (July 1972).

Walum, Laurel. *The Dynamics of Sex and Gender: A Sociological Perspective.* Chicago: Rand McNally & Co., 1977.

Wrong, Dennis. *Population and Society.* New York: Random House, 1968.

Yates, Gayle Graham. *What Women Want: The Idea of the Movement.* Cambridge, Mass.: Harvard University Press, 1975.

Name Index

Subject Index

THE BOOK MANUFACTURE

Composition:	Meridian Graphics, Incorporated Chicago, Illinois
Printing and Binding:	George Banta Company, Inc. Menasha, Wisconsin
Internal Design:	F. E. Peacock Publishers art department
Cover Design:	Sandy Mead Bensenville, Illinois
Type:	Times Roman with Futura Medium Italic and Helvetica Medium display